IMAGES
of America

PINE HILL

ON THE COVER: Pine Hill No. 1 Fire Company was photographed by Henry W. Worrell Jr. in 1964. Pine Hill No. 1 was the first of three fire departments for that town. (Courtesy of Bill Dukes.)

IMAGES
of America

PINE HILL

Les and Ronnie Gallagher

ARCADIA
PUBLISHING

ISBN 978-0-7385-7244-4

Published by Arcadia Publishing
Charleston SC, Chicago IL, Portsmouth NH, San Francisco CA

Printed in the United States of America

Library of Congress Control Number: 2009934914

For all general information contact Arcadia Publishing at:
Telephone 843-853-2070
Fax 843-853-0044
E-mail sales@arcadiapublishing.com
For customer service and orders:
Toll-Free 1-888-313-2665

Visit us on the Internet at www.arcadiapublishing.com

This book is dedicated, with love and appreciation, to our daughters Judith Lerner and Kimberly Palmer and our son Leslie Gallagher Jr.

Contents

ACKNOWLEDGMENTS

We first need to thank our friends in the Pine Hill community. These friends provided us with the knowledge and photographs about Pine Hill to make this book become a reality. We wish to especially thank Mary (Hofacker) Gallagher, Glen (Osborne) Suydam, Mildred Cunningham, Joseph Sheller, Dr. Alfred Osborne Davies, John Elder, Emil Del Conte, Jim Kanuth, Jim O'Neill, Becky Blakeley, Ken Cheeseman, Alice Kennedy, Natalie Maguire, Evelyn Krantz, Bill Dukes, Ida Fieger, Ronnie Meyers, Ellen Kerby, Mary Thumm, and Judd Booker.

This book would not have been possible without the efforts of a dedicated group of family and friends—in particular Judy Lerner, Kimberly Palmer, and Les Gallagher Jr.—without them this work could not have been completed.

Introduction

The history of Pine Hill began over 350 years ago. The earliest known settlers in the Pines were the Lenni Lenape Indians in 1658. As the population of European immigrants to the area increased, the Lenni Lenape Indians were faced with despoilment of their hunting and fishing grounds along with their culture. In March 1940, a joint archeological expedition uncovered remains of one of the Native American settlements. During the expedition, more than 90 items, including arrowheads, flints, pottery, cooking utensils, and wood carvings were unearthed on Branch Avenue.

By 1775, the British occupied both Pine Hill and Philadelphia. Having the highest point—214 feet above sea level—in South Jersey, Pine Hill served as an excellent observation point for the British to track the activities of Philadelphia. The skyline of Philadelphia can still be seen from this point.

One of the earliest settlers of Pine Hill was a gentleman by the name of Isaac Tomlinson. In the 1800s, his family occupied a house located on Blackwood-Clementon Road, a house which still stands. The Borough of Pine Hill purchased the Tomlinson House in November 2000 with a grant from Camden County. The small graveyard behind the house is still owned and maintained by the descendants of Isaac Tomlinson.

Frederick Osborne purchased the Osborne Tract in 1910, which consisted of many acres, covering ground from what is now Sitley Avenue to Fourth Avenue. Also in 1910, Pine Hill's first laundry, located on Clearview Avenue, was managed by Clara and John Reitz. There was no running water, and rainwater was collected in barrels to wash the clothes. Residents had to either go down to the base of the hill and carry buckets of water to their homes or purchase a bucket of water for 5¢ at McLaughlin's General Store, which also served as the town hall. At this time there were only six families living in Pine Hill year-round, but there were many families coming for summer vacations and weekend visits.

Until May 1929, Pine Hill was known as Clementon Heights. It was renamed Pine Hill at the suggestion of Johanna Berton because of all the pine trees and hills throughout the town. Burton also served as Pine Hill's borough clerk.

The depression years of the 1930s were very difficult for the families of Pine Hill, and the majority were on welfare. Help arrived with Pres. Franklin D. Roosevelt's New Deal. The Work Progress program helped the people of Pine Hill by employing them to perform public services, such as repairing rounds. Young men lived in barracks and performed other public jobs as well.

The first school session was held in the basement of the Pine Hill No. 1 Volunteer Fire Company. A two-room wooden schoolhouse was built on West Sixth Avenue in 1917. The children arrived at school in a horse-drawn wagon. That same year, residents made donations to purchase an oil-burning stove to provide heat for the children. The Albert M. Bean Elementary School was built in 1953 and named to honor Dr. Bean, a county school superintendent. The John H. Glenn Elementary School, named after the astronaut and senator John H. Glenn, was built in 1964. In

1969, Overbrook Senior High School was built as part of the Camden County Regional School District. The Pine Hill Middle School was built in 2001. In September 2001, Kenneth P. Koczur, Ed.D, became superintendent of the four schools forming the Pine Hill School District.

In its early years, Pine Hill was known as a health retreat. City doctors would send patients to the area's lakes to relax and rest. People from Philadelphia and surrounding areas made their way to Pine Hill by trolley cars. The trolley went only to the base of the hill, and cars rarely made the trip because of the steep incline of the hill. Reverse was the only option for vehicles of the time, due to the engine delivery systems available.

Pine Hill Lake Park was one of Pine Hill's lakes and was located near what is now Cloverdale Avenue. Patrons paid 10¢ admission fees to use the facilities, such as lockers, showers, and changing rooms. Pine Hill Lake Park was also known as "Stecky's Lake." At this time, Pine Hill was called the "Switzerland of New Jersey" and was a place to dine, dance, and enjoy life.

The highest point in Pine Hill—the land the British once occupied—was developed as Ski Mountain in 1964 by John Early and Emil Del Conte. After Ski Mountain's closing, a water park opened in 1984. When the water park closed, the ground lay dormant for several years, until the 1999 ground breaking for the Pine Hill Golf Club. The golf club was designed by Tom Fazio. The world-famous Pine Valley Golf Course, bordering Pine Hill's Third Avenue, hosted celebrities such as Bing Crosby and Bob Hope in the late 1940s and early 1950s.

Today baseball fields, soccer fields, parks, and playgrounds can be found in Pine Hill. Some of these are named in memory of residents, such as the Joey Green Field, Charlie Bowman Soccer and Football Fields, Stephen Wilz Playground, and most recently, the John F. Maguire Memorial Park, which honors Pine Hill's police officers, firefighters, and EMTs. Pine Hill is a small municipality that continues to grow and improve, with many thanks to lifelong residents.

One

EARLY SETTLERS

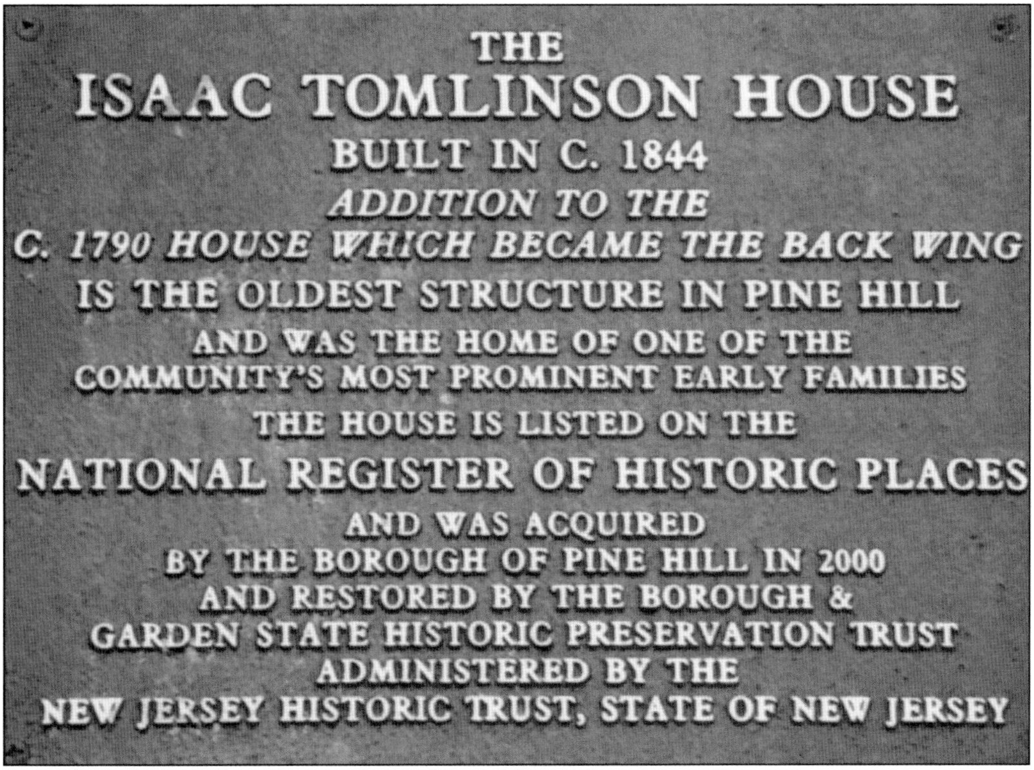

The Isaac Tomlinson House was built by brothers Isaac and Ephraim in 1790. The addition was done in 1844 by James, a nephew who took over the mill when his uncle passed away. This house is located on Blackwood-Clementon Road and is listed on the National Register of Historic Places in the state of New Jersey as the oldest structure in the state that is still standing. (Courtesy of Burt Warren Cheeseman.)

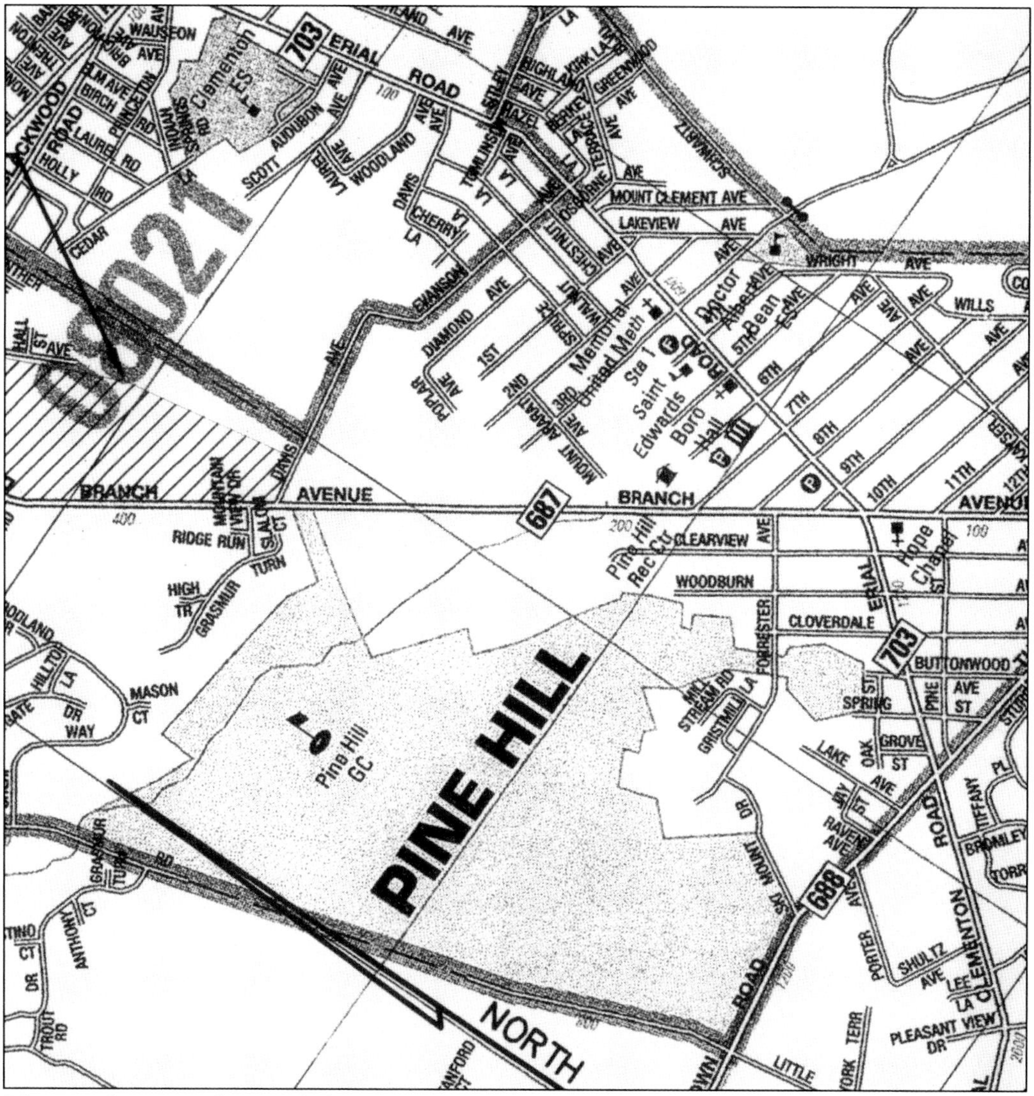

This is only a partial map of what is known as the borough of Pine Hill. Today the town covers 4.1 square miles and is land locked on all sides with no room for expansion. (Courtesy of Les Gallagher Sr.)

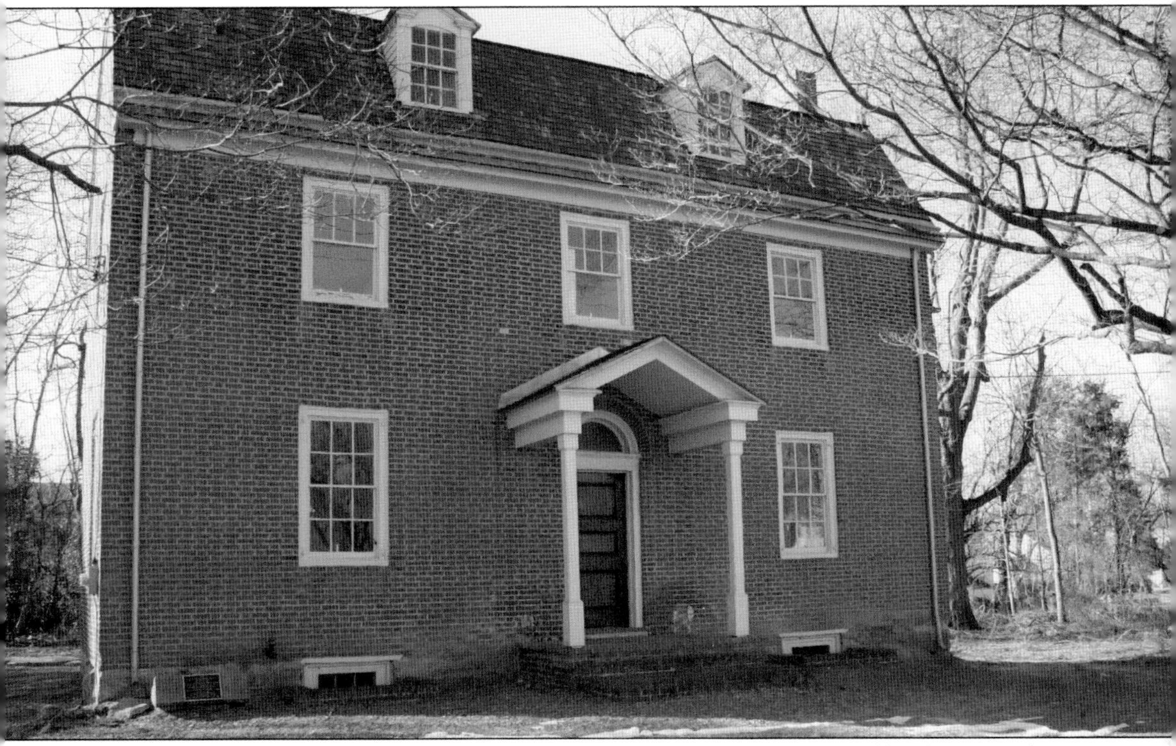

The Tomlinson House was built in 1844 and is the oldest structure in Pine Hill today. It was home to one of the most prominent early families in the community. Isaac Tomlinson established a grist mill on Little Mill Road not far from where the house sits today, and as the economy of the region began to develop, so did his business. A short journey through the woods from the side of the house will lead to the Tomlinsons' graveyard. The Tomlinson family members have been buried there since the early 1800s, and their tombstones can still be viewed today. (Courtesy of Burt Cheeseman.)

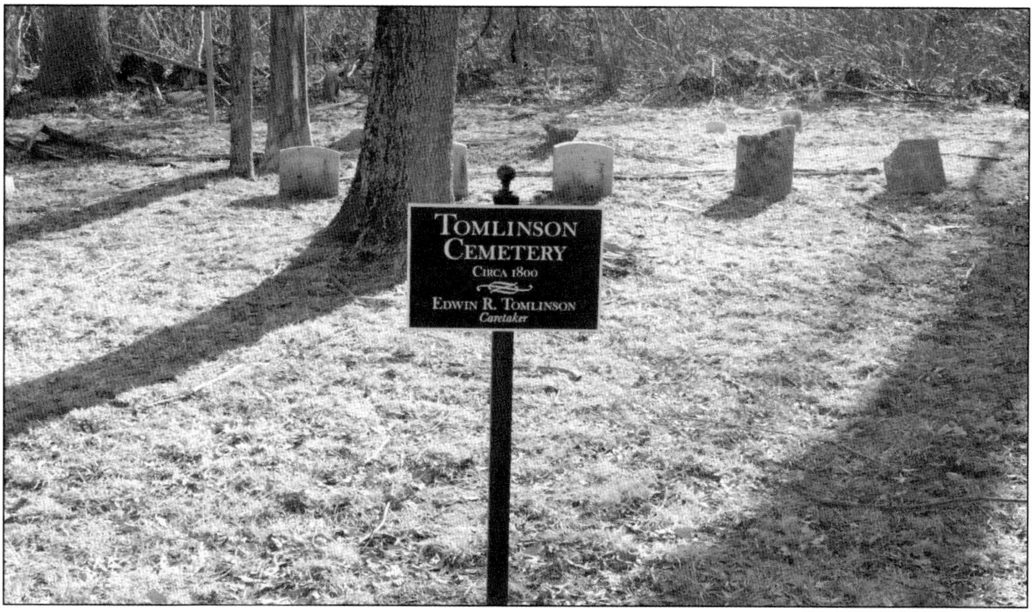

The Tomlinson Cemetery, which is now visible from New Road, is under the care of Edwin R. Tomlinson and Burt Cheeseman. These two men are descendants of Joseph Tomlinson, who was the first member of the family to come to America. The family has been buried at this cemetery since the early 1800s; there are hundreds of graves, but only a few markers remain. (Courtesy of Les Gallagher Jr.)

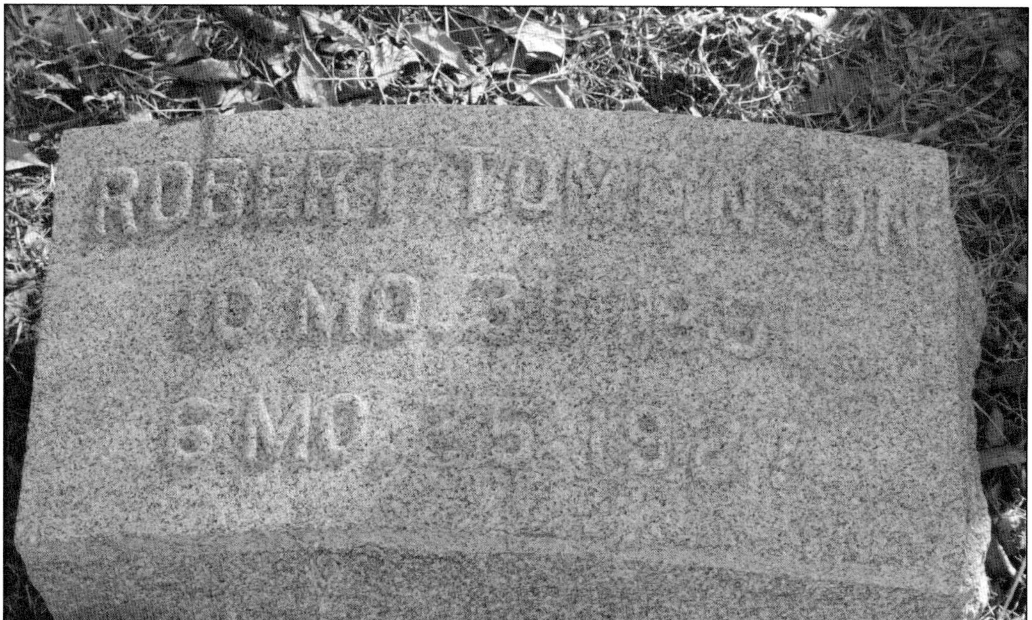

The tombstone of Robert Tomlinson, who was born in October 1851, can be seen very clearly today. Robert was the sixth generation of the Tomlinson family to live in America after his great grandfather three times removed had immigrated to the United States. He was the last registered owner of the property now known as the Tomlinson House. (Courtesy of Les Gallagher Jr.)

Frederick Osborne purchased the Osborne Tract in 1910. The land borders Pine Valley Golf Club and extends from Sitley Avenue to Fourth Avenue. In 1914, Mr. and Mrs. Osborne lived in their home on Spruce Lane. At that time, Pine Hill was Clementon Heights. Mr. Osborne use to call it "the Pines" for short. (Courtesy of Glen Osborne Suydam.)

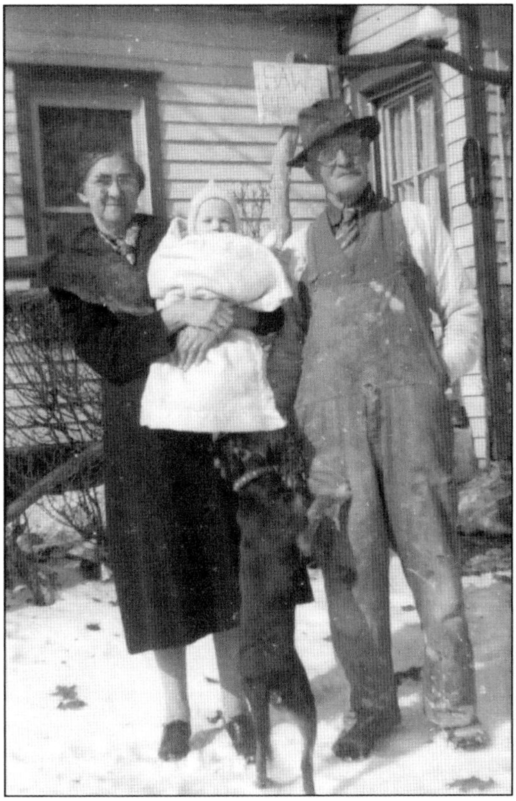

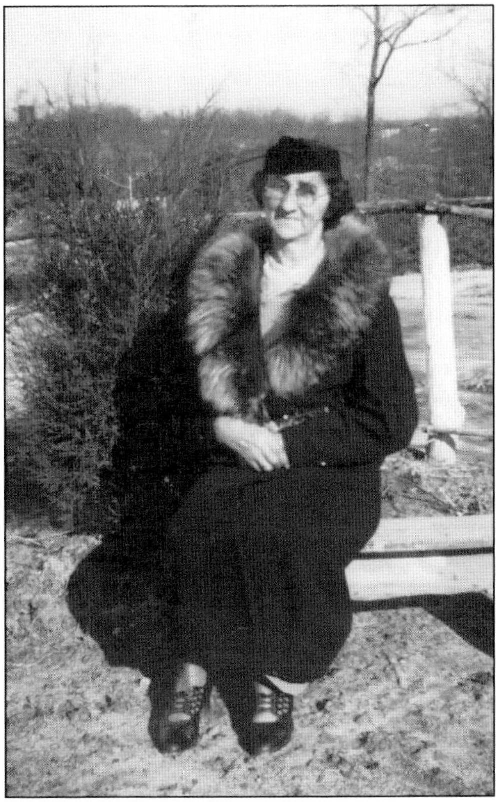

Before the Osborne home was built on Spruce Lane, they lived in a makeshift house with no running water. Mrs. Osborne had to use an outside hand pump for water and carry her water back to the house every day for drinking and laundry. She is pictured at left sitting in her yard in 1914. (Courtesy of Glen Osborne Suydam.)

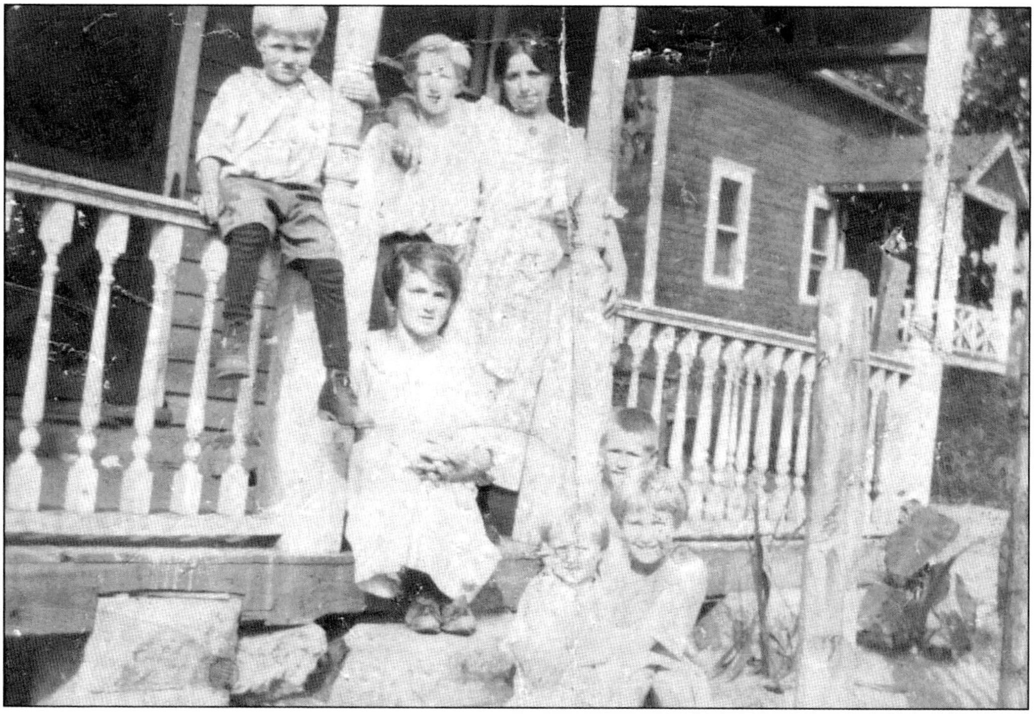

Alice Kennedy and her children pose on their front porch in the 1920s. They lived on Fifth Avenue. The Kennedy family was part of the early settlers who moved to Clementon Heights (Pine Hill). Mr. Kennedy was a volunteer fireman for No. 1 fire department in the 1920s. (Courtesy of Evelyn Krantz.)

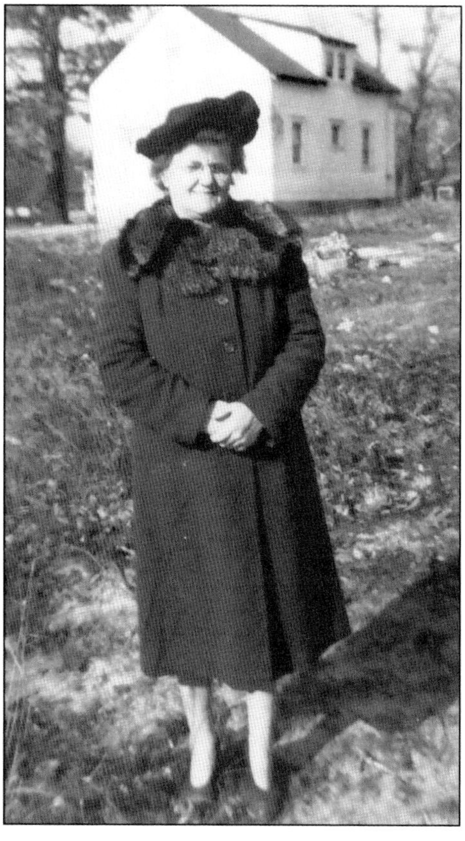

This picture is of Alice Kennedy in her yard on East Fifth Avenue in Pine Hill in 1929. The house in the background was on Fourth Avenue; it had been remodeled. Well into the 1940s, Pine Hill had dirt roads, and many homes were only used as summer vacation retreats. (Courtesy of Evelyn Krantz.)

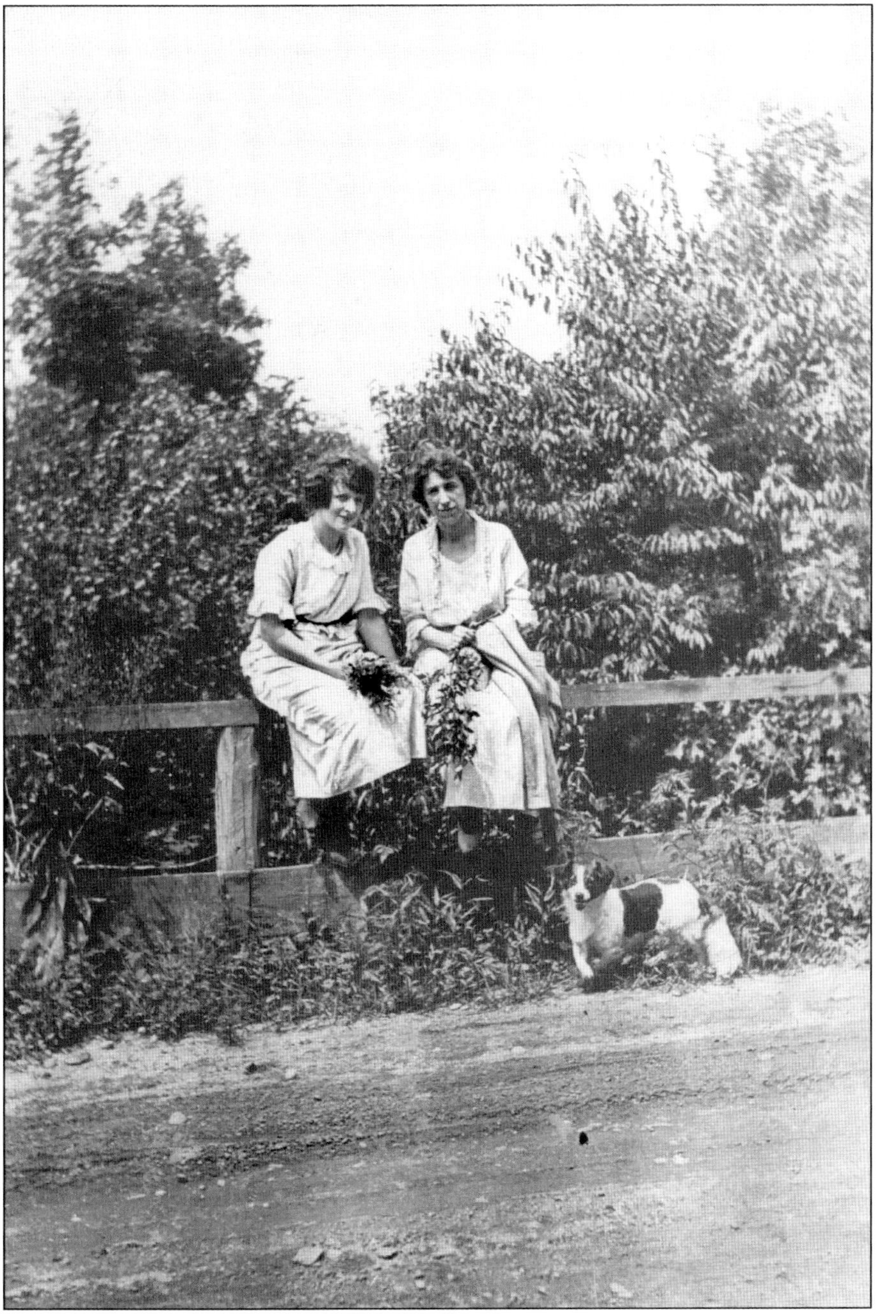

Mary Thumm (left) and Evedine Thumm are on the bridge on West Cloverdale Avenue and Erial Road in the 1920s. A stream passed under the bridge to Stecky's Lake and Pine Hill Park. During the hot summer months, the children of Pine Hill would go to park at the lake to stay cool and have fun. The entry fee was 10¢, which entitled one to use the lockers, showers, changing rooms, and the lake to have fun and cool off. The stream was also a good place to go fishing for brown trout. To this day, it is the only area in South Jersey where brown trout are found in a natural habitat, but no one can fish for that particular fish because they are endangered. (Courtesy of Mable Thumm.)

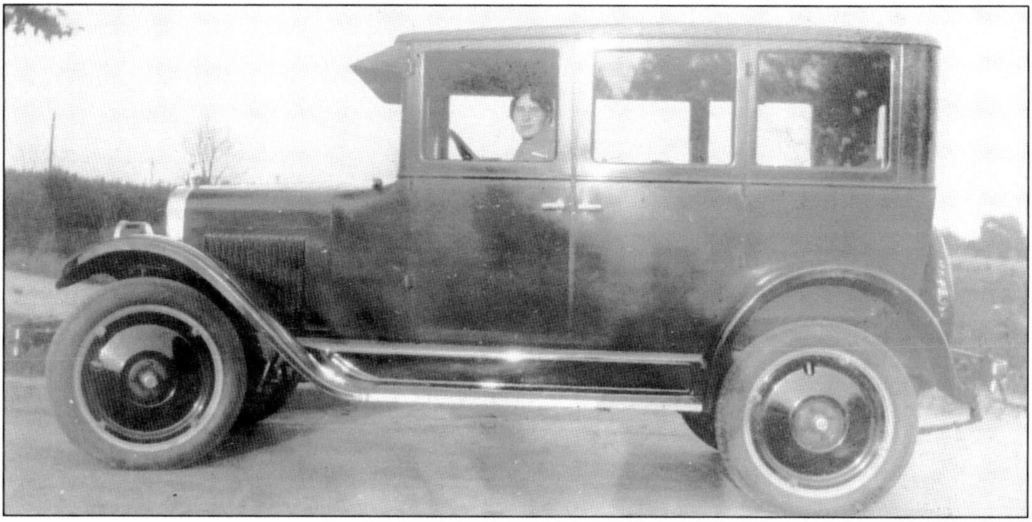

In the 1920s, not many people in town had cars. Here is Mrs. Smith in her 1924 Ford. The Smiths farmed part of the Osborne Tract that stretched from Sitley Avenue to Third Avenue and ran along the border which is now Pine Valley. To farm, one needed a vehicle to pick up the much-needed supplies to keep the farm going, so most farmers had some kind of transportation. (Courtesy of Mary Gallagher.)

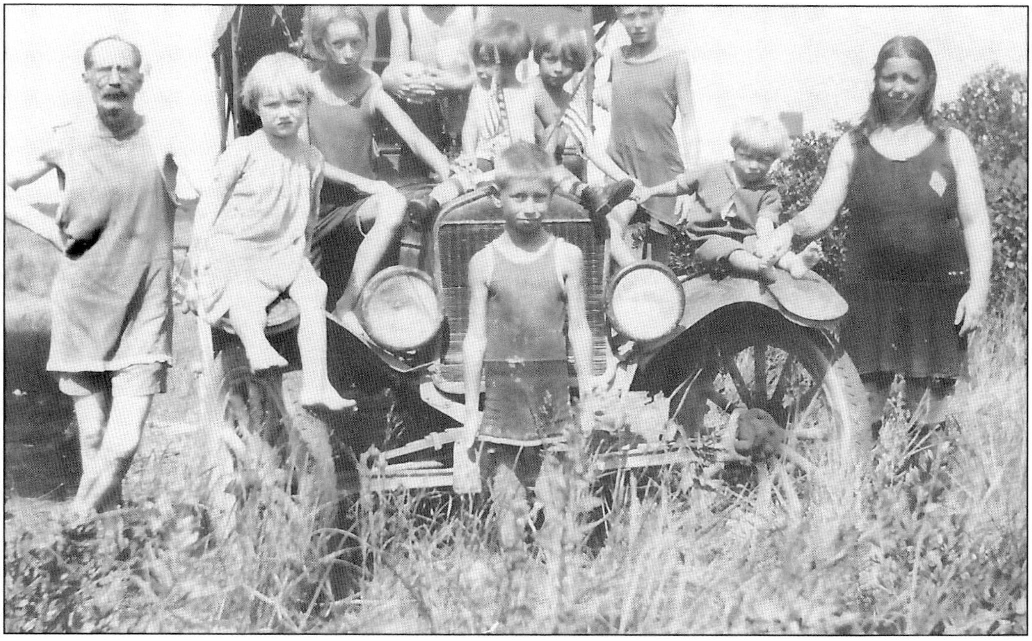

In 1926, on a hot summer day, three families prepare for a day at Stecky's Lake. Dressed in their swimsuits, Mr. Dick is on the left side of the car with Mrs. Baer on the right, and in the middle, mostly seated on the front of the car, are the children from the Dick, Baer, and Kennedy families. (Courtesy of Mary Gallagher.)

Elly Fisher stands at the edge of the water at Stecky's Lake in 1928. A dam was erected to form the lake by Mr. Osborne's and Captain Hudson's home in the early 1900s. With the development of the lake located on West Cloverdale Avenue, tourism came to Pine Hill. The lake had lockers, showers, and changing rooms for use with a 10¢ admission fee. (Courtesy of Ida Fisher.)

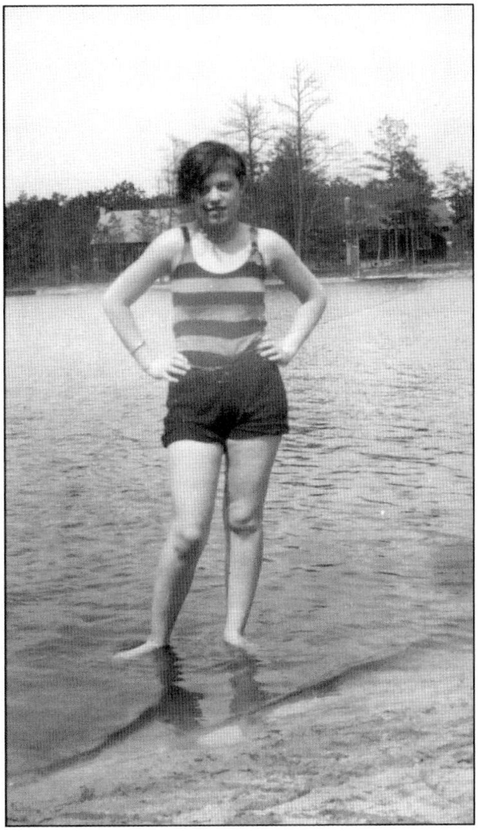

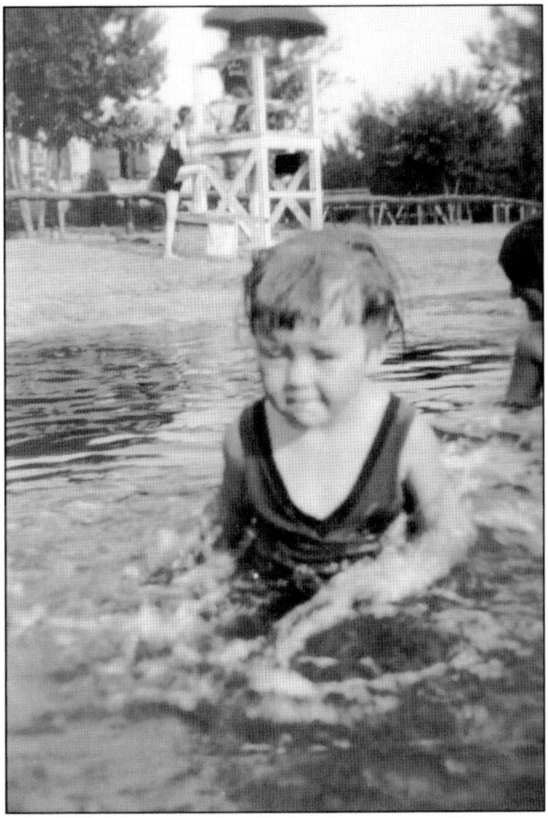

Mary Elizabeth Hofacker can be seen at left splashing around the lake at the age of three (July 1932). Mary remembers the summers to be so much fun. Pine Hill capitalized on tourism in the 1930s with the development of Stecky's Lake on Cloverdale Avenue. It proved to be a popular resort until a fire destroyed it in 1945. (Courtesy of Mary Gallagher.)

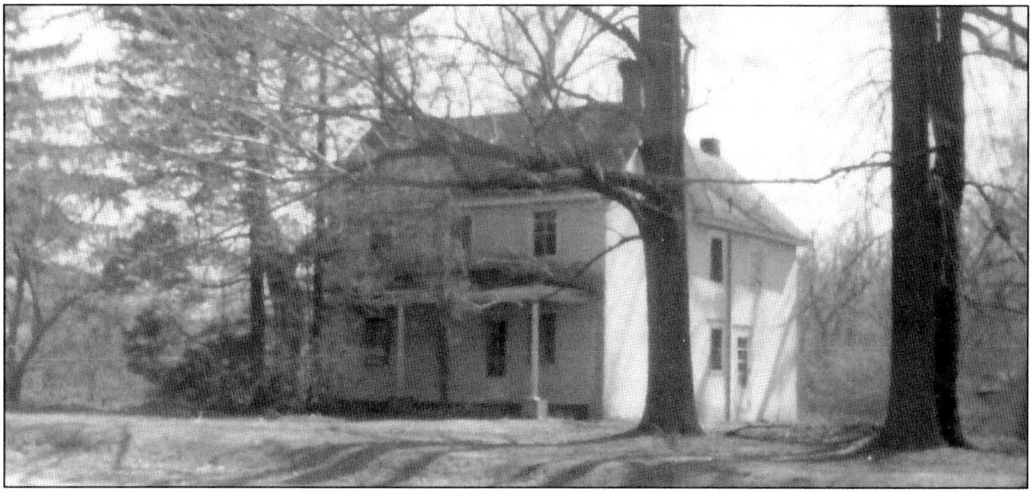

Warren (Burt) Cheeseman was born in this house in 1930; the house was located a stones throw from the Tomlinson House on Blackwood-Clementon Road. Burt's mother was Sara B. Tomlinson Cheeseman, a direct descendant of Isaac Tomlinson. She married Nelson Cheeseman in the early 1900s and built the house where they raised their family. (Courtesy of Warren Burt Cheeseman.)

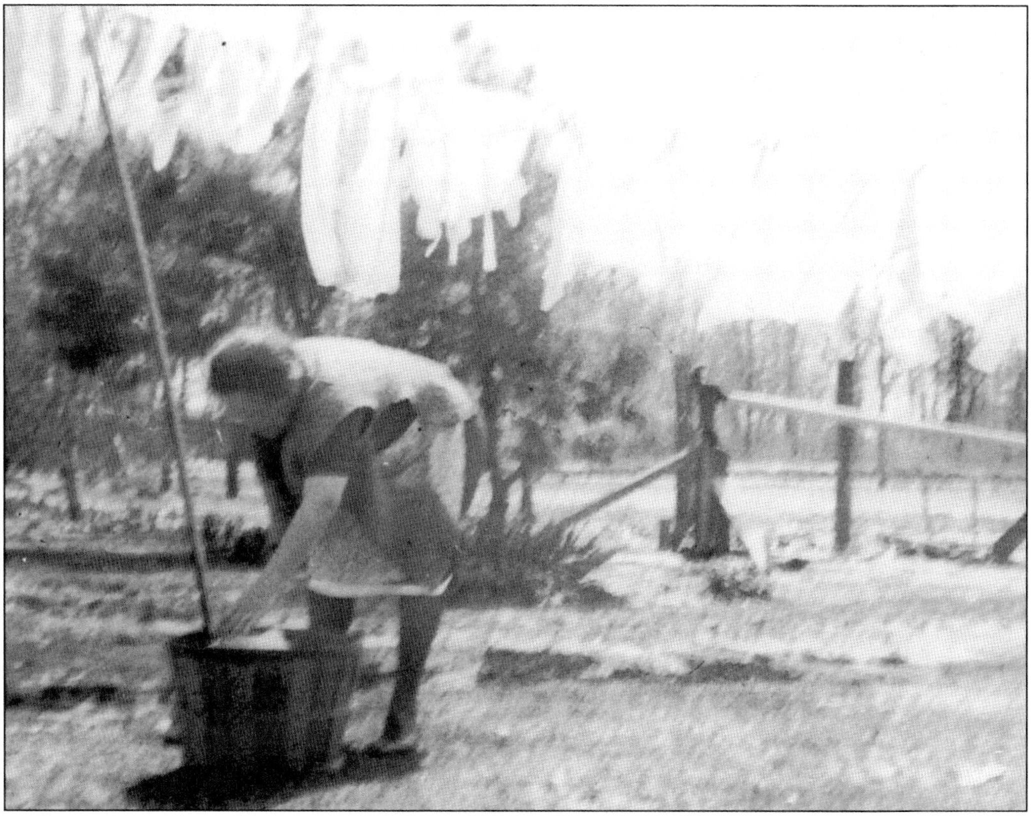

In 1937, Florence Fisher was in her yard hanging the laundry to dry in the breeze. The clothesline had to stretch so far that one had to use a clothes pole to hold up the weight of the wet clothes. The hand pump can be seen in the back near the fence. There was no indoor plumbing; instead, water was carried inside. (Courtesy of Ida Fieger.)

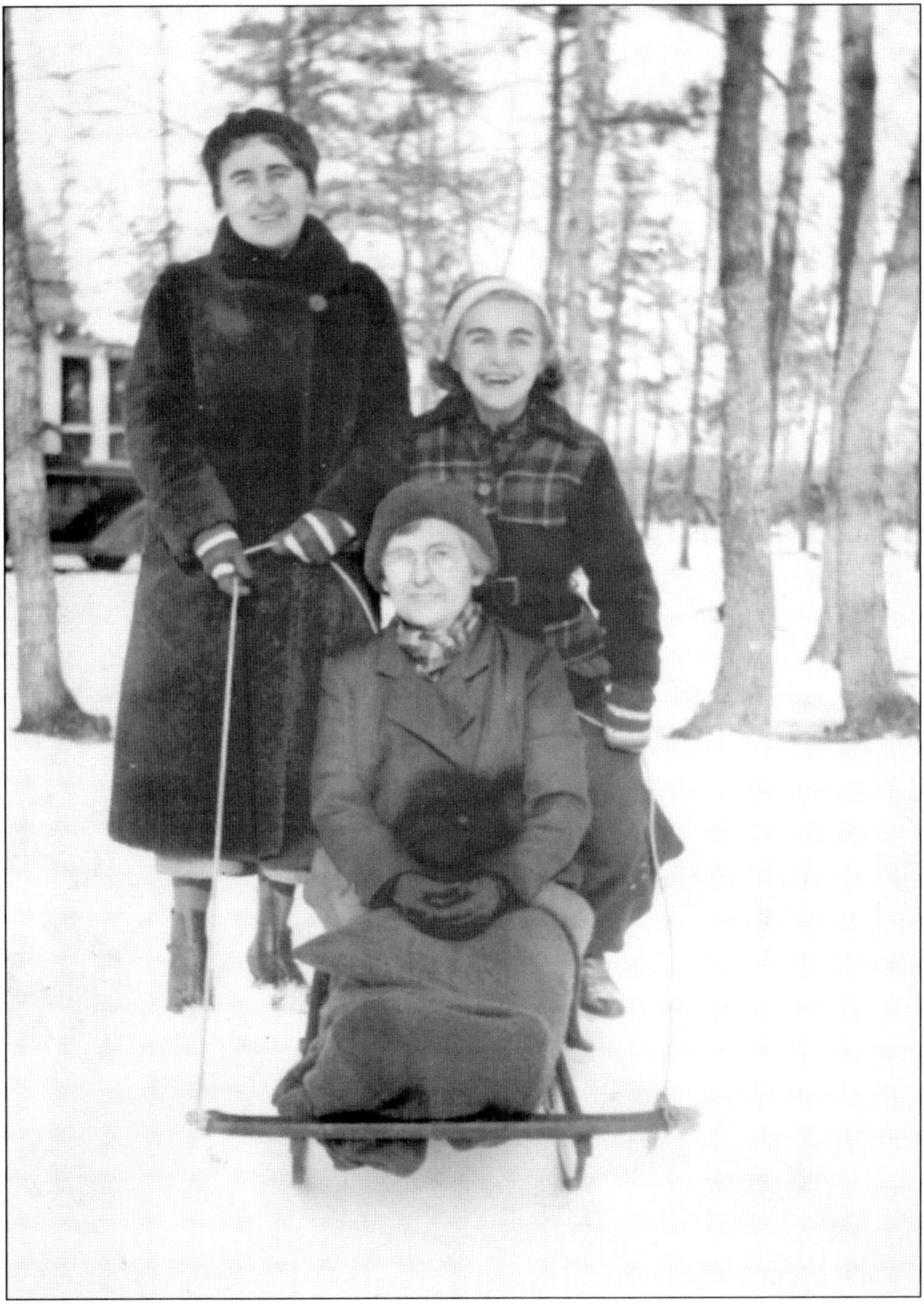

This photograph shows the Meinhardt family on Third Avenue getting ready for sledding during the winter of 1936. The snowstorm made it unsafe to drive up the hills coming into town, so the borough blocked off Branch Avenue at the top of the hill for sledding. It was too dangerous to sled down Erial Road, because it was way too steep. Even grandma Meinhardt was ready to go sledding with her big smile. The local store on the corner did not close during storms, because they knew that residents would walk there even when it snowed. (Courtesy of Mary Gallagher.)

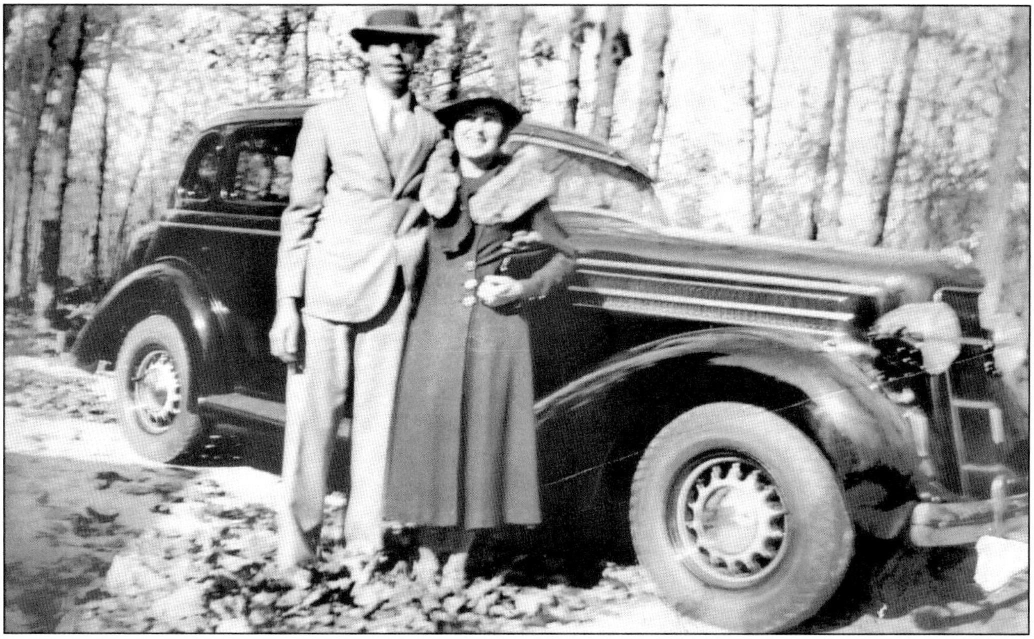

Mr. and Mrs. Meinhardt are shown in this 1946 photograph by their 1935 Plymouth. After returning from a drive through the countryside, they had to drive up Erial Road backwards, as the hill coming into town was so high that only the four-cylinder Dodge and Chevy could make it up the hill going forward. The hill on Erial Road was so steep that they later cut off the top and lowered the road. (Courtesy of Mary Gallagher.)

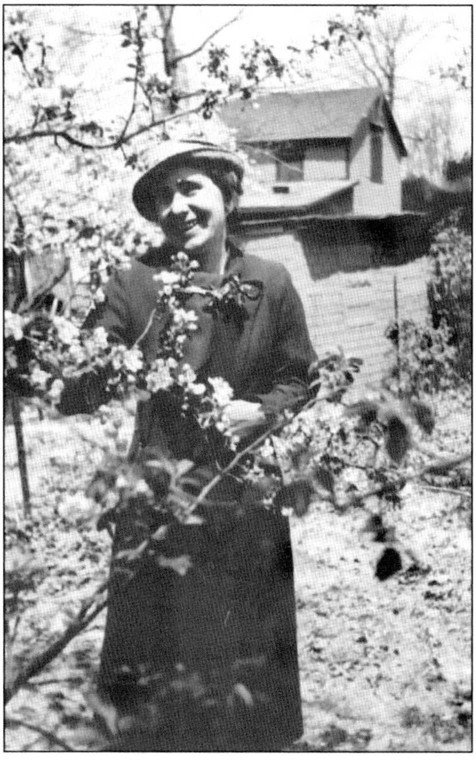

This photograph was taken of Mrs. Meinhardt in her backyard on East Third Avenue in May 1938. Some say springtime is the best time of the year in Pine Hill with the smell of the fresh air and sweet flowers in bloom. The house in the background was a summer cottage where families came to stay in the summer. (Courtesy of Mary Gallagher.)

The Meinhardt sisters are posing in front of a tree in July 1939 on East Third Avenue. The sisters loved those hot summer days going to Stecky's Lake. Pine Hill was a great town to grow up in because it came to life in the summertime. People came from all over to visit those who owned summer homes in town, and the lake would come to life with residents and visitors. (Courtesy of Mary Gallagher.)

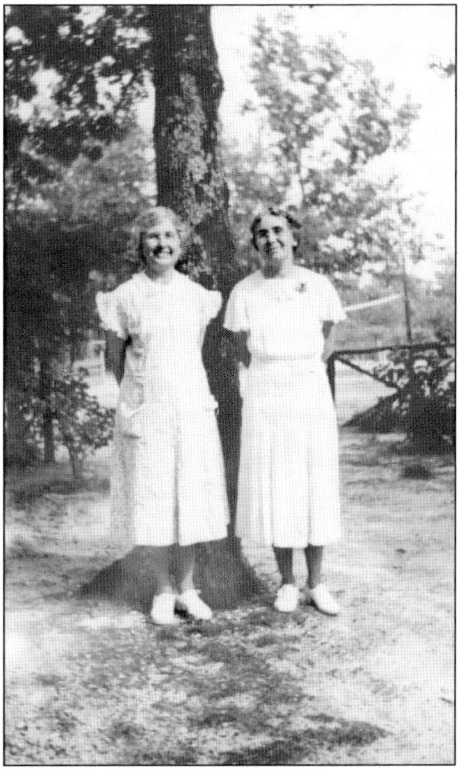

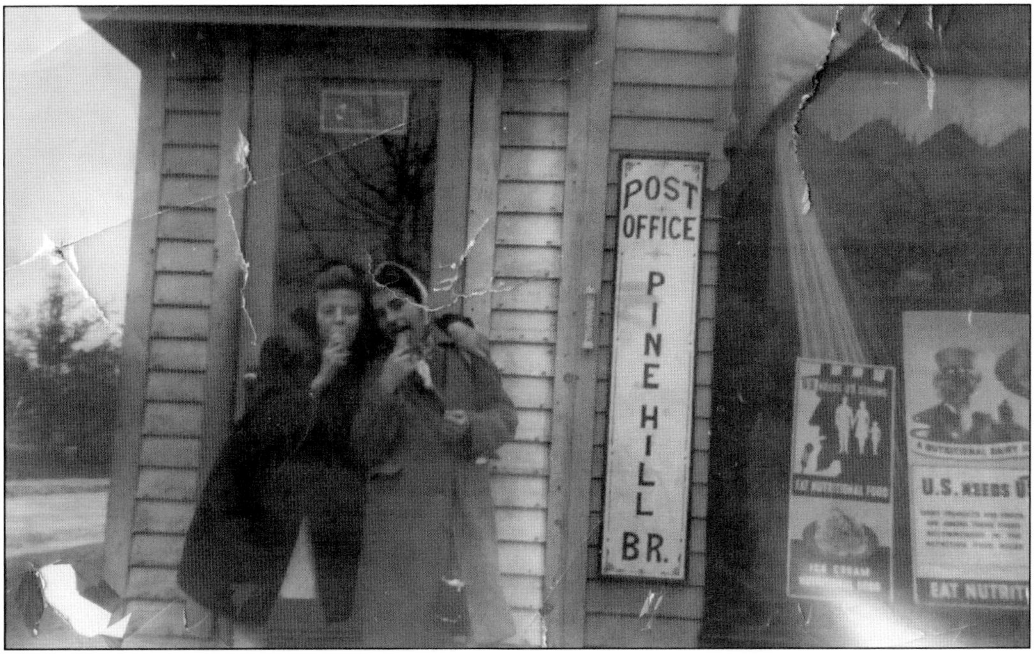

In 1939, Dot Thumm (left) and Pearl Kergides enjoying ice cream in front of the Pine Hill Post Office on West Ninth Avenue. Johanna and Gus Berton owned the post office and the Berton Store. They sold stamps, money orders, and individual P.O. boxes, and everyone could also enjoy ice cream and fountain sodas. (Courtesy of Ellen Kerby.)

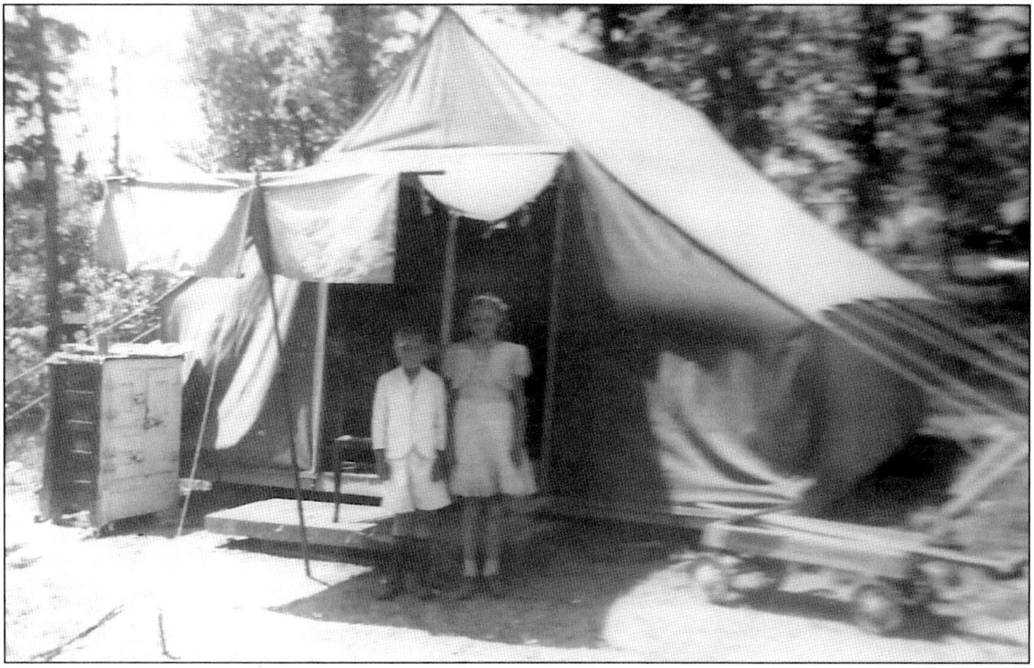

In May 1939, the Keifer family had to pitch a tent on the land that they purchased from Mrs. McFeely. They had to live in the tent while Ed Keifer (the father) built their home. They used an icebox outside the tent to store food. The property was located on East Woodburn Avenue. The children had fun playing in the woods and white sand while their parents built the house. (Courtesy of Ellen Kerby.)

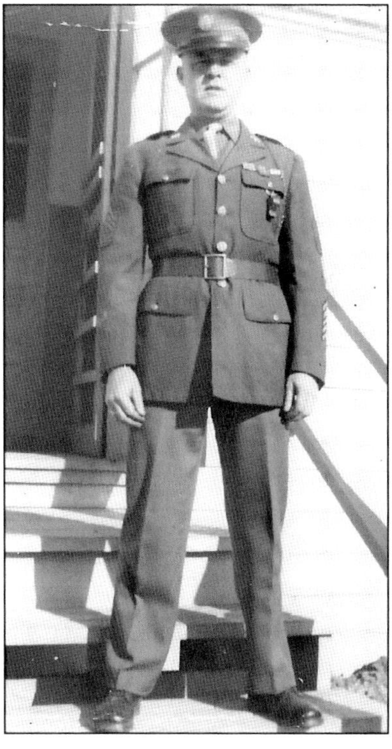

This photograph shows George Hofacker home on leave from the army in the 1940s. He was one of the World War II servicemen from Pine Hill. He lived on East Fourth Avenue, and at that time, his family was only one of the 506 families who lived in town full time. The other residents only lived in Pine Hill in the summer. (Courtesy of Mary Gallagher.)

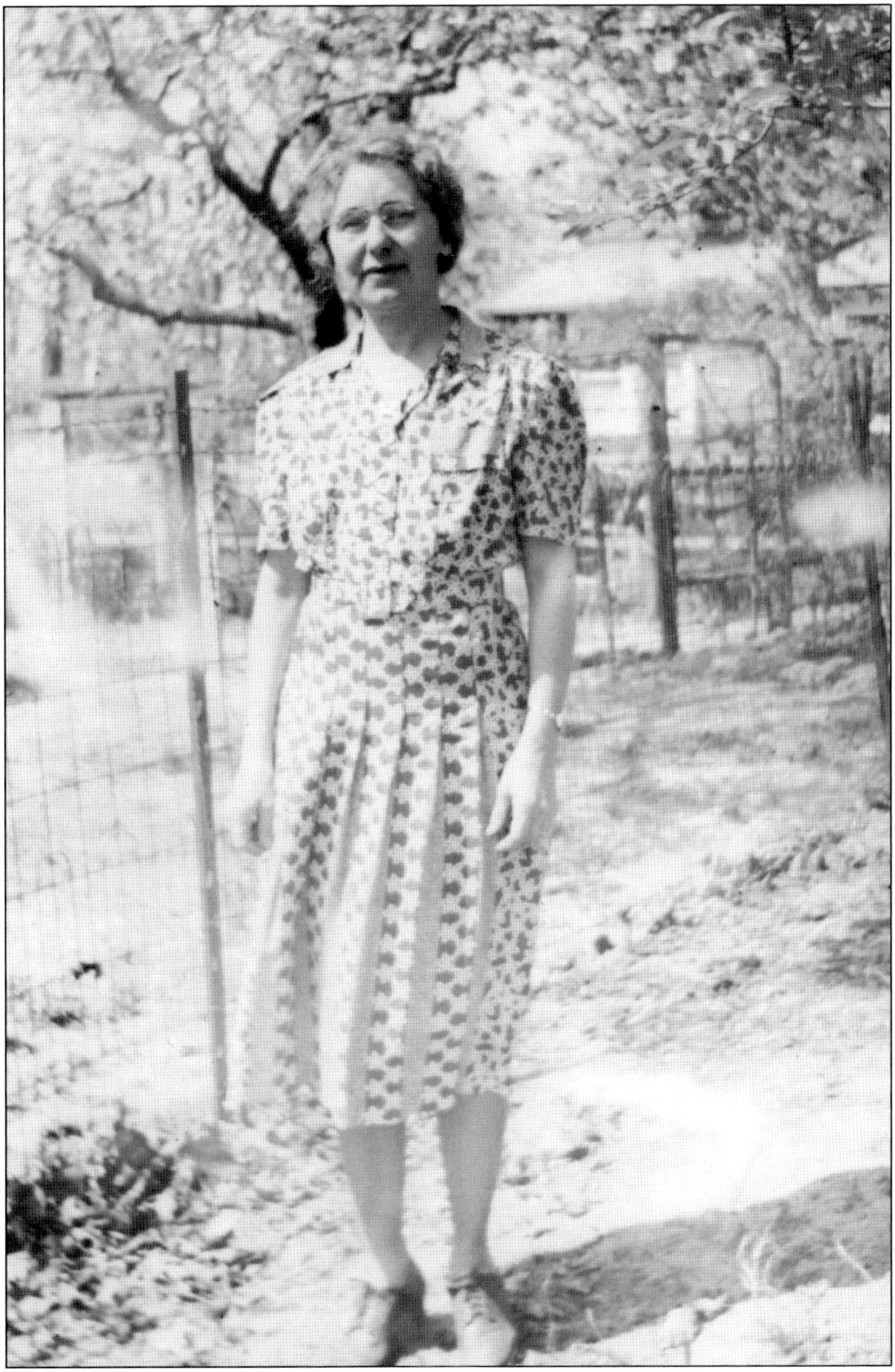

In her backyard on Third Avenue in Pine Hill stands Mrs. Meinhardt in the early 1940s. The white sand in Pine Hill made it hard to grow grass and difficult to grow a garden, so Mr. Van Dexter would deliver fresh fruit and vegetables from his homegrown garden by horse and buggy. (Courtesy of Mary Gallagher.)

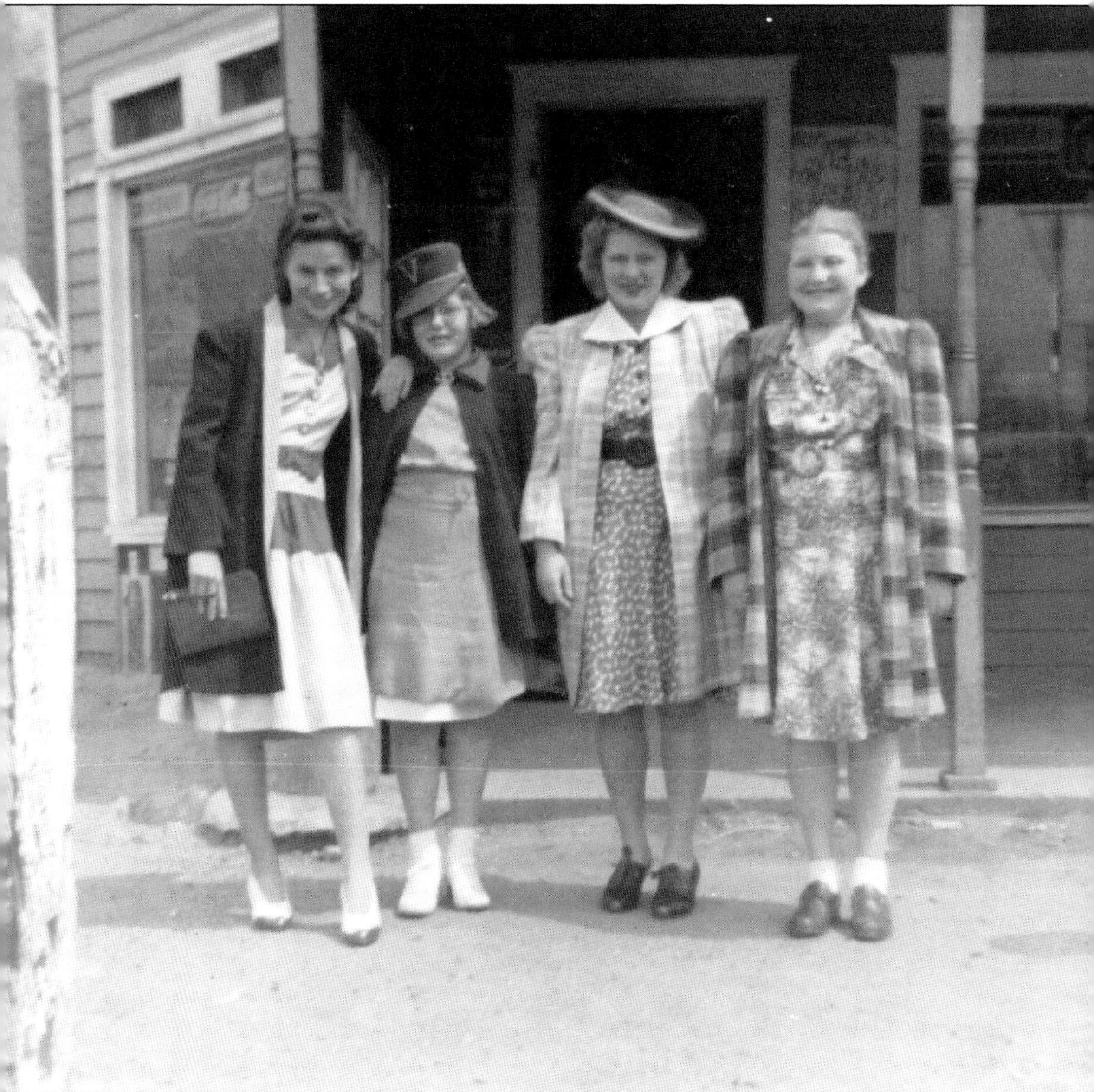

Standing from left to right in front of Johnson's Store in 1942 are Dot Thumm, Harriett Johnson, Zudggie Schreiver, and June Johnson. Located on Branch and Erial Road, Johnson's was the local hot spot for teens to gather when not at the lake. Everyone went to Johnson's Store to buy candy and hang out with friends for good times and good laughs. At that time, the roads were not paved but were mainly dirt and cinder. The old corner store has since been replaced, first with Mulligans, which had penny candy and some other conveniences, and now with a WaWa convenience store, where candy costs much more than a penny. (Courtesy of Mabel Thumm.)

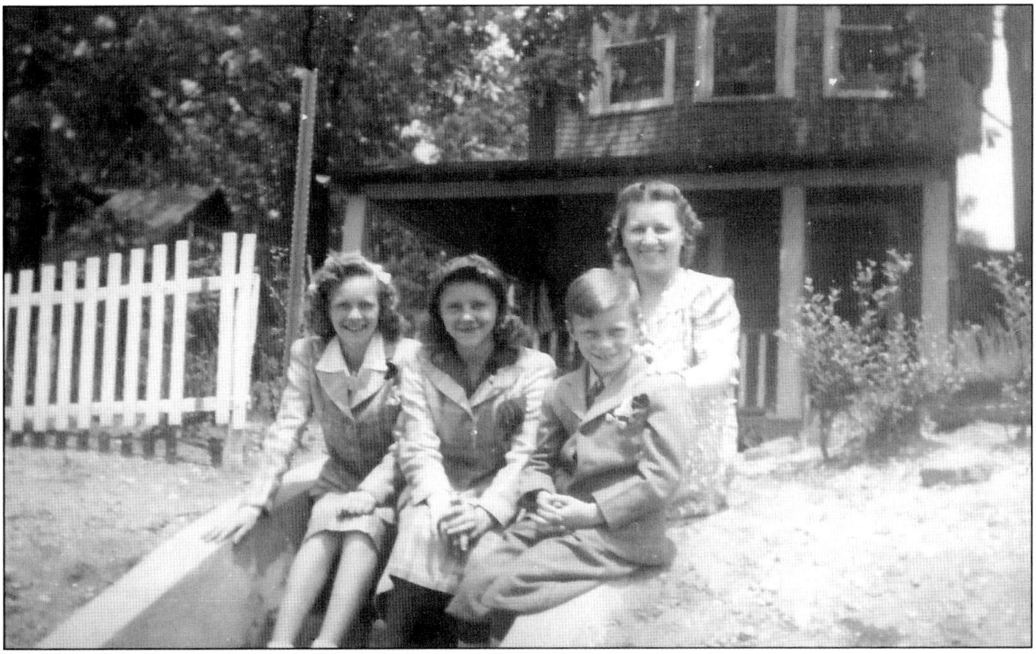

This photograph shows the Hofacker family posing in front of their home in 1943 on West Fourth Avenue in Pine Hill. Mary Hofacker is sitting on her front step with her children, from left to right, Mary, Georgeanna, and George Jr. Mary Hofacker still remembers enjoying that nice spring day with her family. Mary still resides in that home today. (Courtesy of Mary Gallagher.)

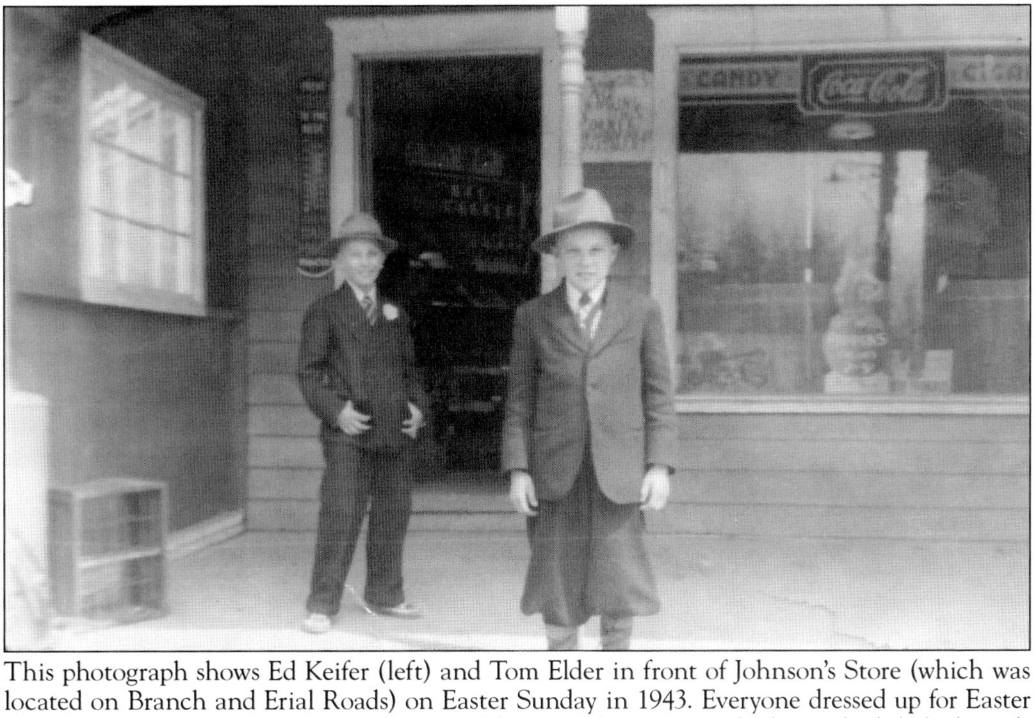

This photograph shows Ed Keifer (left) and Tom Elder in front of Johnson's Store (which was located on Branch and Erial Roads) on Easter Sunday in 1943. Everyone dressed up for Easter church services, and after church, they would go to Johnson's to take home fresh baked goods from the bakery. (Courtesy of Ellen Kerby.)

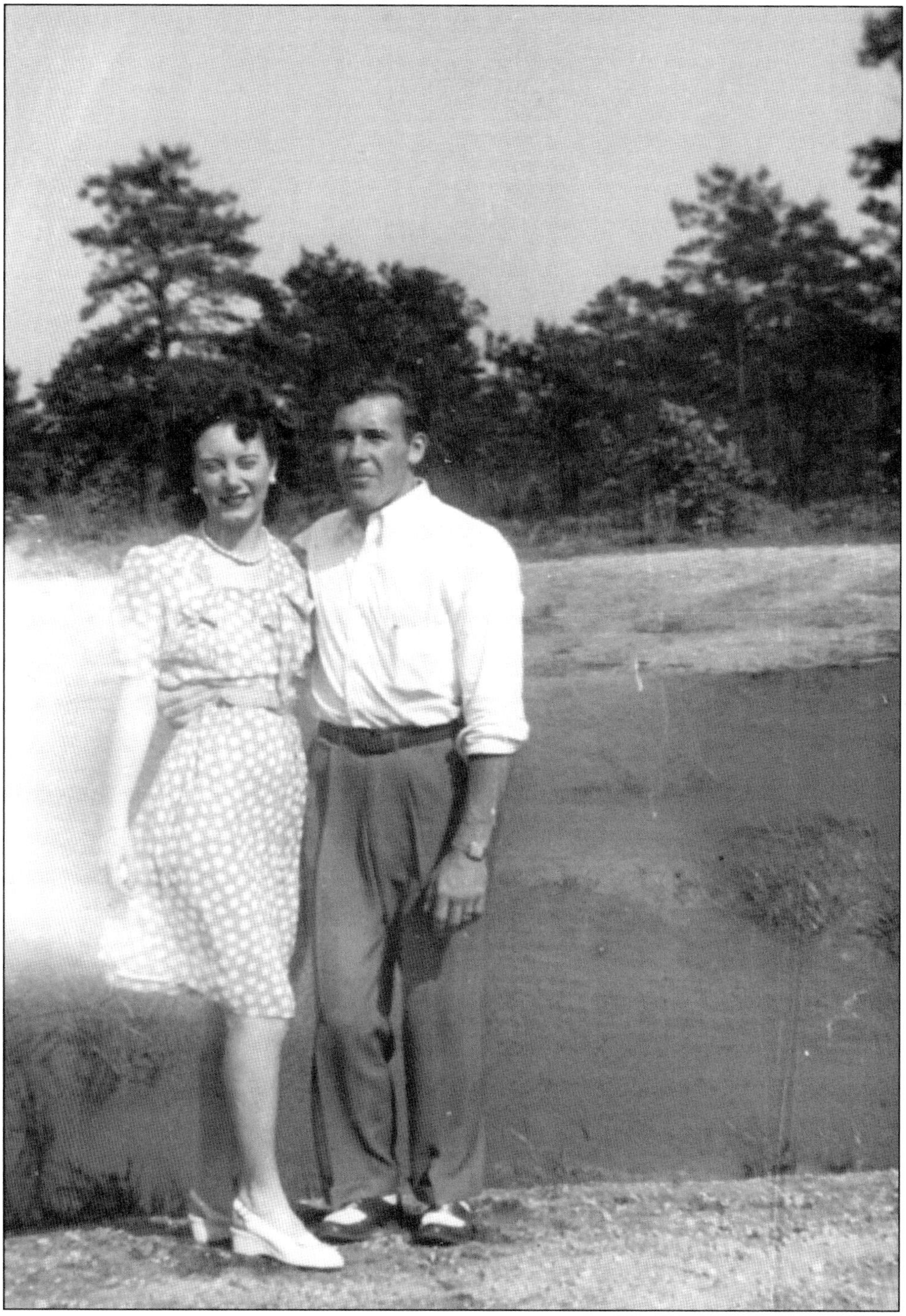

Ida Fisher and Walt Fieger stand at the gravel pit on the corner of Branch and Turnersville Roads. In the 1940s and 1950s, it was where all the teens gathered to hang out and swim. It was filled in not long after Joey Green caught an infection that killed him from swimming there. In Joey's memory, there was a little league field built down the road for the children of Pine Hill to enjoy. (Courtesy of Ida Feiger.)

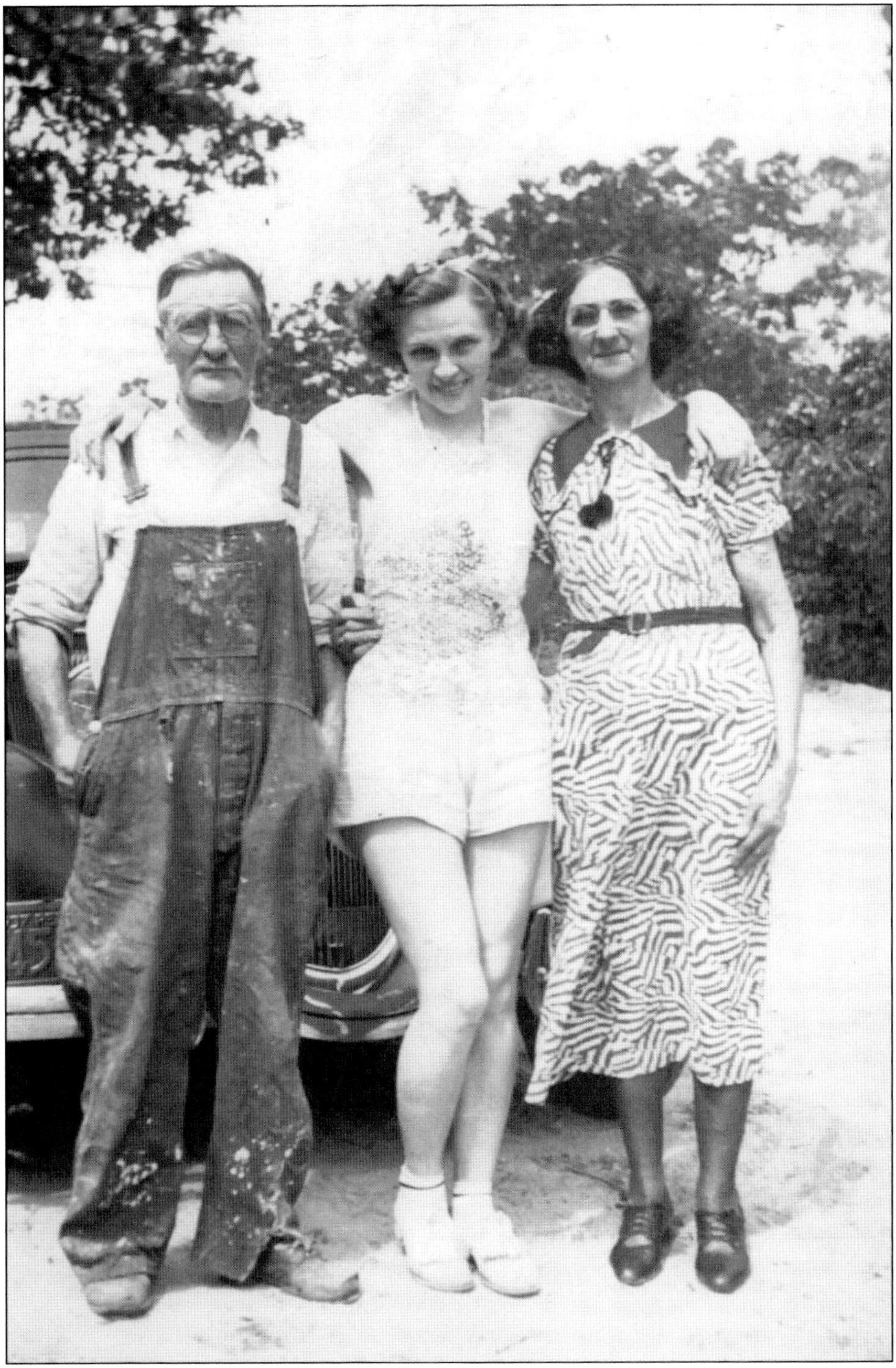

Glen Osborne stands between her mother and father in front of their four-cylinder Dodge in 1950 on Spruce Lane. The car may have been old but it got them where they needed to go. Her father liked the car because when they first arrived at Pine Hill he could drive forward up the hill and did not have to drive up in reverse like others. (Courtesy of Glen Osborne Suydam.)

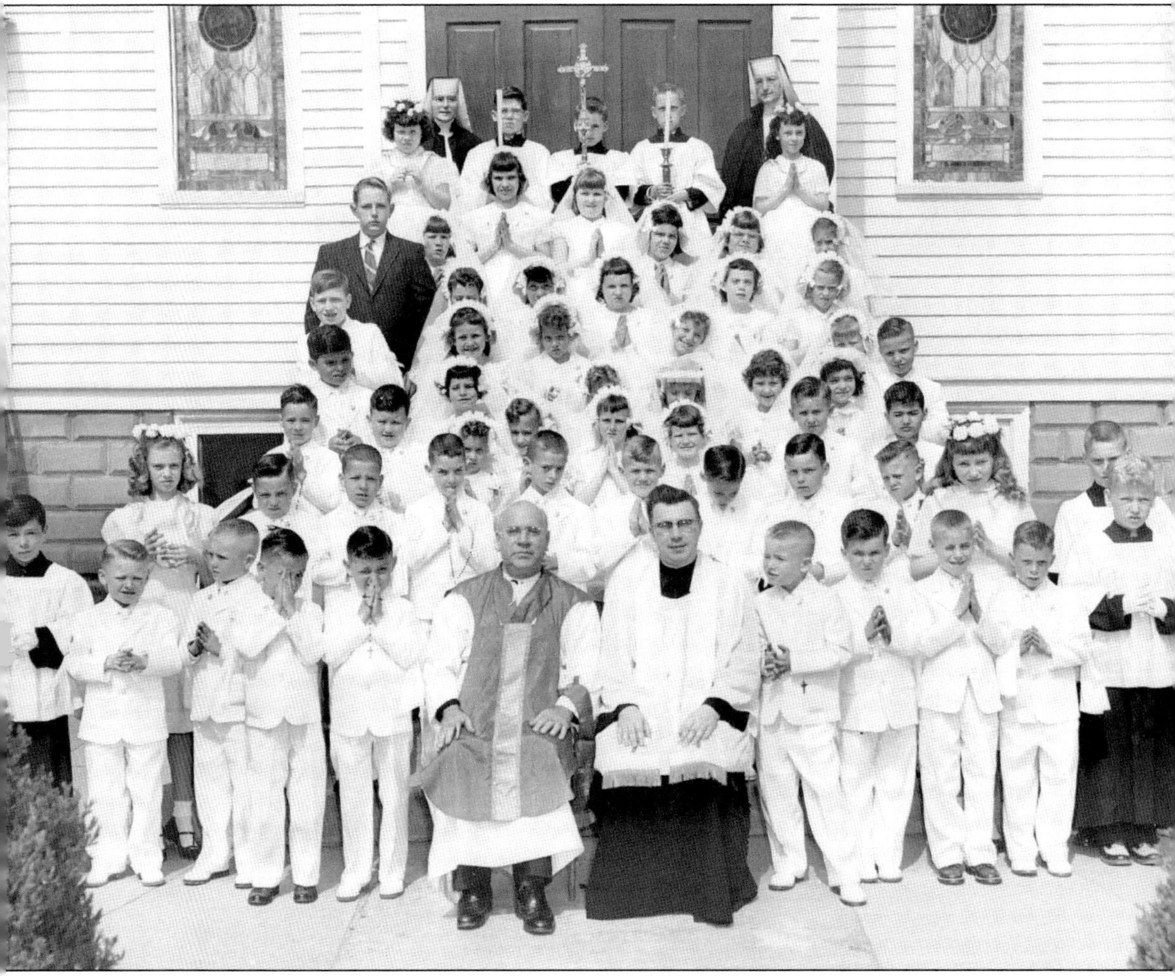

In May 1959, the first communion class of Saint Edward's Catholic Church is pictured at 500 Erial Road. Father Kirk is in the first row with the gray robes. Everyone called him "Father Tut-Tut." Sister Patricia Ann (left) and Sister Ann Stephen are standing in the eighth row. This was the old church that is no longer there. The new church that is standing today was constructed on November 5, 1977. (Courtesy of Mable Thumm.)

Two

FIRE DEPARTMENTS

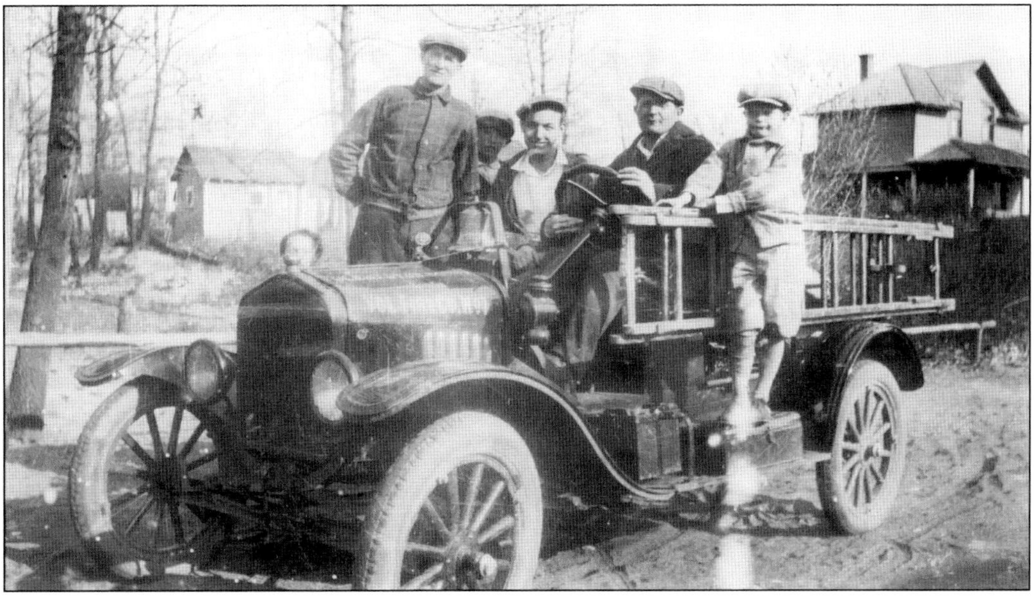

On September 17, 1917, the Pine Hill Fire Department was created. At the time the borough was actually a part of Clementon Township. Thus the first name of the fire department was Clementon Heights No. 1 Volunteer Fire Company. The original firefighting vehicle was a Model-T chemical wagon carrying 85 gallons of soda acid. Pictured on the truck are, from left to right, Sam and Ray Kennedy, Bob Pickup, Charlie Berkey, and one of his children. Farthest left, his head barely visible, is another of Berkley's children. (Courtesy of Evelyn Krantz.)

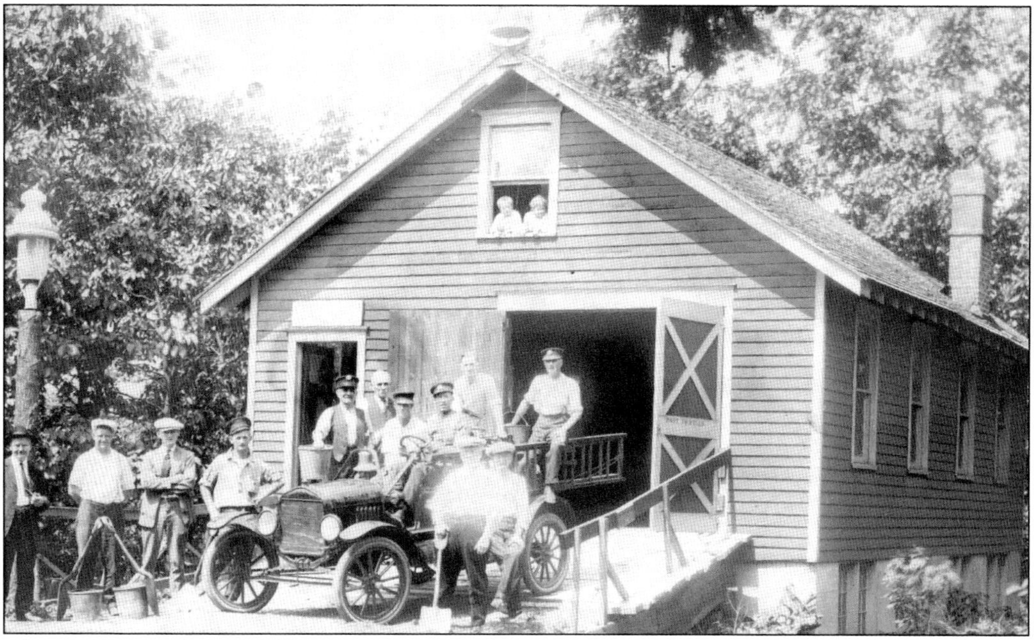

This picture is of Pine Hill No. 1 Fire Station in 1917, which was a one-bay, barn-style building located in the 300 block of Erial Road. This photograph shows the Kennedy children in the small window at the top of the barn. The Kennedy family was one of the first settlers in Pine Hill. (Courtesy of Alice Kennedy.)

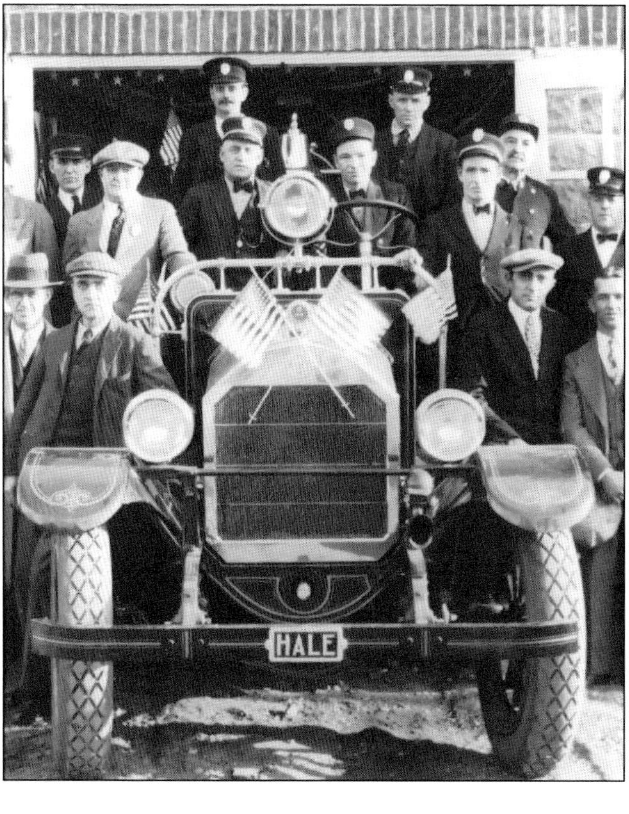

In early 1926, Clementon Township purchased three new Hale 250 GPM rotary gear pumpers. The cost of each unit was approximately $1,200. Somerdale, Marlton, and Clementon Heights companies each received a unit in 1927. This was Pine Hill's first new truck and was painted the customary red, which was damaged the first day out when it ran off the road into the woods. (Courtesy of Bill Dukes.)

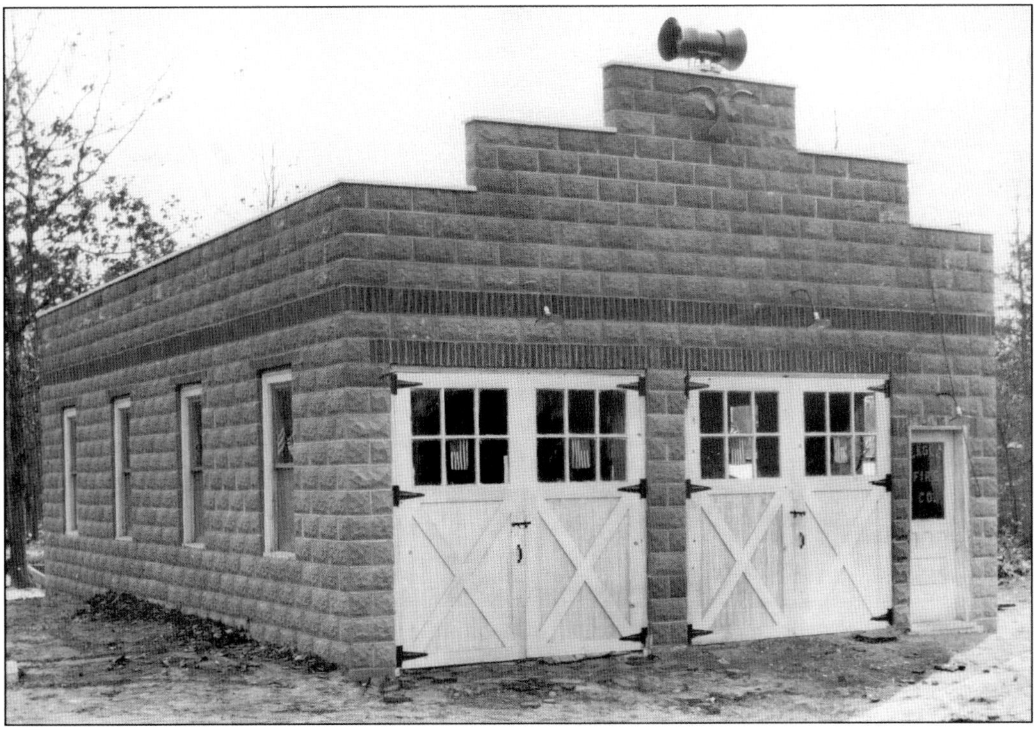

In 1927, the membership split, and a second fire department called Eagle Fire Company was created. Eagle's members constructed the barn-style building on a hillside platform within the 1100 block of Erial Road. The current Pine Hill Fire Company now sits on this site. (Courtesy of Bill Dukes.)

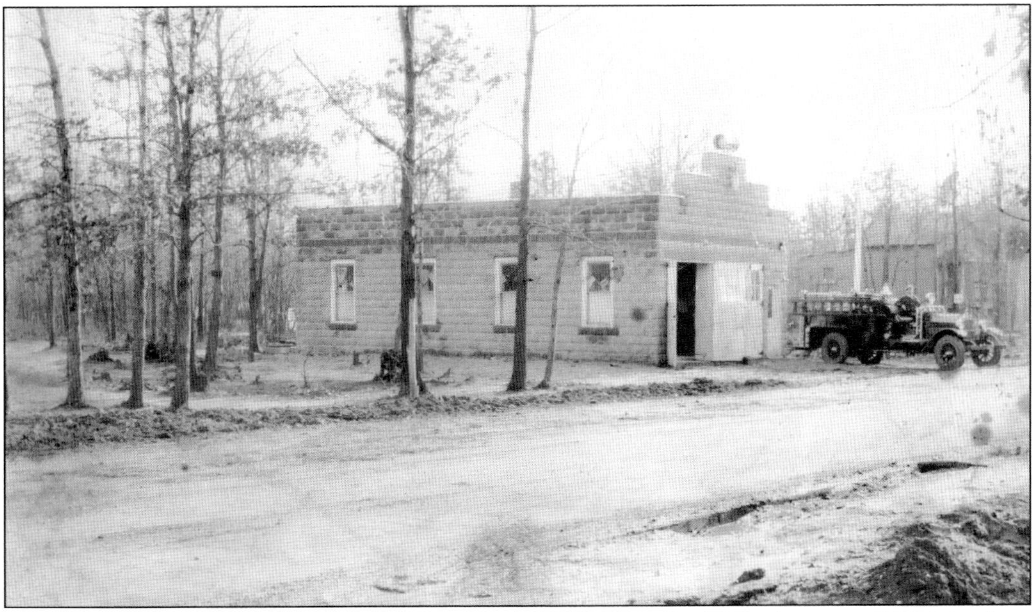

The new Hale fire truck was relocated from Pine Hill No. 1 to Eagle's firehouse in 1928. Members of No. 1 were not using it properly, and the town fathers gave the Eagle Company a chance to do it right. This 1928 photograph shows the 1927 Hale outside of the Eagle Fire Company on Erial Road. (Courtesy of Jim O'Neill.)

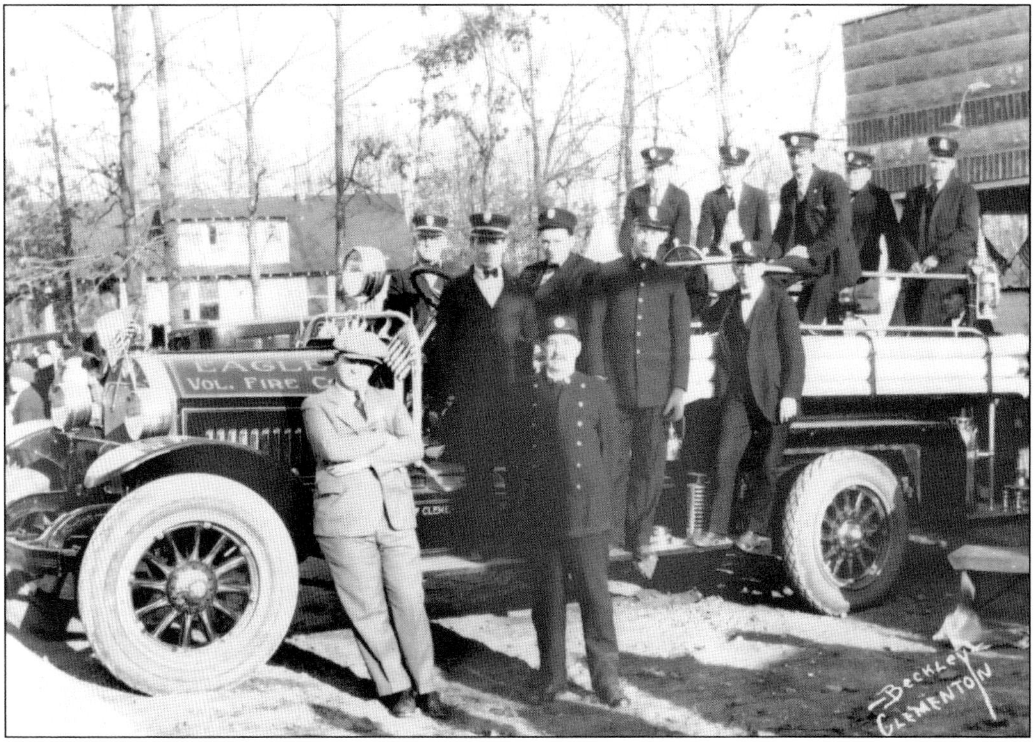

The Borough of Pine Hill seceded from Clementon Township in 1929. However, the Clementon Heights Fire Company maintained its name until May 1936, when the membership voted to become the Eagle Volunteer Fire Company and Pine Hill No. 1. During the 1930s and 1940s, the two fire companies survived on a small appropriation provided by the borough and fund-raisers. Equipment other than the Hale included used units, military surplus, or some home-built apparatus made by members. (Courtesy of Bill Dukes.)

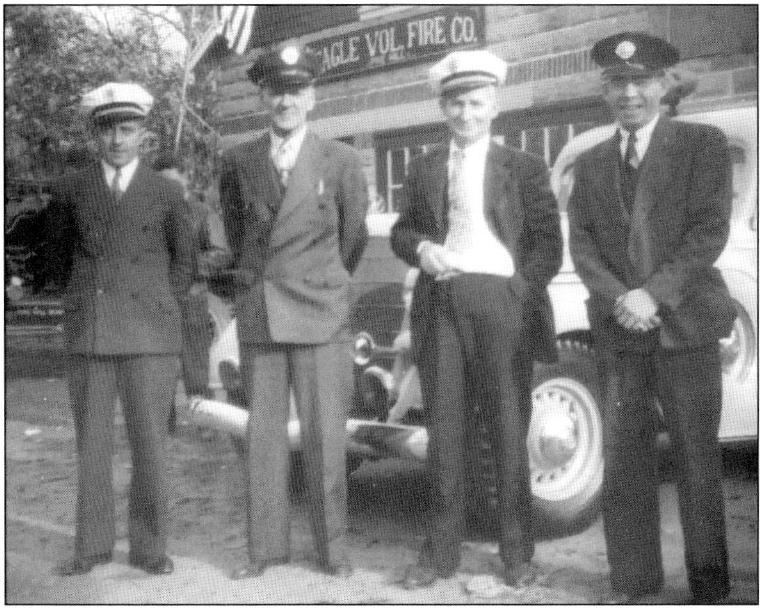

Standing outside Eagle Volunteer Fire Company in 1942 are, from left to right, volunteers Emin Schuller, John Rietz, Walt Hurbert, and unidentified. The department also provided residents with emergency medical services and emergency transportation to the hospital. During social events, the trucks and equipment were moved outside the hall. (Courtesy of Mabel Thumm.)

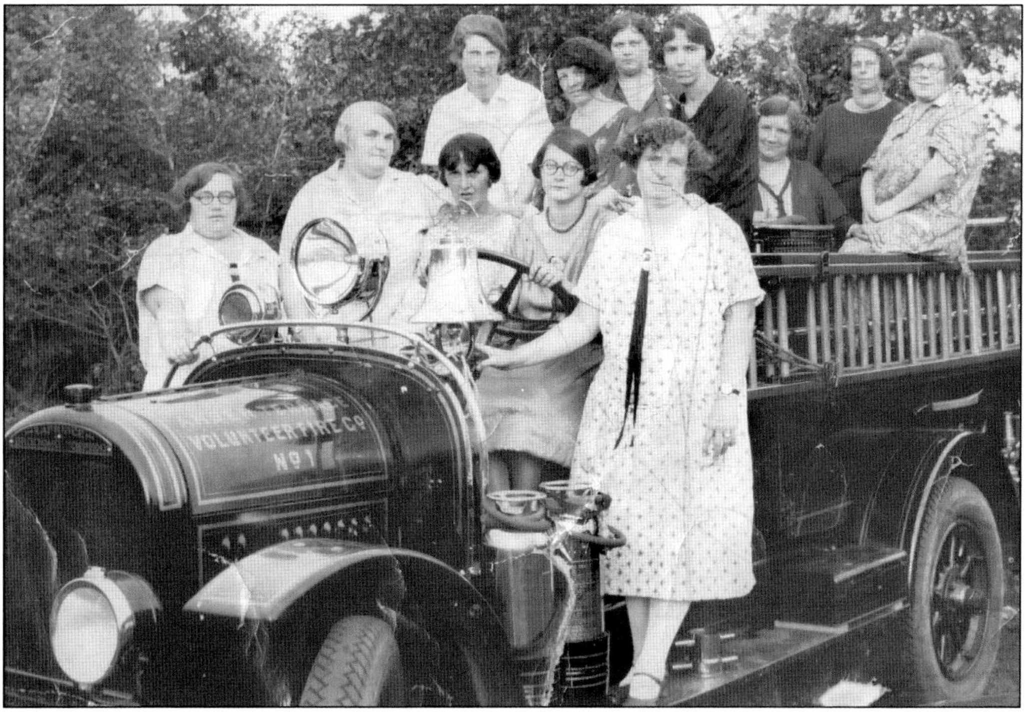

In 1943, a group of citizens living in the far western section of the borough, known as the Amber Terrace section, decided to improve the fire protection of their neighborhood. Amber Terrace Volunteer Fire Company was born. The original fire station was a one-bay station that was actually attached to the Pine Hill Municipal Building, which was then located at the intersection of West Branch Avenue and Cross Road. (Courtesy of Jim Knauth.)

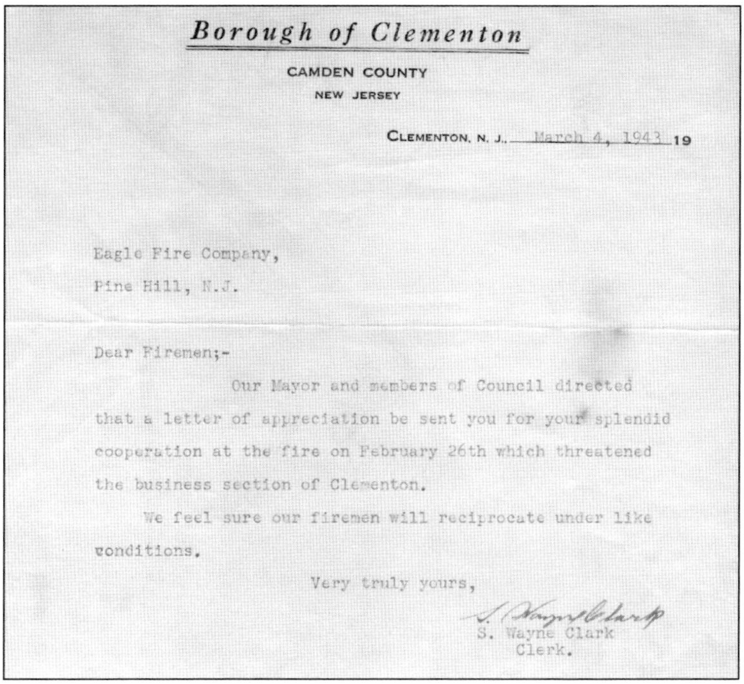

Borough of Clementon

CAMDEN COUNTY
NEW JERSEY

CLEMENTON, N. J., March 4, 1943 19

Eagle Fire Company,
Pine Hill, N.J.

Dear Firemen;-

Our Mayor and members of Council directed that a letter of appreciation be sent you for your splendid cooperation at the fire on February 26th which threatened the business section of Clementon.

We feel sure our firemen will reciprocate under like conditions.

Very truly yours,

S. Wayne Clark
S. Wayne Clark
Clerk.

In 1943, Eagle Fire Company of the borough of Pine Hill came to the aide of the borough of Clementon to fight the fire that was endangering their business section. This is a letter sent to the fire company signed by the borough clerk of Clementon on March 4, 1943, to show their appreciation. (Courtesy of Les Gallagher.)

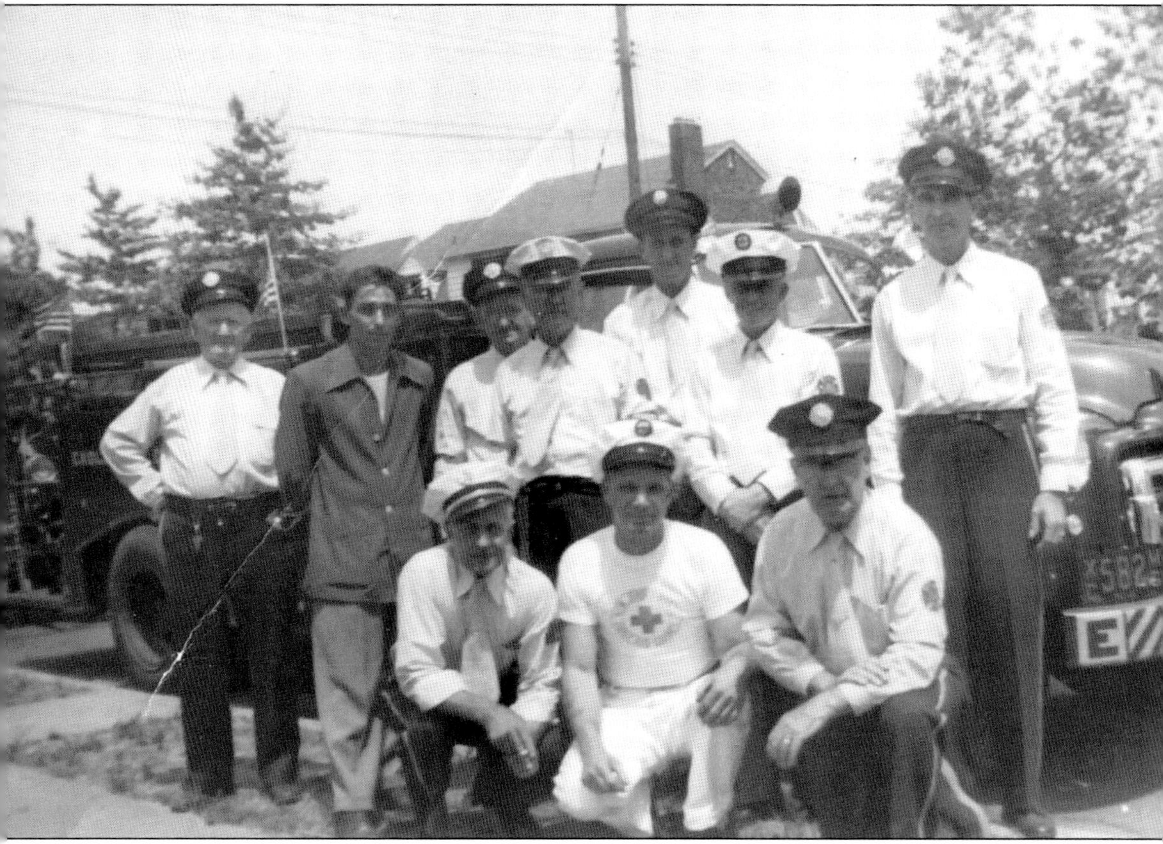

In 1949, volunteer members of the Eagle Fire Company and First Aid Squad stood in front of the company's GMC Pumper. Members in the white hats were the officers, and those in the dark hats were other members. The ambulance driver is in the center with the hospital cross on his shirt. (Courtesy of Jim O'Neill.)

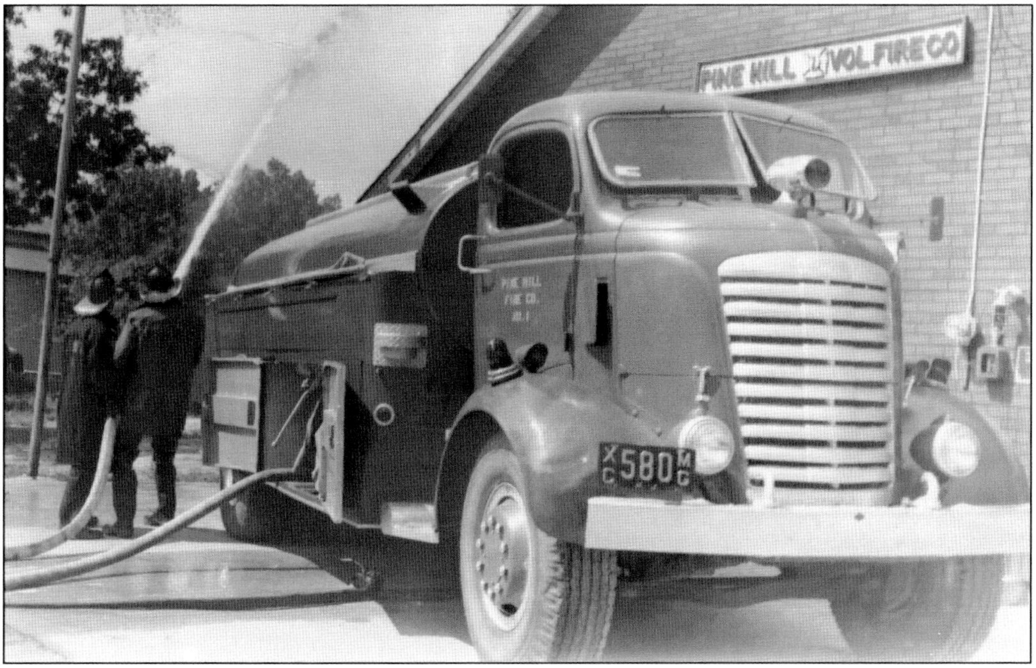

Pictured is the 1949 ESSO oil truck for which the fire station paid $500. The problem was that there was no room in the station to house it, so the truck was actually kept under a large oak tree next to the fire station. The truck was kept filled in the summer and empty in the winter, filling it from an Erial Road hydrant when needed. (Courtesy of Bill Dukes.)

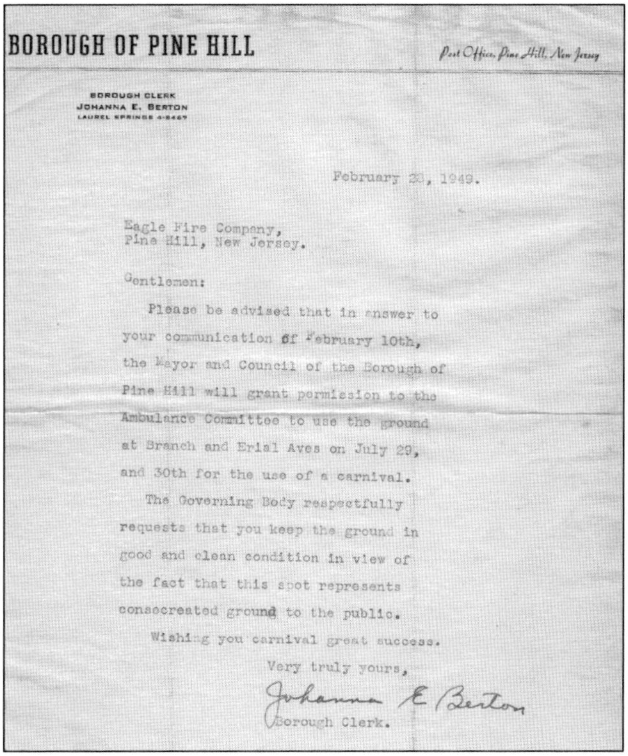

BOROUGH OF PINE HILL

Post Office, Pine Hill, New Jersey

BOROUGH CLERK
JOHANNA E. BERTON
LAUREL SPRINGS 4-8467

February 28, 1949.

Eagle Fire Company,
Pine Hill, New Jersey.

Gentlemen:

Please be advised that in answer to your communication of February 10th, the Mayor and Council of the Borough of Pine Hill will grant permission to the Ambulance Committee to use the ground at Branch and Erial Aves on July 29, and 30th for the use of a carnival.

The Governing Body respectfully requests that you keep the ground in good and clean condition in view of the fact that this spot represents consecreated ground to the public.

Wishing you carnival great success.

Very truly yours,

Johanna E. Berton
Borough Clerk.

Pictured at right is a letter dated February 28, 1949, and signed by the borough clerk, Johanna Berton. The letter is giving permission from the mayor and council to the ambulance committee to host a carnival as part of fund-raising efforts. The carnival was to be held at Branch and Erial Roads, which is the monument location. (Courtesy of Les Gallagher.)

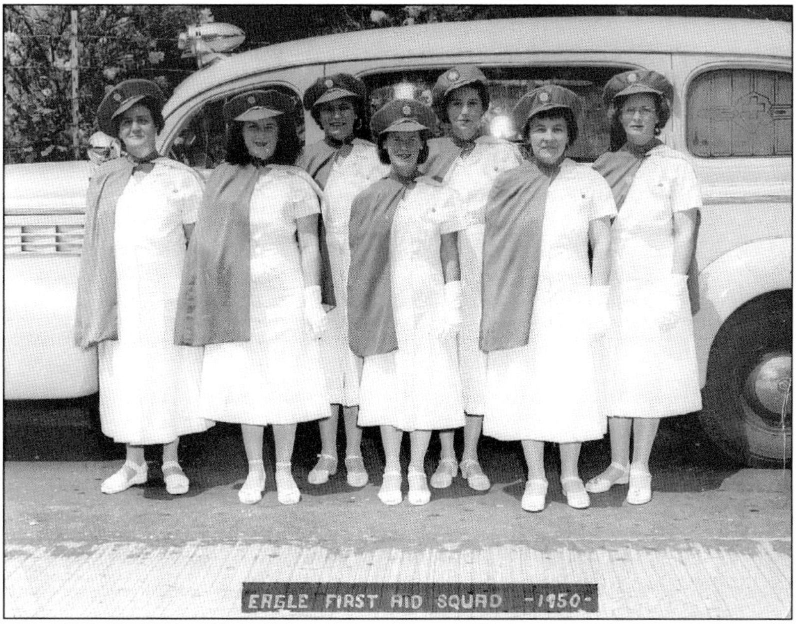

This picture of Eagles First Aid Squad in the 1950s shows them wearing white dresses and red capes. They were the only first aid squad in Pine Hill at that time. Those identified are, from left to right, three unidentified women, Marie O'Neill, Sis Hickman, Dorothy Hamilton, and Evelyn Blakeley. (Courtesy of Jim O'Neill.)

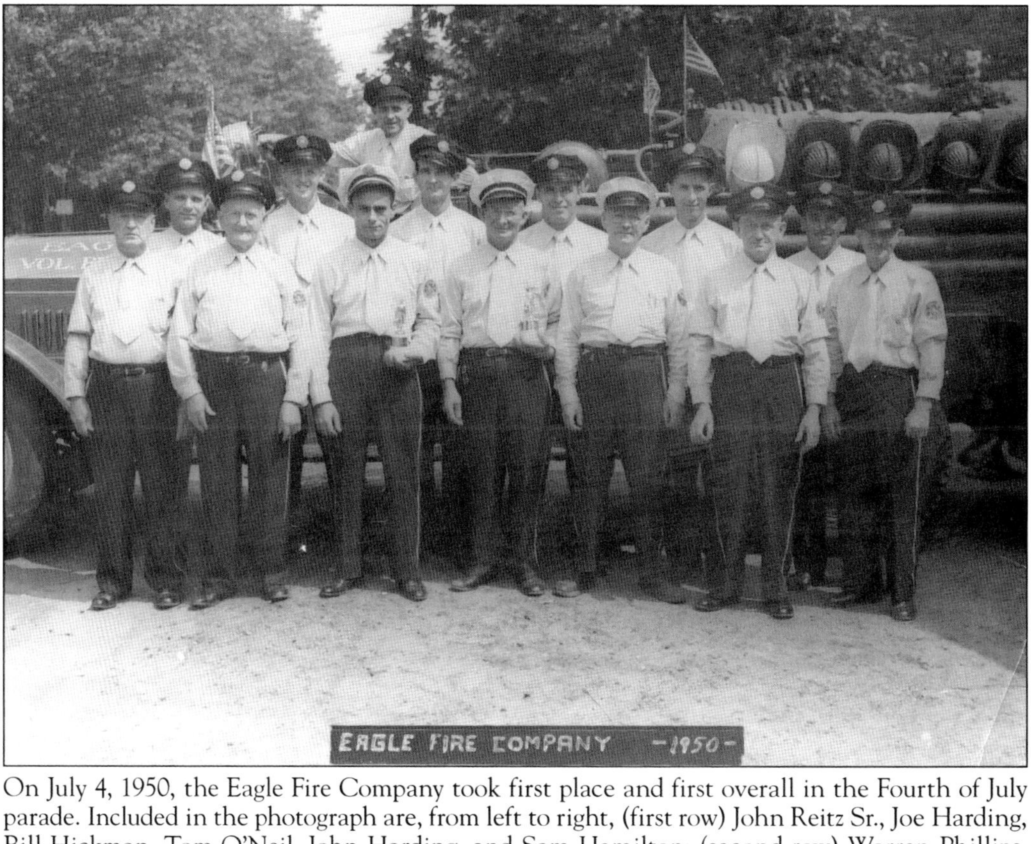

On July 4, 1950, the Eagle Fire Company took first place and first overall in the Fourth of July parade. Included in the photograph are, from left to right, (first row) John Reitz Sr., Joe Harding, Bill Hickman, Tom O'Neil, John Harding, and Sam Hamilton; (second row) Warren Phillips, Jackie Cathcart, Hank Ballentine, Burt Johnson; and in the driver's seat is John Reitz Jr. (Courtesy of Jim O'Neill.)

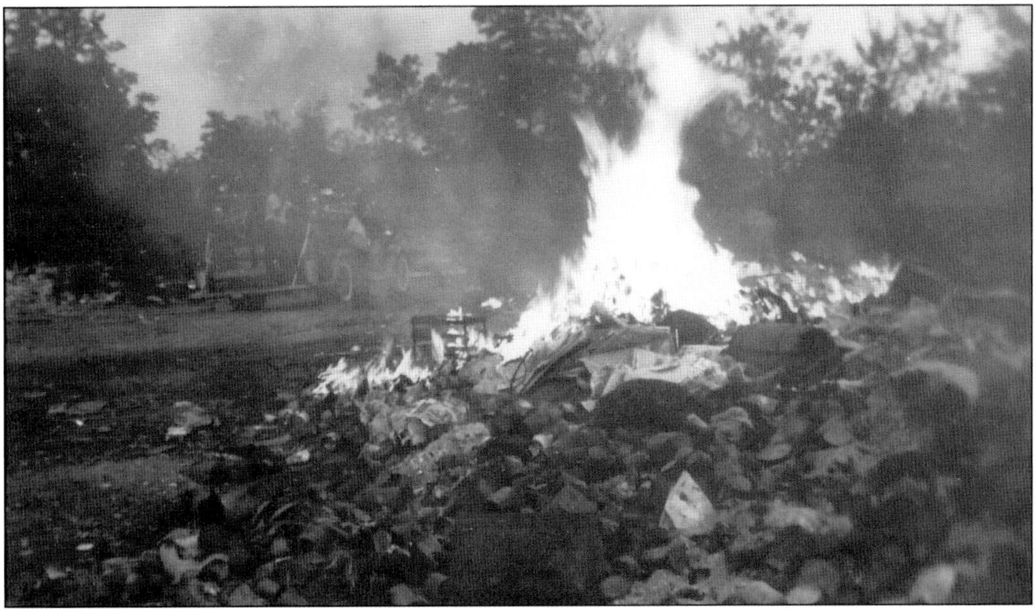

The Pribramsky family home at 45 West Woodburn Avenue caught fire at 10:30 pm on January 26, 1950. Milton Pribramsky and his four children fled to safety after smelling smoke. Pribramsky tried to fight the fire himself with a garden hose. The cause of the fire was unknown. Winifred Pribramsky collapsed after returning from a friend's house and seeing her house ablaze. (Courtesy of Jim Knauth.)

The remains of the Pribramsky home after firefighters from the borough's three companies battled for an hour and a half before getting it under control. Four firemen suffered from smoke inhalation (Emil Broschart—52, George Laird—52, Raymond Hamilton—18, and Mr. Kerper—42). The firemen were treated by Eagle Fire Company Ambulance. Neighbors helped carry out furniture during the blaze. (Photograph by Henry Worrell Jr.; courtesy of Jim Knauth.)

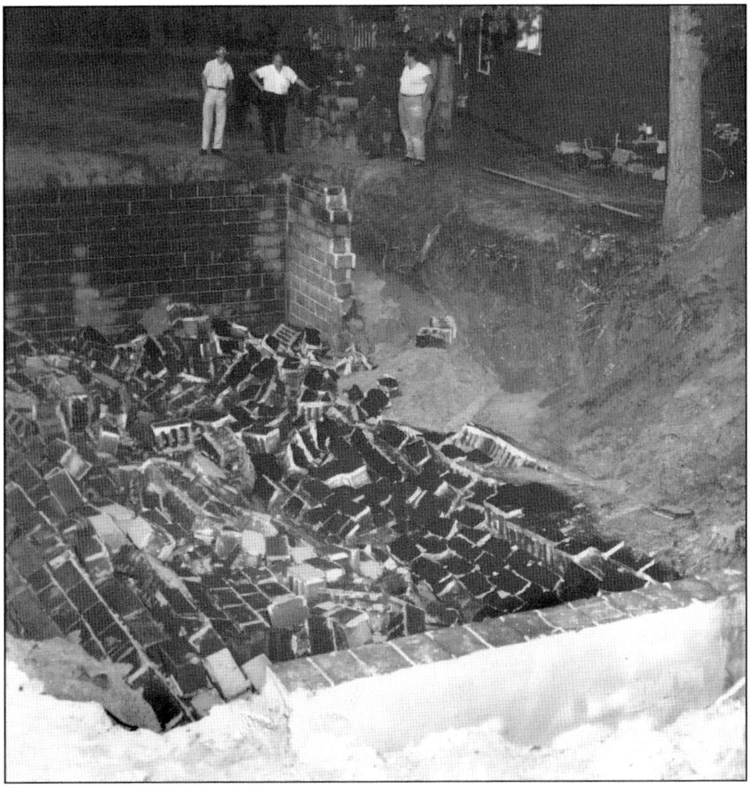

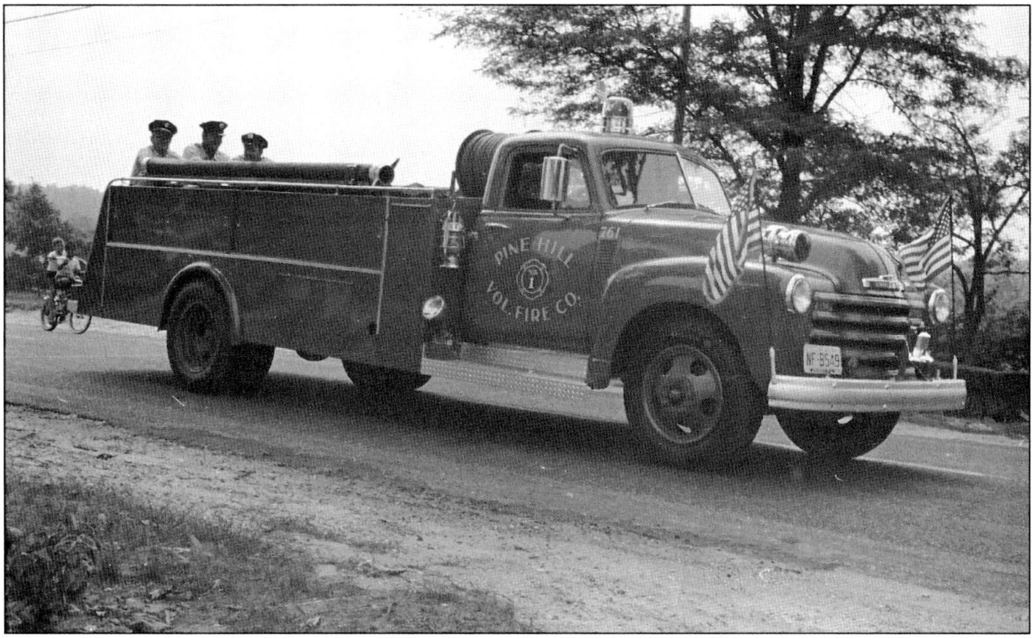

During the 1950s, with the war behind them, all three fire companies had an assurance. In 1953, the No. 1 fire company purchased a brand-new Chevrolet truck/bus chassis. A body design was derived and built by members that included side compartments, rear ladder storage, and a 500-gallon tank. The pump was to be a 70 GPM-PTO driven unit. (Courtesy of Bill Dukes.)

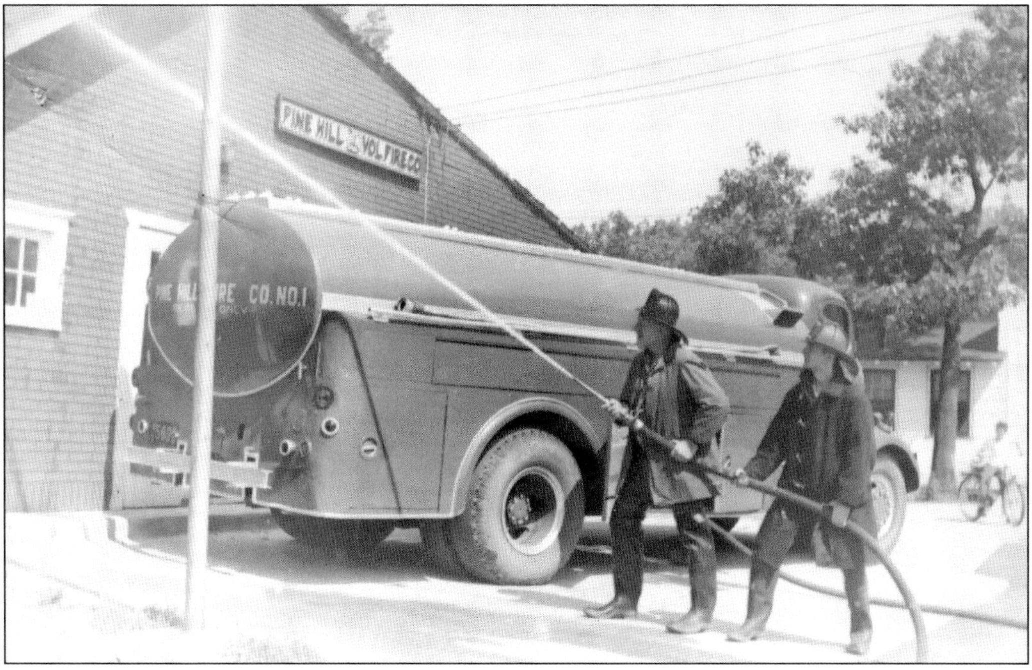

Big Art and Les Moser manning the hose during a fire drill in the 1950s. They were using the 1953 Chevrolet tanker truck for their water supply. All members were volunteers, and they had a drill once a month to keep them skilled and prepared to fight fires. When the fire whistle blew, day or night, firemen would drop what they were doing and respond. (Courtesy of Bill Dukes.)

In 1957, two unidentified boys came to get water from the fire trucks during a snowstorm after the water system froze. The firemen are deputy chief James La Grande Sr. (far left) and Clarence and Bill Buchoffer standing on the truck. (Courtesy of Jim Knauth.)

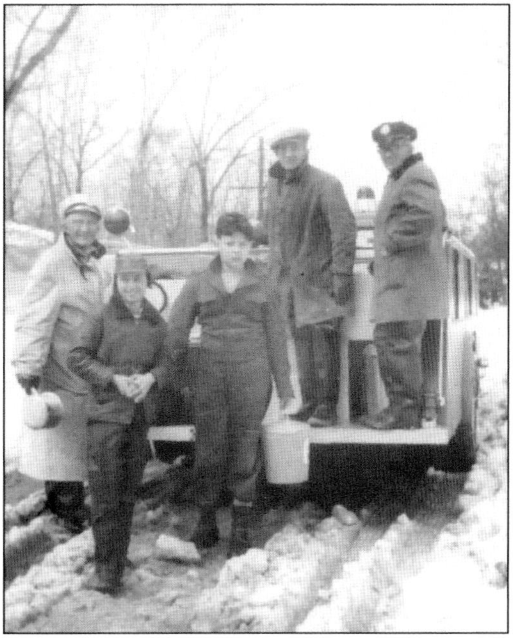

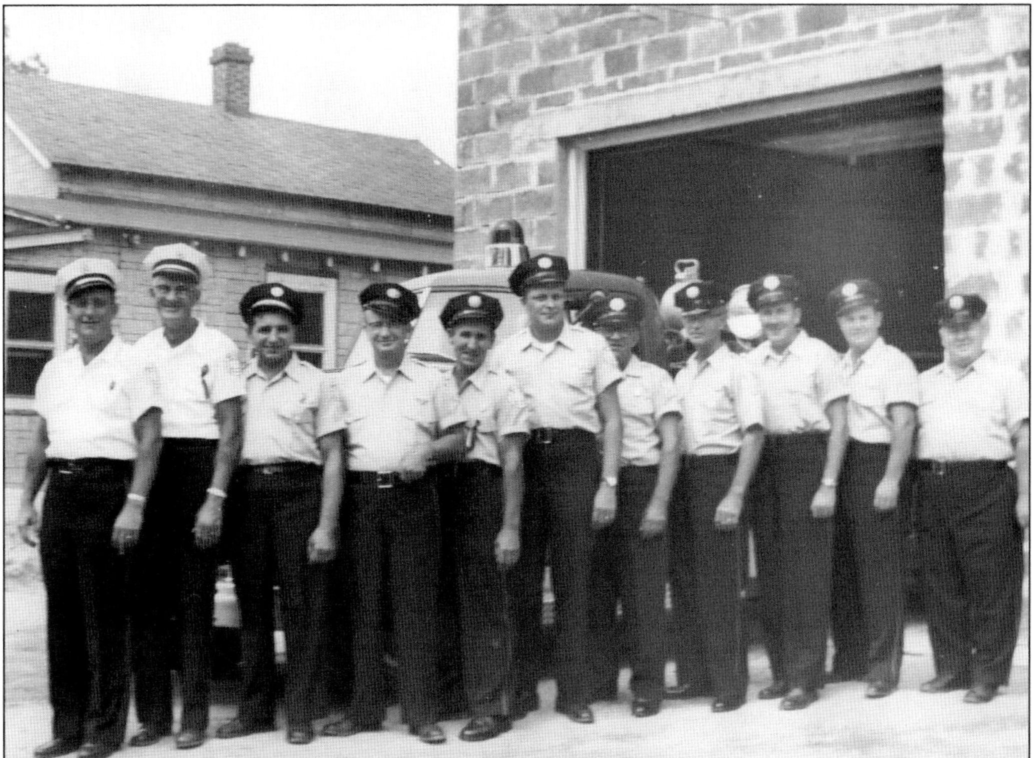

This photograph was taken around 1958 in front of Pine Hill Fire Company No. 1. The firemen are, from left to right, John Schmidt, James La Grande Sr., Roy Porter, Mike Yaworski, Bill Garrison, James La Grande Jr., William Buchoffer, Herb Appenzeller, Jack Brown, Jim Taylor, and Frank Cole. (Courtesy of Bill Dukes.)

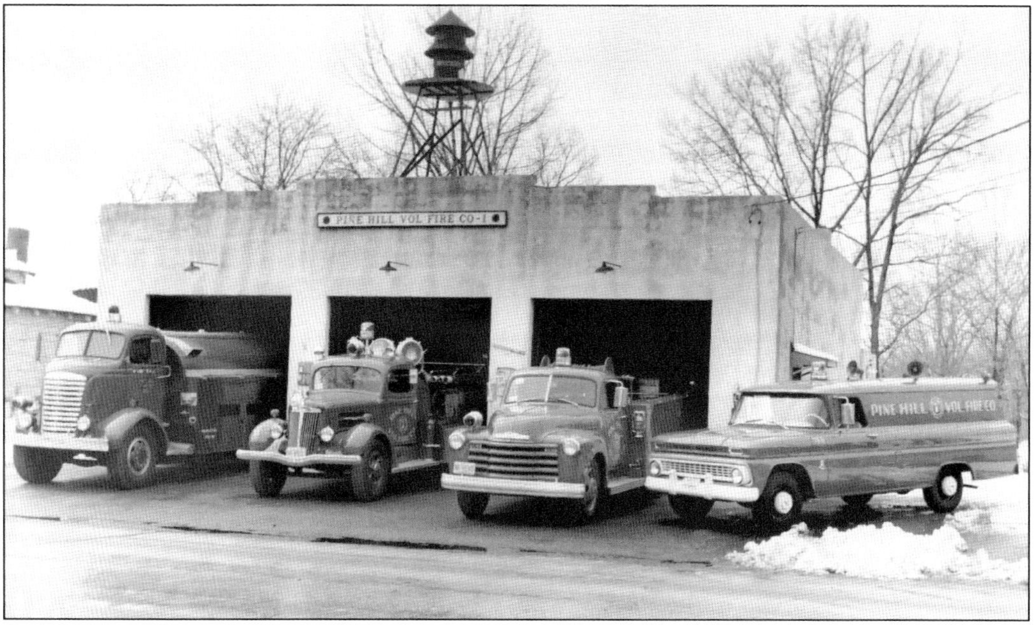

As shown on the cover, the trucks of Pine Hill No. 1 Fire Company are shown in tip-top shape in 1964. This building still stands but no longer serves as a firehouse. (Courtesy of Bill Dukes.)

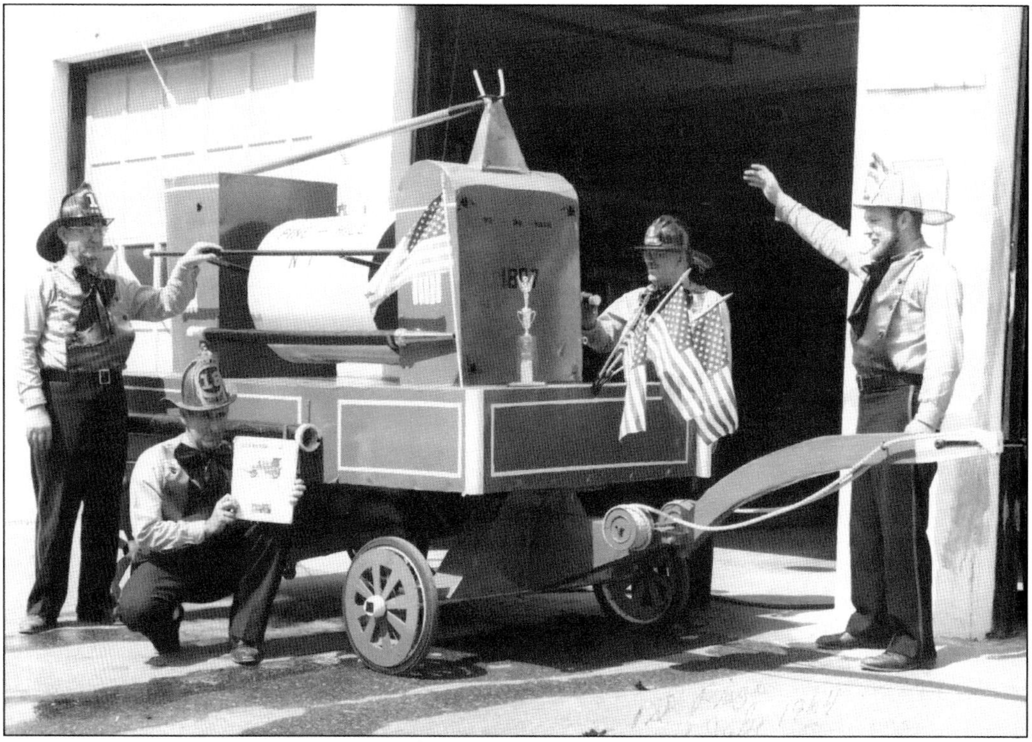

The float of the Pine Hill No. 1 Fire Department won first prize in the Fourth of July parade in 1964. The men made this float with cardboard, paint, and a bicycle. Included in the photograph are the following: John Mangaro (with an arm in the air), Bill Garrison (kneeling), Bill Buchoffer (behind the float by the flags), and Emil Busher. (Courtesy of Bill Dukes.)

A roster shows the members responsible for taking care of the fire company property when affairs were held. Volunteers would help take care of the hall by moving the equipment, cleaning, and setting up for different occasions. Social affairs would often take place at the firehouse, including weddings, dances, and holiday parties. (Courtesy of Les Gallagher.)

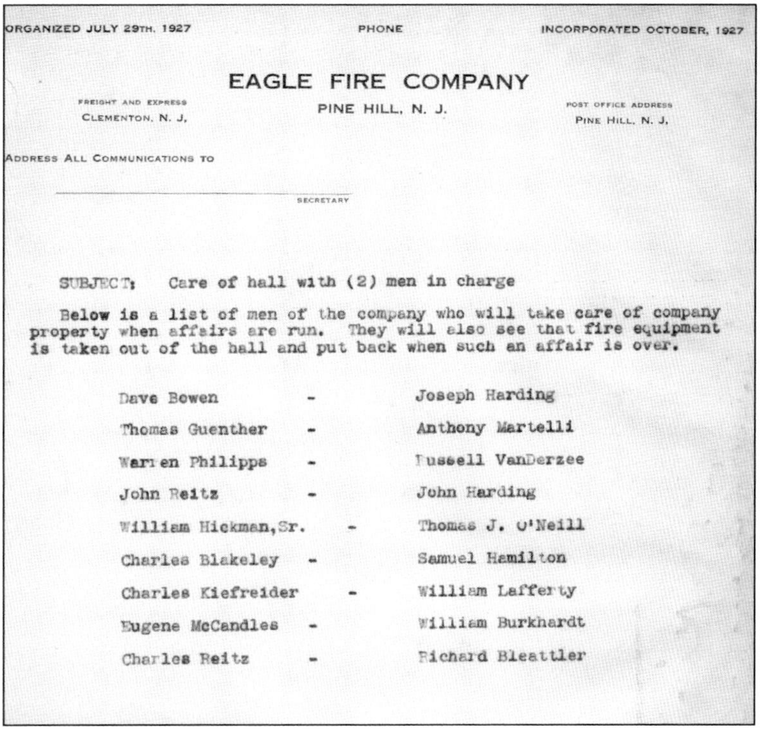

ORGANIZED JULY 29TH, 1927 PHONE INCORPORATED OCTOBER, 1927

EAGLE FIRE COMPANY

FREIGHT AND EXPRESS CLEMENTON, N. J. PINE HILL, N. J. POST OFFICE ADDRESS PINE HILL, N. J.

ADDRESS ALL COMMUNICATIONS TO

SECRETARY

SUBJECT: Care of hall with (2) men in charge

Below is a list of men of the company who will take care of company property when affairs are run. They will also see that fire equipment is taken out of the hall and put back when such an affair is over.

Dave Bowen	-	Joseph Harding
Thomas Guenther	-	Anthony Martelli
Warren Philipps	-	Russell VanDerzee
John Reitz	-	John Harding
William Hickman, Sr.	-	Thomas J. O'Neill
Charles Blakeley	-	Samuel Hamilton
Charles Kiefreider	-	William Lafferty
Eugene McCandles	-	William Burkhardt
Charles Reitz	-	Richard Bleattler

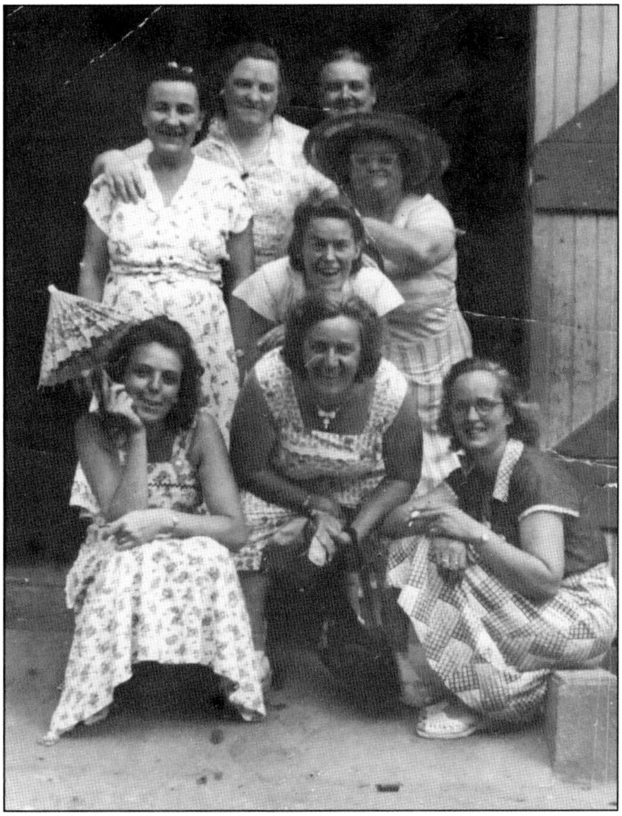

This photograph shows the Ladies Auxiliary in front of Eagle Fire Company. They just came back from a bus trip to Riverview Park. Included in the photograph are Monica Harding, Sis Hickman, Dorthy Hamilton, Cass Bleattler, Evelyn Blakeley, and three unidentified women. (Courtesy of Becky Blakeley.)

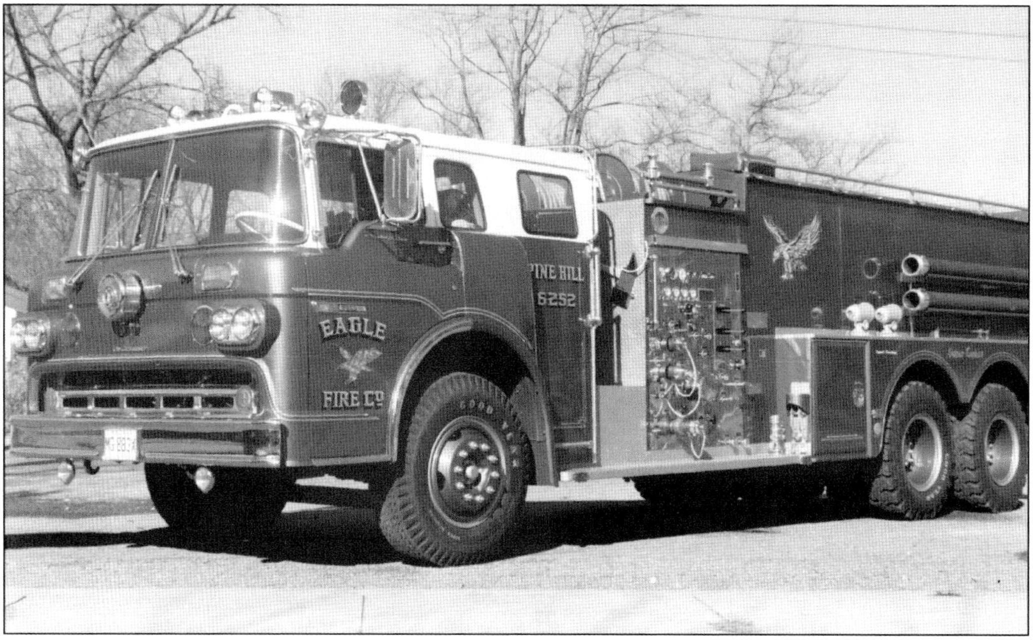

In 1972, the Eagle Fire Company received a new tanker. It was a Great Eastern truck with a Ford cab. Each company in Pine Hill had its own area of town to cover and its own personality that showed in the color of its trucks. Even though the companies had some differences, when the heat of fire came into play, they covered each other's back. (Courtesy of Jim Knauth.)

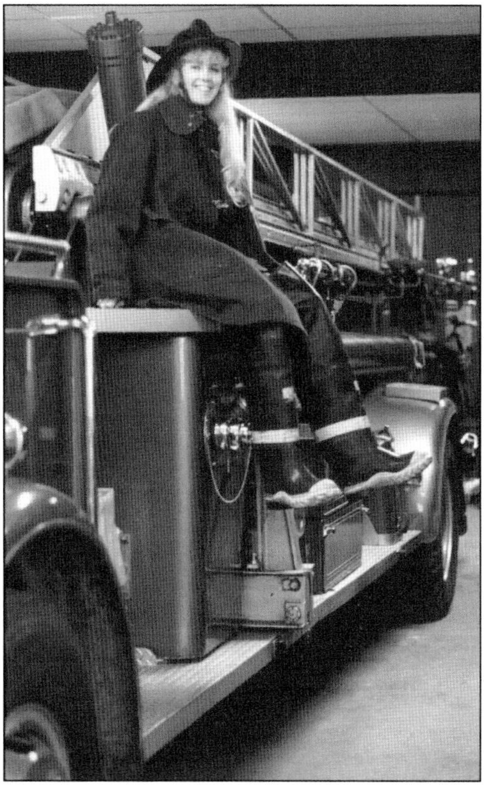

Eagle Fire Company had the first female volunteer firefighters in South Jersey. In 1972, firefighters' wives jumped into action to fill the void from lack of male volunteers. The women were trained, performed drills, and fought fires alongside the men. Some of the female firefighters were Marie O'Neill, Peggy Knauth, Mary Moore, Alice McEwen, Ricky Schmidt, and Ronnie Gallagher (shown at left). (Courtesy of Ronnie Gallagher.)

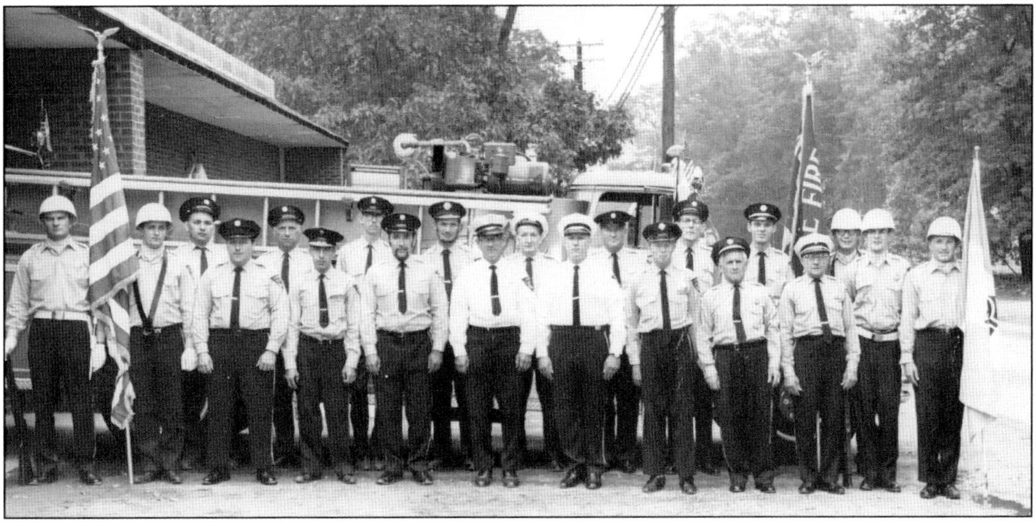

This photograph shows the first color guard outside of Eagle Fire Company in 1973 on Erial Road. From left to right are (first row) Joe Popow, Les Gallagher Sr., Walt Franks, Bob Yenetta, Bill Taylor, Jim O'Neill (chief), Joe Sladek (assistant chief), Bill Korsley, Jim Spicer, John Reitz, Stanley Kilokowski, and Bill Alcott; (second row) Sonny Messner, Sam Morris, Charlie Reitz Jr., Dave Pluck, Joe Franklin, Bill McManus, Tom Gunther, John Michaels, and Frank Lonsdale. (Courtesy of Jim O'Neill.)

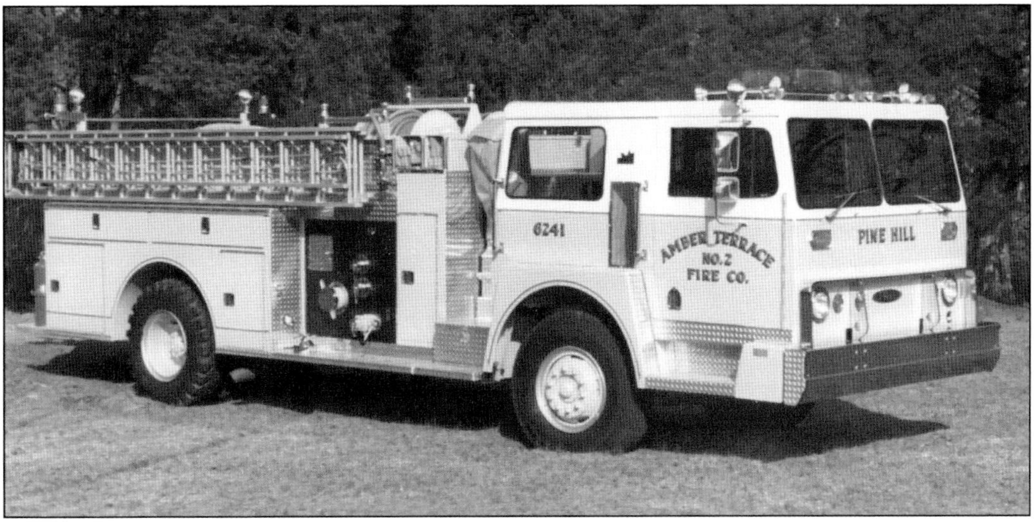

This photograph shows Amber Terrace No. 2 Fire Truck in 1980s. Amber Terrace Fire House was located at 14 De Cou Road. During the late 1950s, all three Pine Hill fire companies made significant improvements to their facilities. Amber Terrace constructed a full masonry, three-bay building with a pre-cast roofing assembly. The No. 1 fire company also decided to expand. (Courtesy of Bill Dukes.)

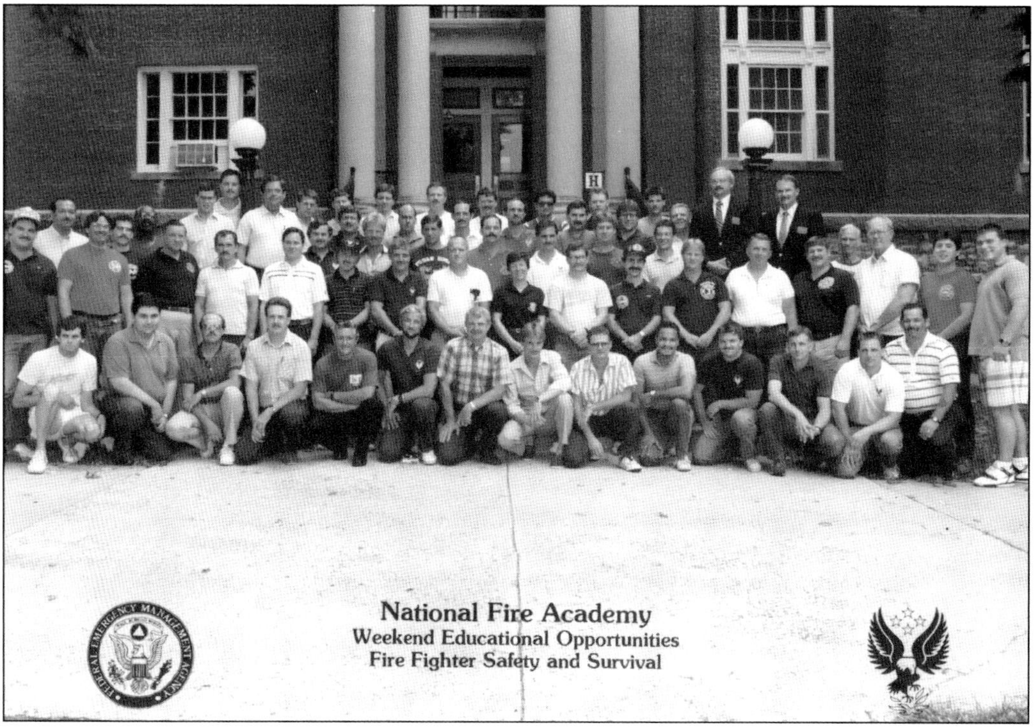

In 1988, Pine Hill sent one member from each of the fire companies to the National Fire Academy. No. 1 sent one fireman, as did Eagle and Amber Terrace. In this picture are the firefighters who attended the safety and survival class that weekend. Les Gallagher is in the first row, fifth from left. He was the member from Eagle Fire Company. (Courtesy of Bill Dukes.)

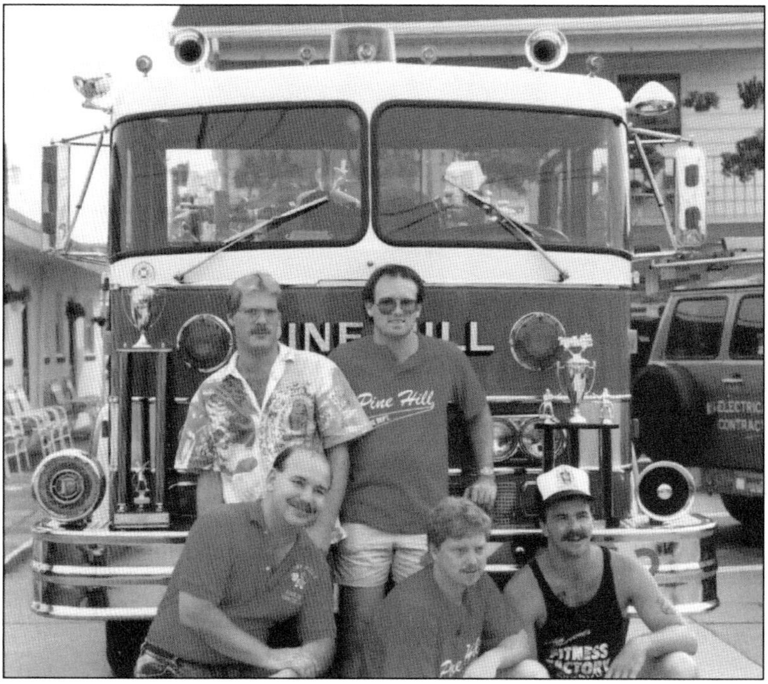

The Pine Hill No. 1 Fire Company won first prize in 1989 in Wildwood at the New Jersey State Firemen Convention. Volunteers put a lot of time into washing and waxing their trucks for the annual convention. Pictured from left to right are (first row) Bob Miller, Joe Hunter, and Wayne Reehle; (second row) Norman Sears and Chris Green. (Courtesy of Bill Dukes.)

This photograph shows Pine Hill No. 1 Fire Company in September 1990 with the vice president of the United States, Dan Quayle. Firemen included in the photograph are, from left to right, Capt. Ray Muller, past chief Bill Kohler, Steve Rabchuck, Scott Metzger, Joe Hunter, and Mike Houston. (Courtesy of Bill Dukes.)

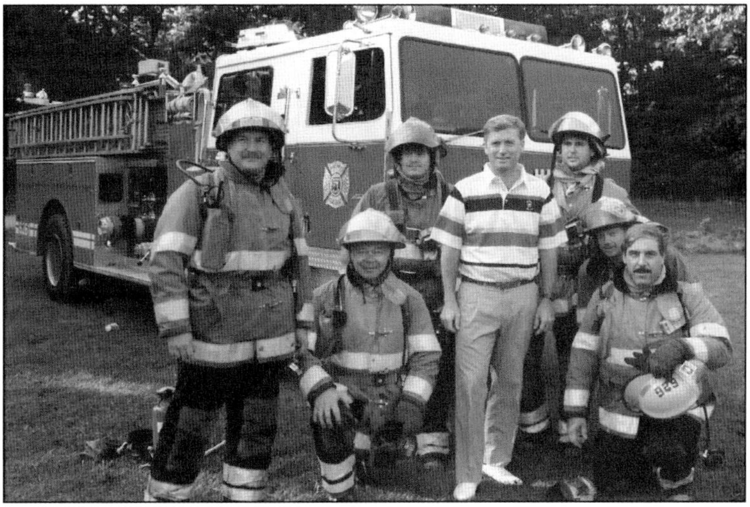

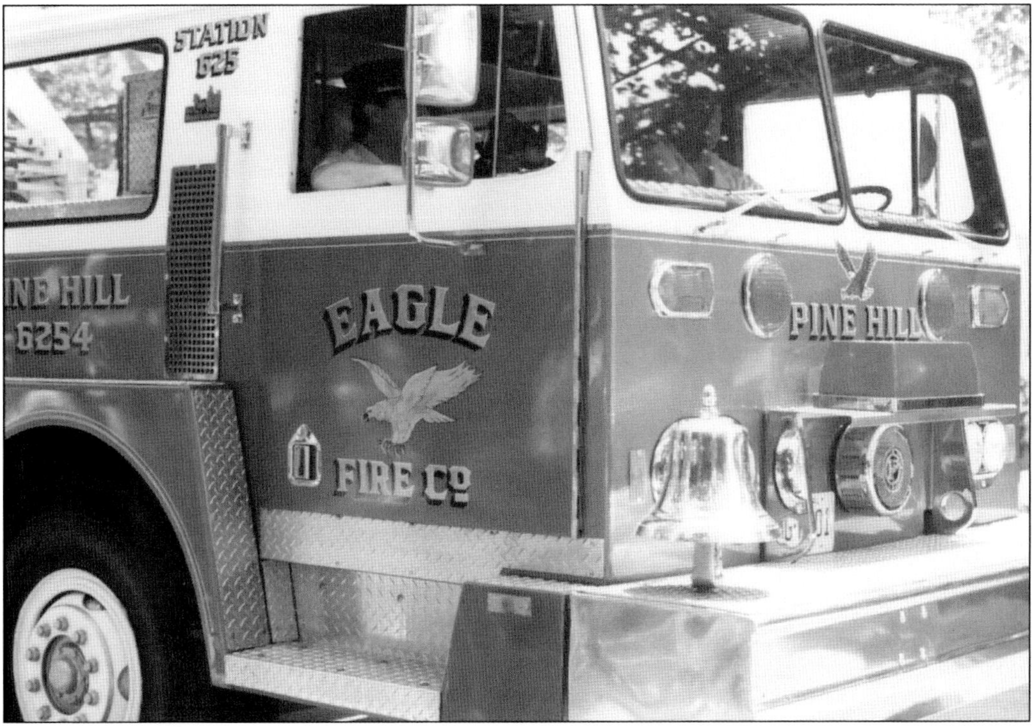

In 1990, the Eagle Fire Truck was still green prior to all the trucks being painted red once again. Around 1999, Pine Hill went back to having only one fire company in an effort to save money. The new Pine Hill Fire Company has two paid firemen and the rest are volunteers. (Courtesy of Les Gallagher.)

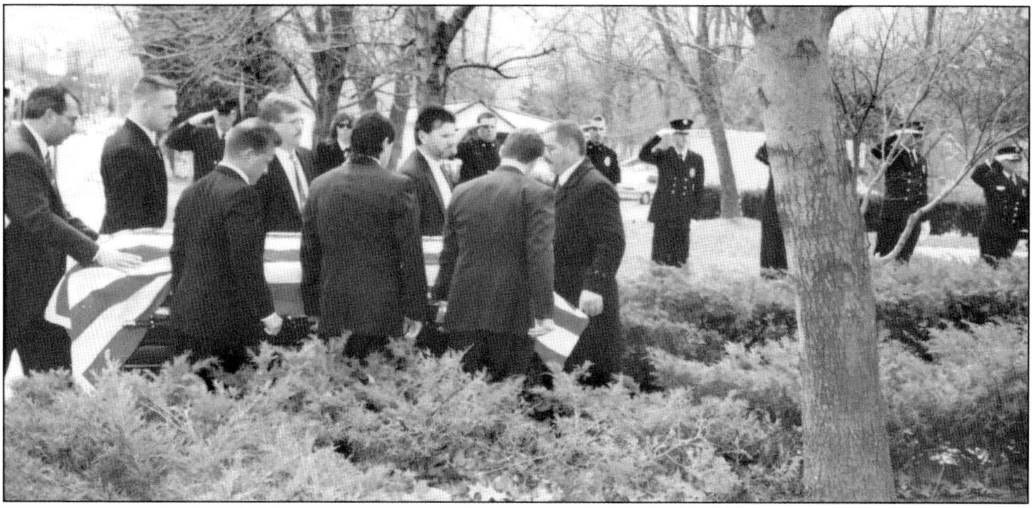

Councilman John Maguire was put to rest on March 27, 1999. Maguire was an outstanding member of the community who also served as an assistant Scout leader, volunteer fireman, member of the American Legion Post No. 286, and treasurer of the fire commission. The firemen stand at attention in dress uniform to honor their fellow man as his coffin is draped with the American flag. (Courtesy of Natalie Maguire.)

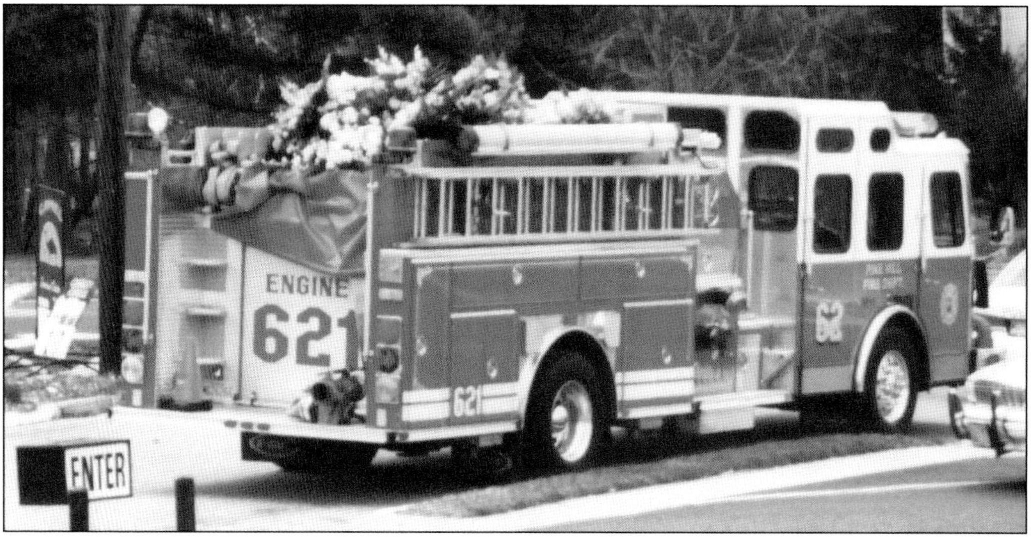

In 1999, Engine 621 is in front of Ora L. Wooster Funeral Home, where firemen are loading the flowers to be carried to John Maguire's gravesite. A procession of police and fire vehicles lead family, friends, and members of the American Legion Post No. 286 to the cemetery in Berlin to pay homage to their comrade. (Courtesy of Natalie Maguire.)

Three

Police Department

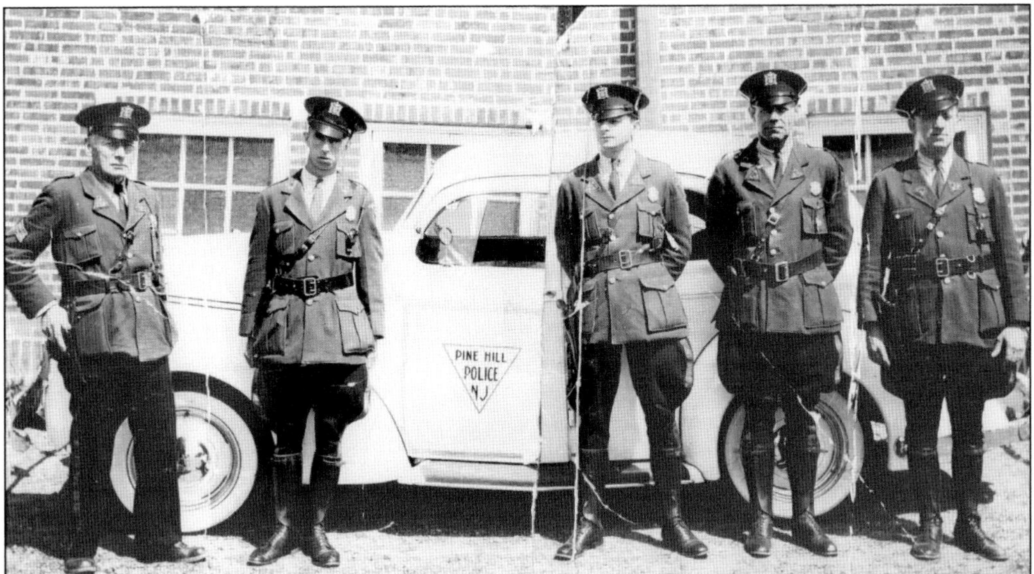

The Pine Hill Police Department in 1938 consisted of a chief, sergeant, and three patrolmen. Standing in front of their first police car are, from left to right, chief Joe Smith, patrolman Allen Bill, patrolman Ed Potts, patrolman Edward Hackit, and Sgt. Harry Knoll. The car was only used when needed, because the borough only allotted $10 a week for gas. The first police officer of Pine Hill was Herb McClintock. (Courtesy of chief of police Ken Cheeseman.)

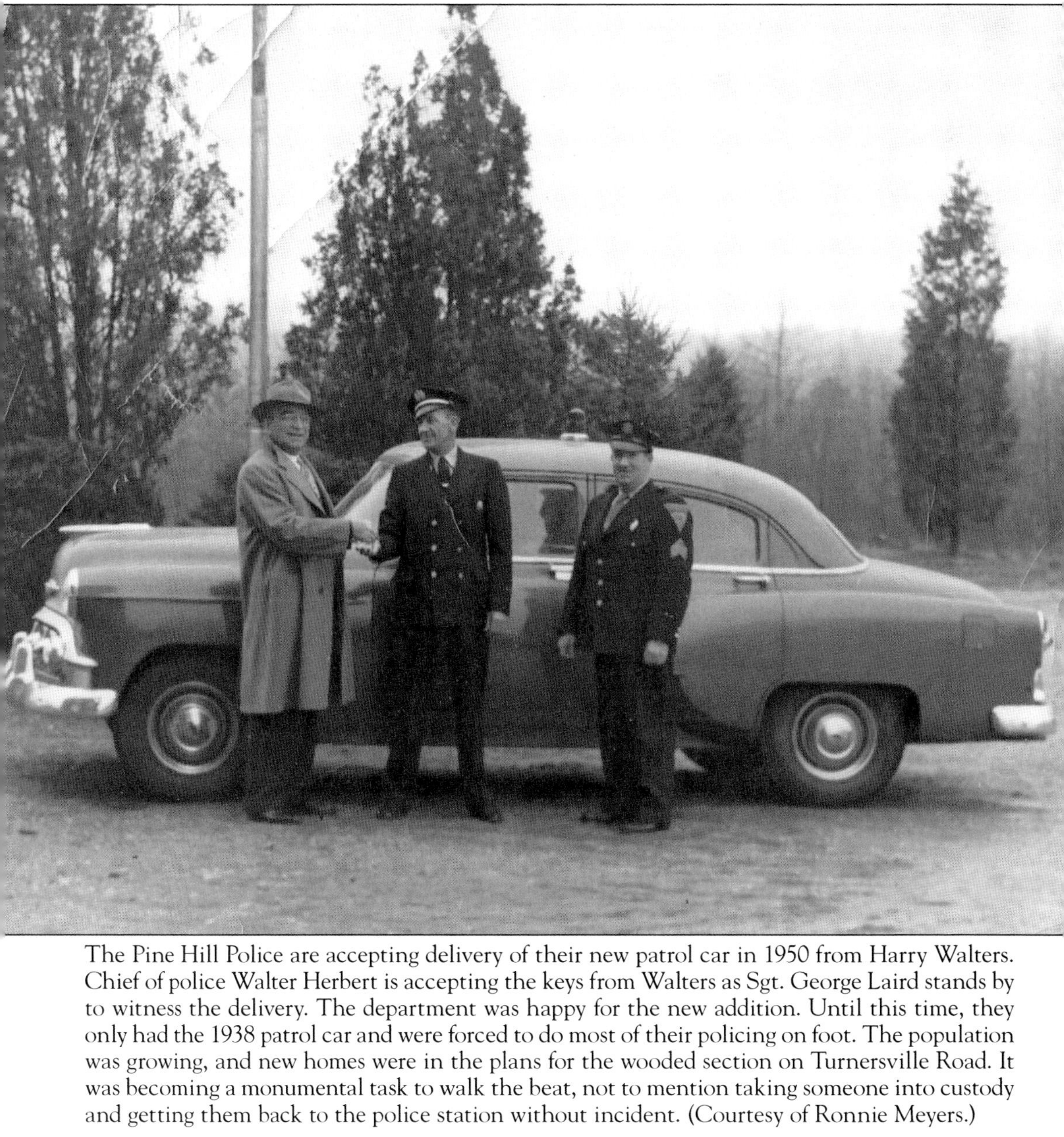

The Pine Hill Police are accepting delivery of their new patrol car in 1950 from Harry Walters. Chief of police Walter Herbert is accepting the keys from Walters as Sgt. George Laird stands by to witness the delivery. The department was happy for the new addition. Until this time, they only had the 1938 patrol car and were forced to do most of their policing on foot. The population was growing, and new homes were in the plans for the wooded section on Turnersville Road. It was becoming a monumental task to walk the beat, not to mention taking someone into custody and getting them back to the police station without incident. (Courtesy of Ronnie Meyers.)

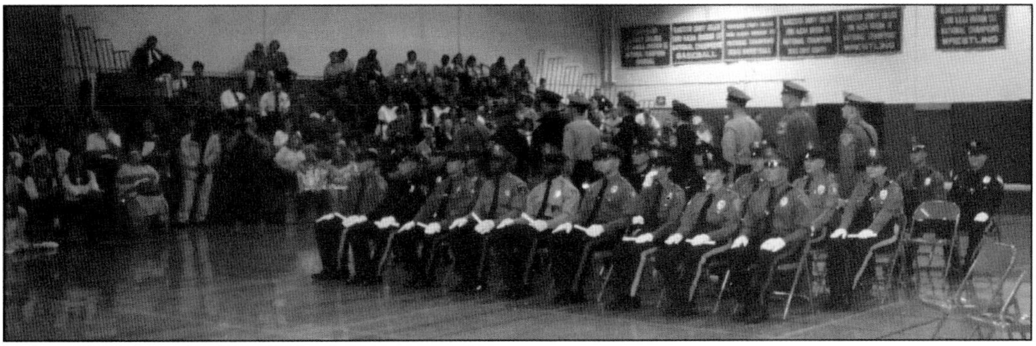

Pine Hill proudly announces the graduation of the 11th Special Officer Class of the New Jersey Police Academy; three of the graduates were to become Pine Hill police officers. These officers endured training that was very grueling and demanding, and not all of their classmates were able to complete the course to become officers. (Courtesy of Natalie Maguire.)

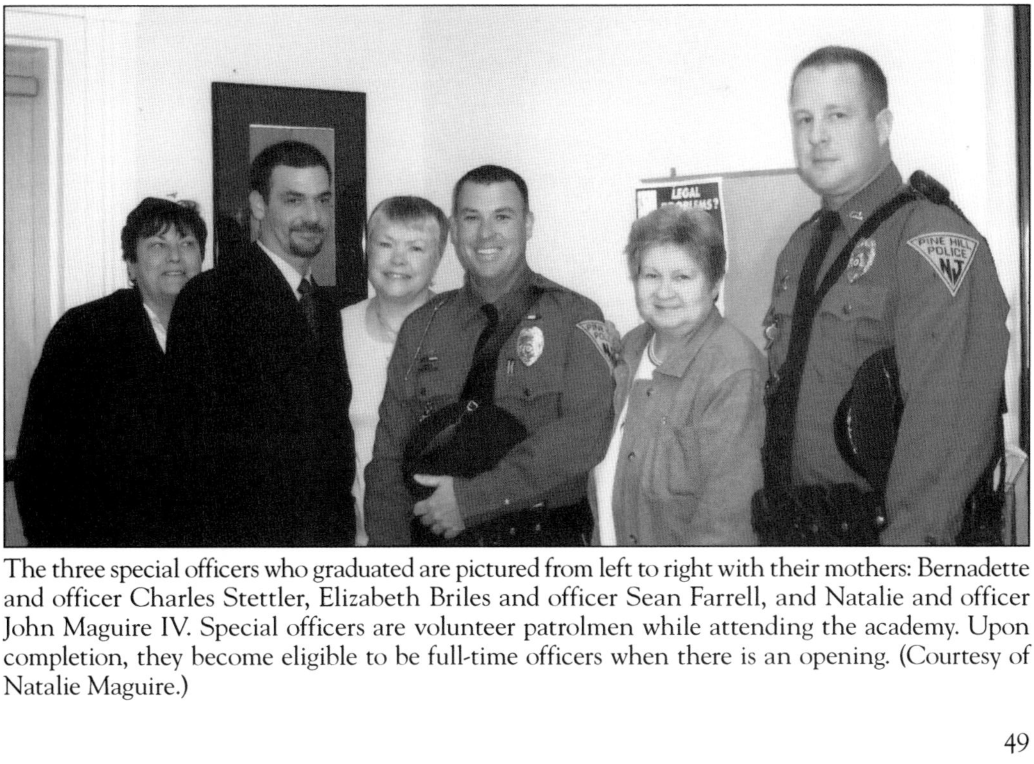

The three special officers who graduated are pictured from left to right with their mothers: Bernadette and officer Charles Stettler, Elizabeth Briles and officer Sean Farrell, and Natalie and officer John Maguire IV. Special officers are volunteer patrolmen while attending the academy. Upon completion, they become eligible to be full-time officers when there is an opening. (Courtesy of Natalie Maguire.)

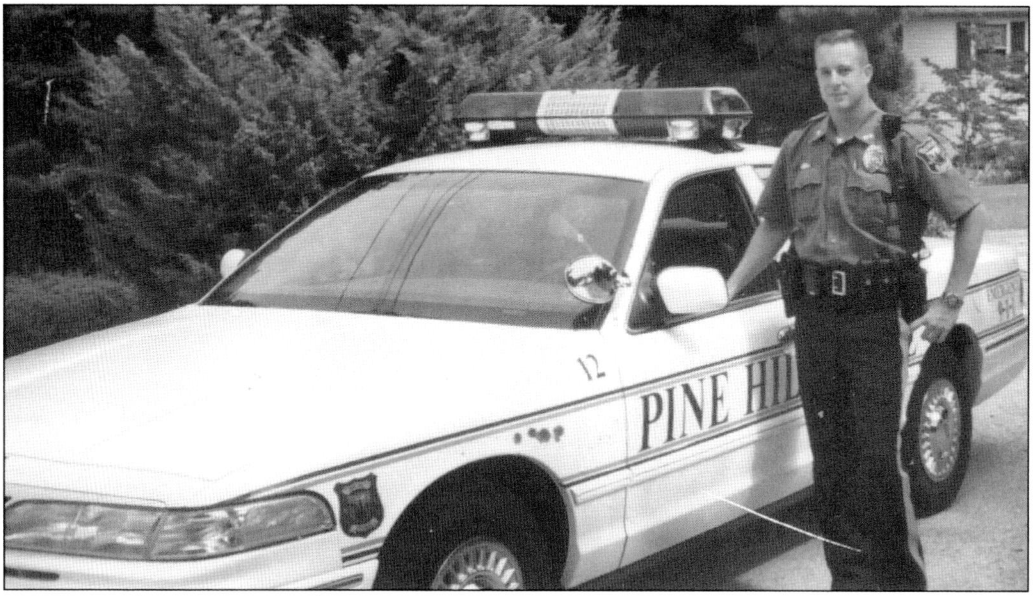

Patrolman John Maguire IV, a lifelong resident of Pine Hill, stands by his patrol car. His grandfather Max Henshke moved here when John's mother, Natalie, was very young, and he continues the family tradition today as he and his wife, Wendi, raise their family here in town. John attended Dr. Albert Bean Elementary School and graduated from Overbrook Senior High School in Pine Hill. (Courtesy of Natalie Maguire.)

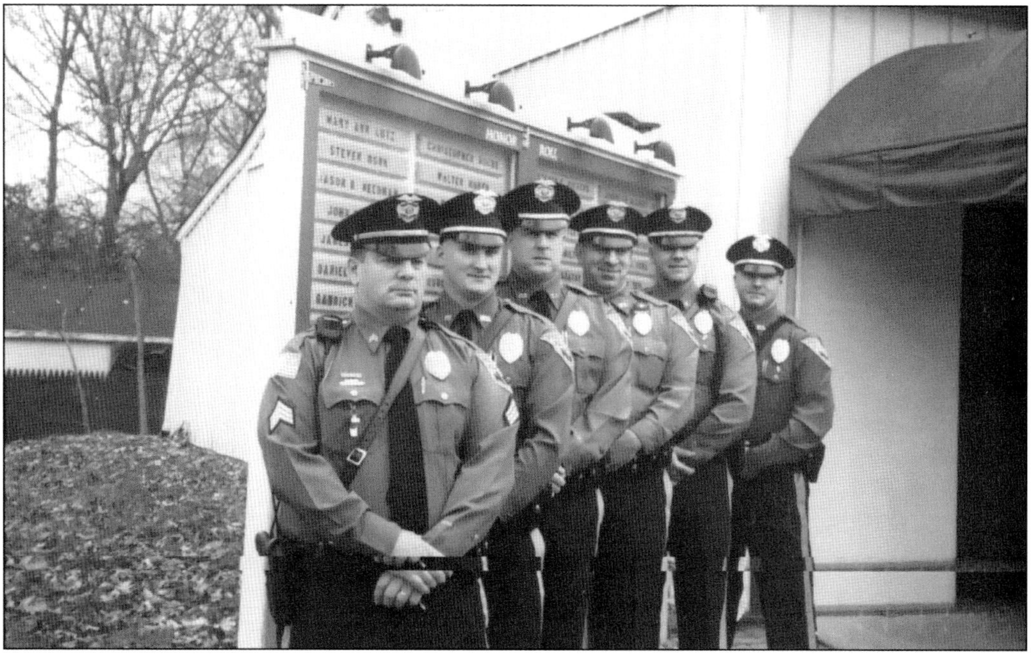

Here are some of Pine Hill's finest posing for a picture outside the American Legion after the veterans ceremony on a damp November day. Pictured from left to right are Sgt. Richard Annacone, patrolman William Heron, patrolman John Maguire, patrolman Ronald Raynore, patrolman Robert Booker, and patrolman Jason Rowello. (Courtesy of the Pine Hill Police Department.)

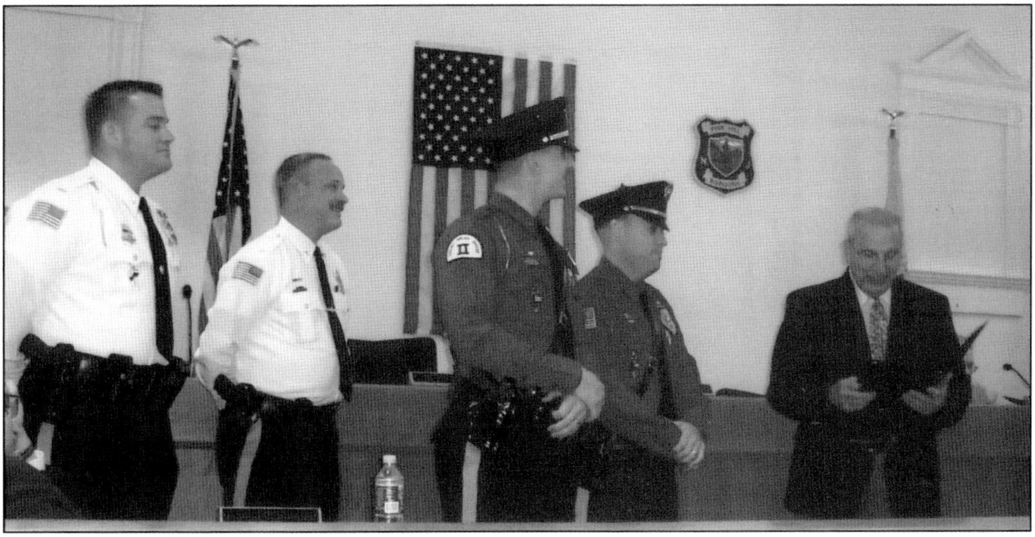

Officer Farrell and special officer Kramer are being honored by Mayor Fred Costintino for their excellent job in law enforcement. The officers rescued four children and returned them unharmed to their mother. The children were abducted by an adult male who violated a restraining order. The officers took him into custody without incident. Chief Ken Cheeseman (second from left) and Lt. Chris Winters (farthest left) were on hand for the presentation. (Courtesy of Natalie Maguire.)

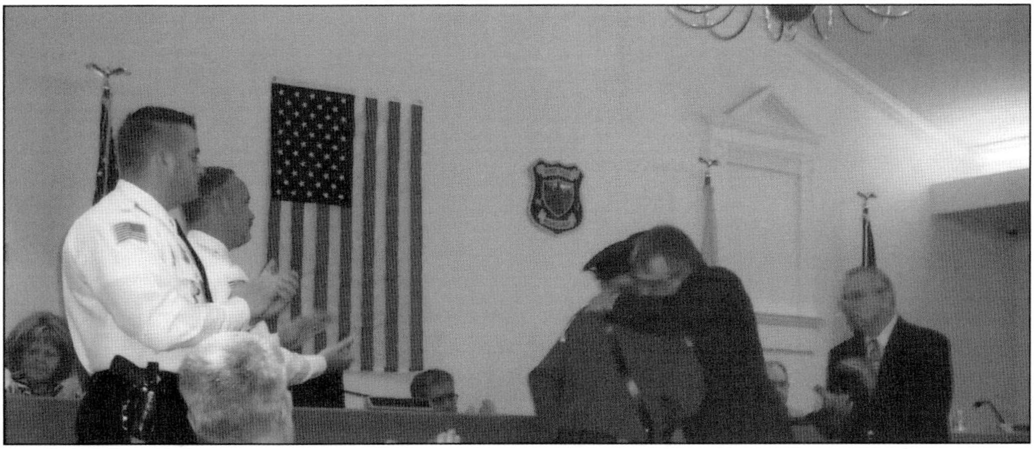

Councilman Chuck Warrington, director of public safety, consoles officers Sean Farrell and Ronald Raynore who were recognized for their outstanding effort. They were dispatched on a difficult call, a small child had fallen into a pond and drowned. Both officers are certified emergency medical technicians and had initiated CPR to resuscitate the child, but after he was airlifted to Cooper Hospital, he sadly succumbed to the drowning. (Courtesy of Natalie Maguire.)

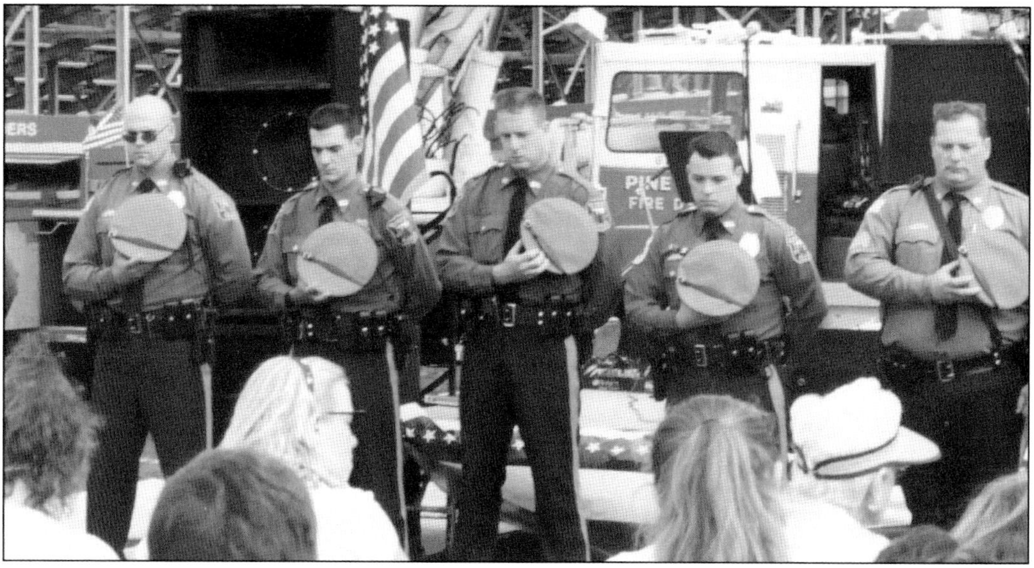

On October 14, 2001, Pine Hill police officers observe a moment of silence during a fund-raiser to help families who lost loved ones during the September 11, 2001, tragedy at the World Trade Center. Some of the local first responders helped during the search and recovery at Ground Zero. From left to right are patrolmen Robert Booker, Charles Stettler, John Maguire, Sean Farrell, and Sgt. Richard Annacone. (Courtesy of Natalie Maguire.)

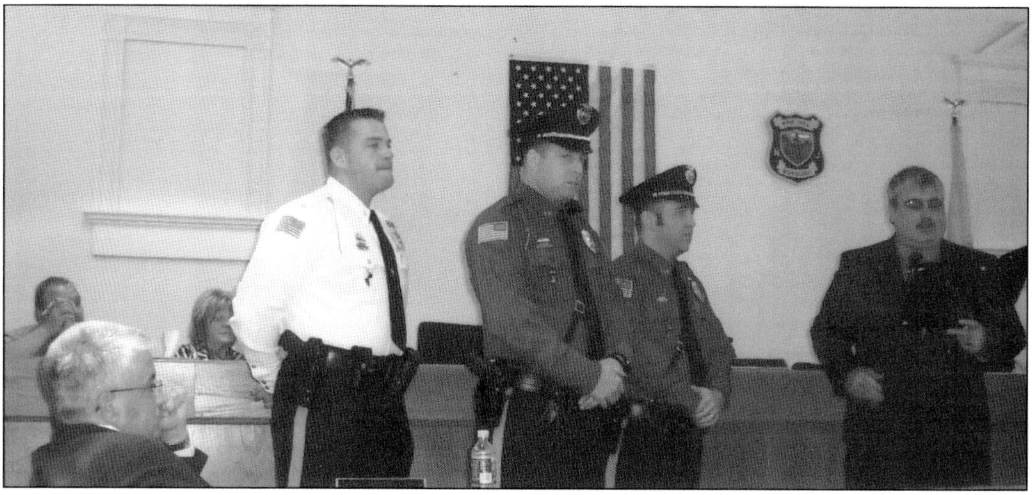

Councilman Chuck Warrington, director of public safety, reads the commendation that was presented to officers John Maguire and Timothy McElroy for their professionalism, resourcefulness, and ability to act quickly in the apprehension of two burglary suspects without incident. Standing from left to right are Lt. Chris Winters, officer John Maguire, officer Timothy McElroy, and councilman Chuck Warrington. Seated in the background are councilman Ross DelRossi and secretary Loretta Buchanan. (Courtesy of Natalie Maguire.)

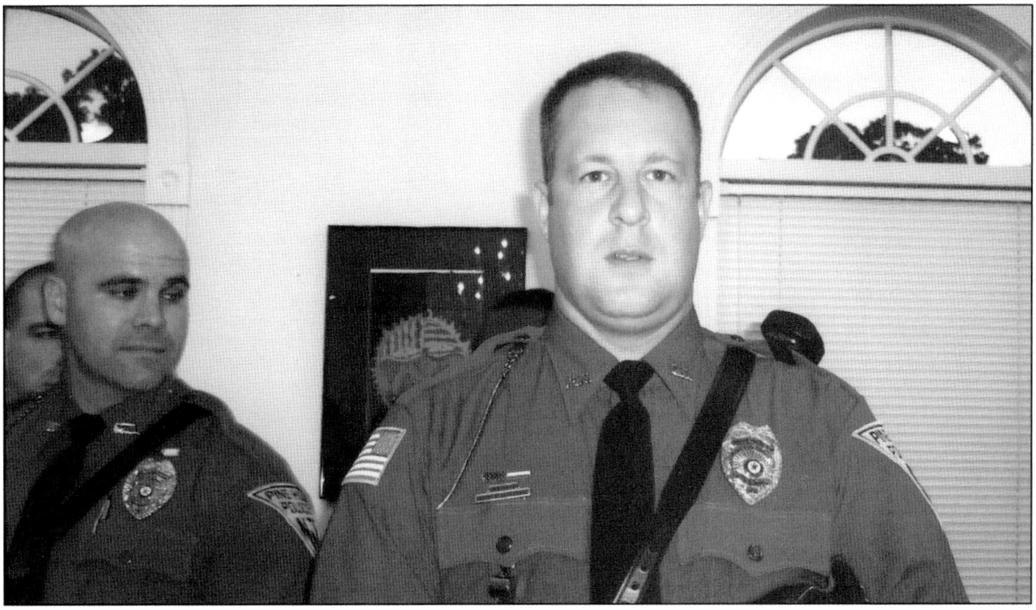

Pictured here from left to right are officers Ronald Raynor, Robert Booker, and John Maguire VI, awaiting the commendation ceremony of officer Booker for his drive and determination in saving the life of a young woman who was attempting suicide and assisting in the emergency birth of a healthy baby girl. (Courtesy of Natalie Maguire.)

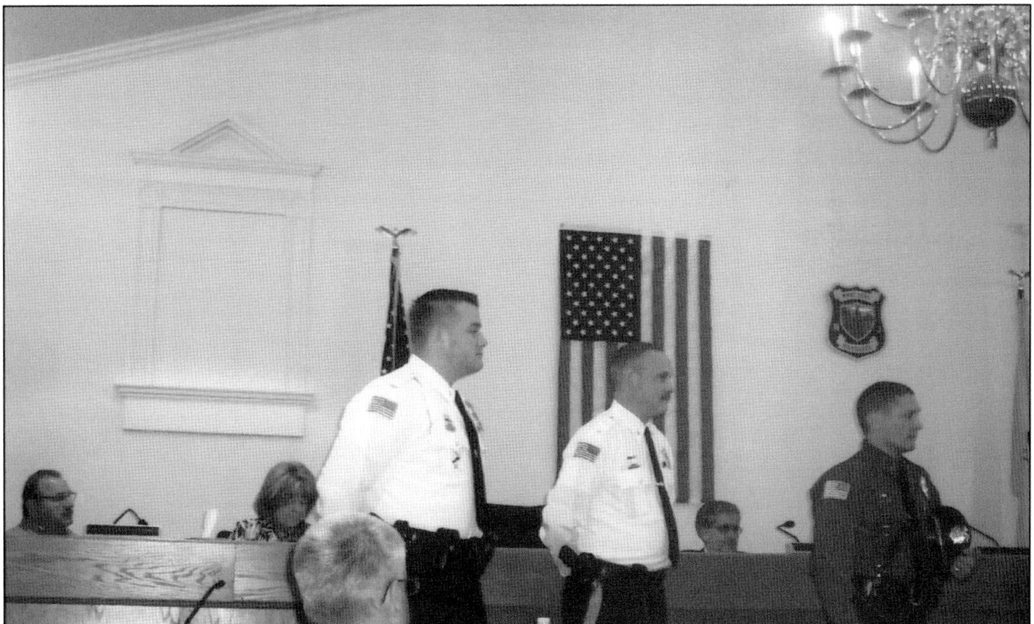

Patrolman Matthew Pierson, aka "Officer Dynamo" (in blue), stands at attention as Mayor Fred Costintino reads the commendation he received. Officer Pierson single handedly relieved two males of their guns and confiscated their marijuana while controlling six other men at the scene without incident. He also worked undercover with the DEA and assisted in confiscating $300,000 in cash, motorcycles, and drugs while bringing down 16 drug dealers. (Courtesy of Natalie Maguire.)

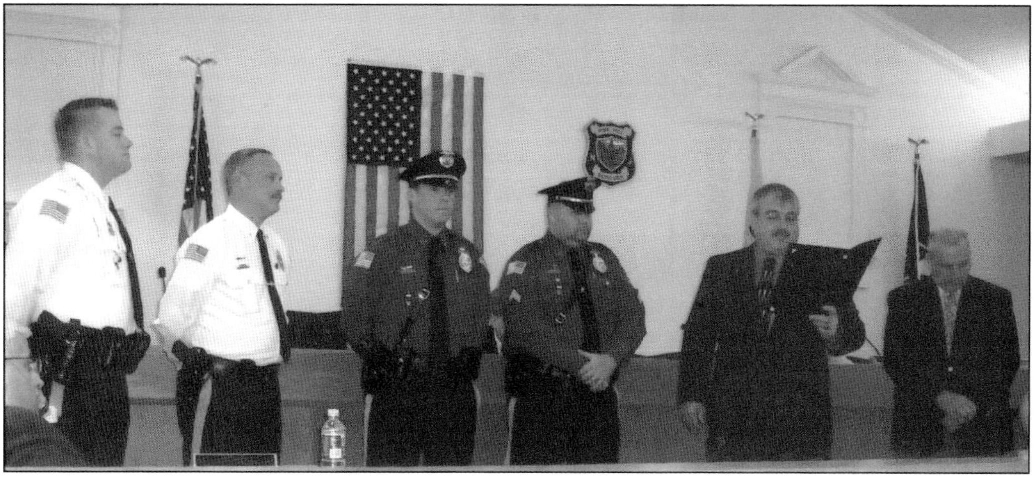

Pictured here are, from left to right, Lieutenant Winters, Chief Cheeseman, patrolman Robert Smuda, patrolman Christopher Witts, councilman Chuck Warrington, and Mayor Fred Costintino. Warrington is reading a commendation that recognized the work of officers Smuda and Witts in apprehending a wanted male, who was seen scaling a chain-link fence, without further incident. (Courtesy of Natalie Maguire.)

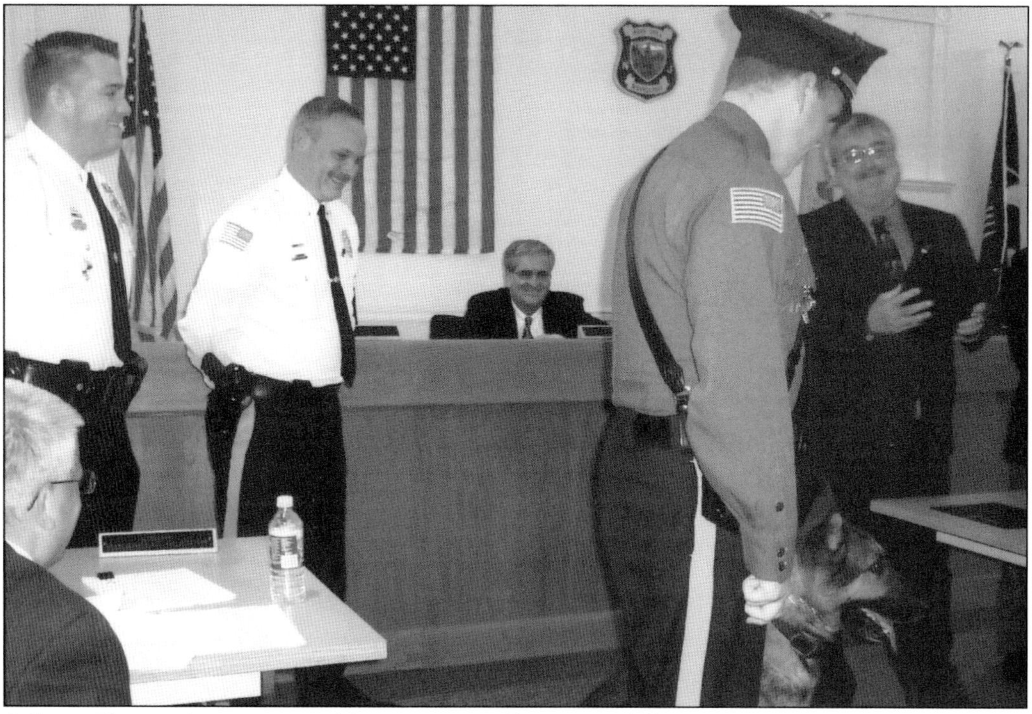

Officer Christopher Witts and his partner, officer K9 Cliff, receive commendation for a job well done. While on patrol, they responded to an alarm at a local business and found the front window broken and a suspect fleeing. The suspect was apprehended, and the stolen merchandise was returned. Officer Cliff was also recognized for his work in uncovering drugs that were well hidden in a vehicle and packaged for distribution. (Courtesy of Natalie Maguire.)

Four

AMERICAN LEGION

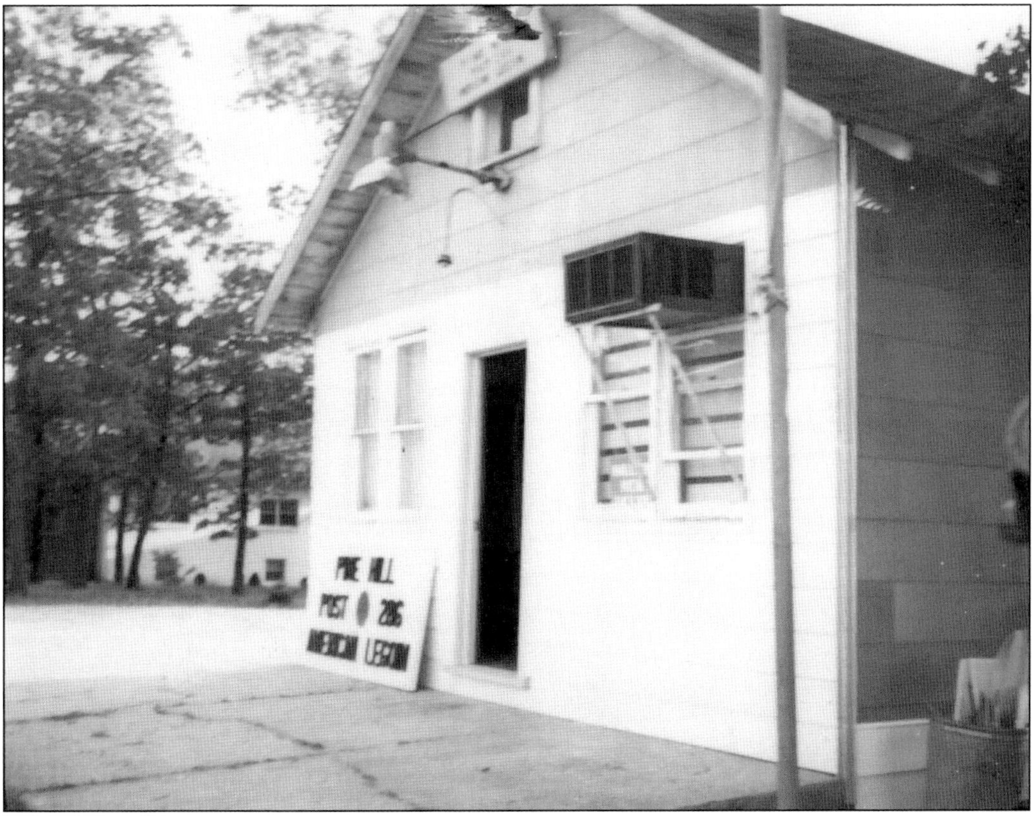

American Legion Post No. 286 almost lost its building in 1947 to outstanding debts. Under the leadership of commander John Thumm, the members rescued the structure from a tax sale by requesting tax relief from the mayor and council. Tax exemption was granted at a meeting between finance officer Michael Hoppenthaler and borough clerk Jessie Davies. The last debt was paid in 1948 and the deed placed in a safe deposit box. (Courtesy of Post No. 286.)

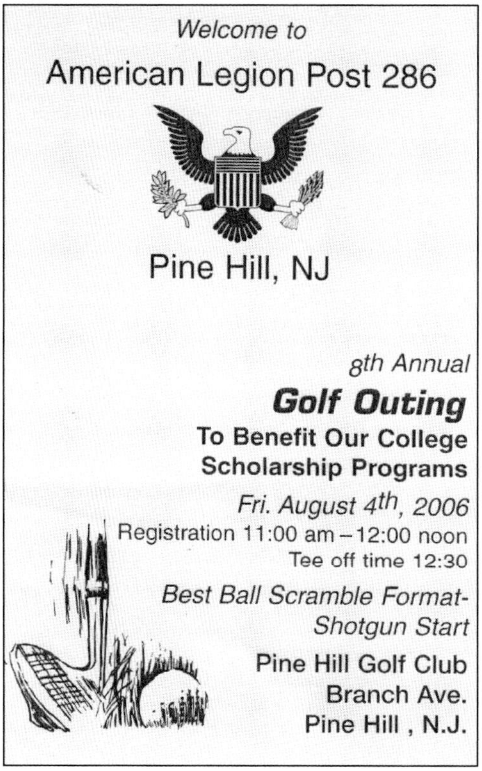

In 1941, the American Legion Post No. 286 was organized by local World War I and World War II veterans dedicated to honoring the servicemen of Pine Hill. Post No. 286 has run many fund-raisers to assist local veterans and the children of their community. They have a "Golf Outing" each year to benefit their college scholarship program, which awards scholarships to local graduating seniors who demonstrate their idea of Americanism through a written essay. (Courtesy of Post No. 286.)

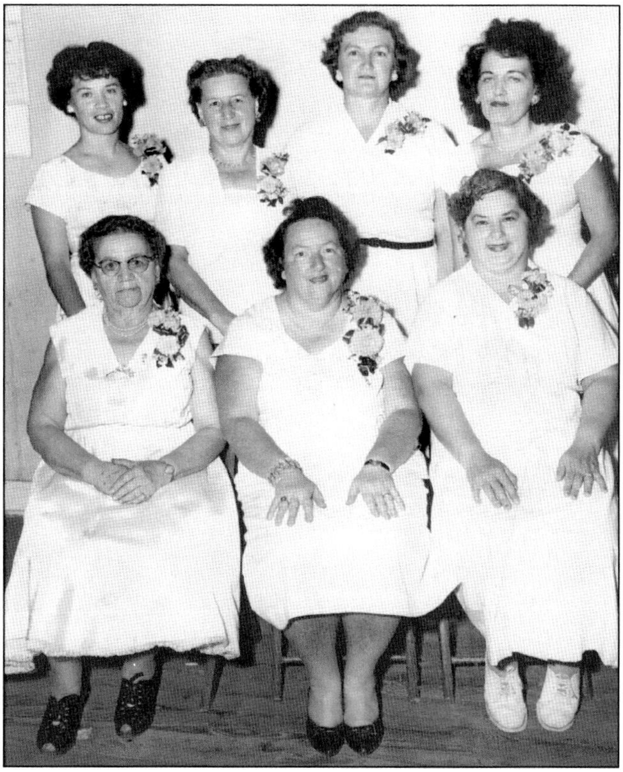

This photograph shows the Ladies Auxiliary installation dinner in May 1950. Newly elected officers are (first row) secretary, Josephin Boer; president, Theresa McNamara; and sergeant at arms, L. Gibson; (second row) finance officer, Sis Owens; historian, Mary Hofacker; vice president, Evelyn Krantz; and chaplain, Theresa Gibson. The women of the auxiliary are dedicated to preserving the memory of those who have served their country and paid the ultimate sacrifice (their life) while in the military. (Courtesy of Mary Gallagher.)

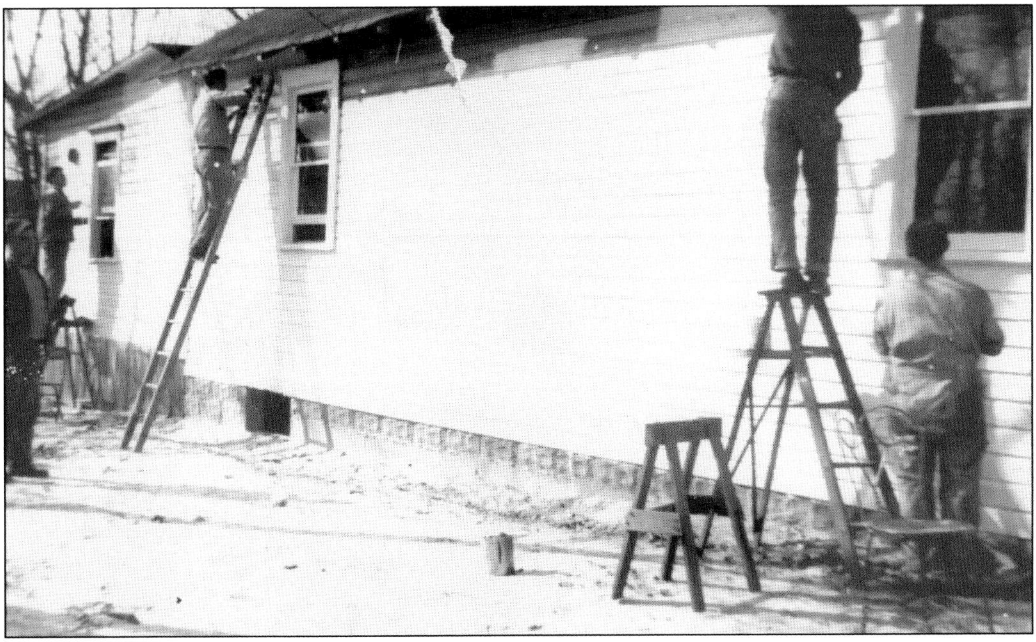

In fall 1956, members of American Legion Post No. 286, under the direction of George Hofacker and Richie Berkey, completed the enlargement of their building. This new addition included a new kitchen and appliances. The addition gave the post another venue for fund-raising, and they now would have a community breakfast to help raise funds for children and youth. (Courtesy of Post No. 286.)

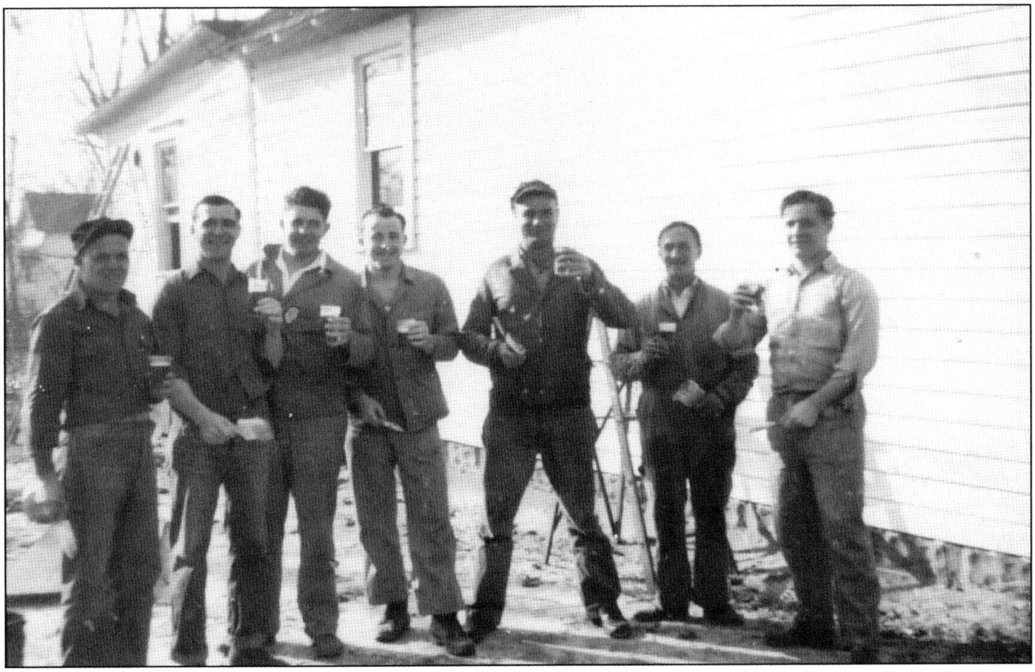

The finishing touches are made on the addition when the siding is complete. This made the building look uniform, and veterans are all about looking good. It was hard work, but it all paid off in the end, as some of the members celebrate their good work with a cool drink. (Courtesy of Post No. 286.)

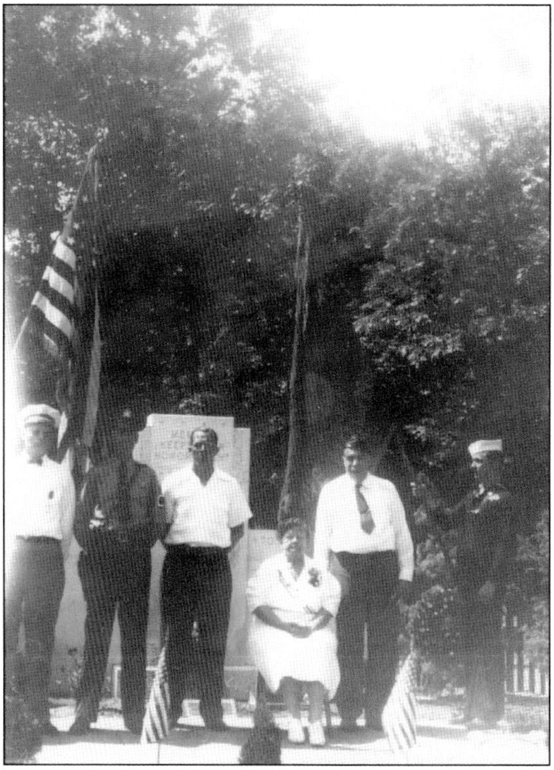

After the unveiling of the new monument, Mrs. Jefferson, a "Gold Star Mother," who lost her son in the war is seated next to American Legion commander DeBrosse. Also standing are members of the police department, fire department, town council, and the honor guard. (Courtesy of Mable Thumm.)

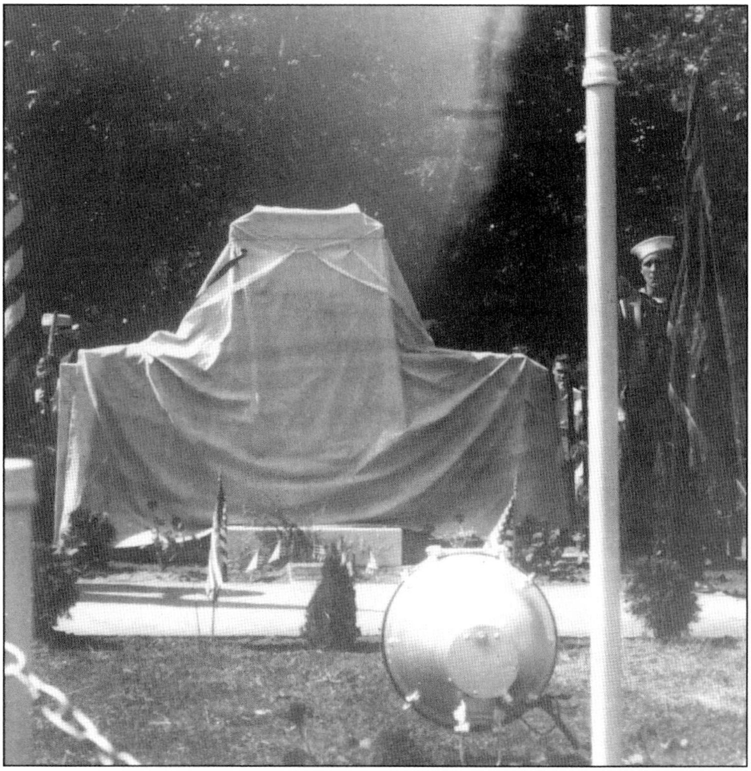

In 1955, an honor guard stands watch over the covered new stone monument at the corner of Branch and Erial Roads, which replaced the wooden honor roll that stood at the corner of Sixth Street and Erial Road since 1944. They are waiting for the unveiling of those citizens of Pine Hill who proudly served in the military during World War II. (Courtesy of Post No. 286.)

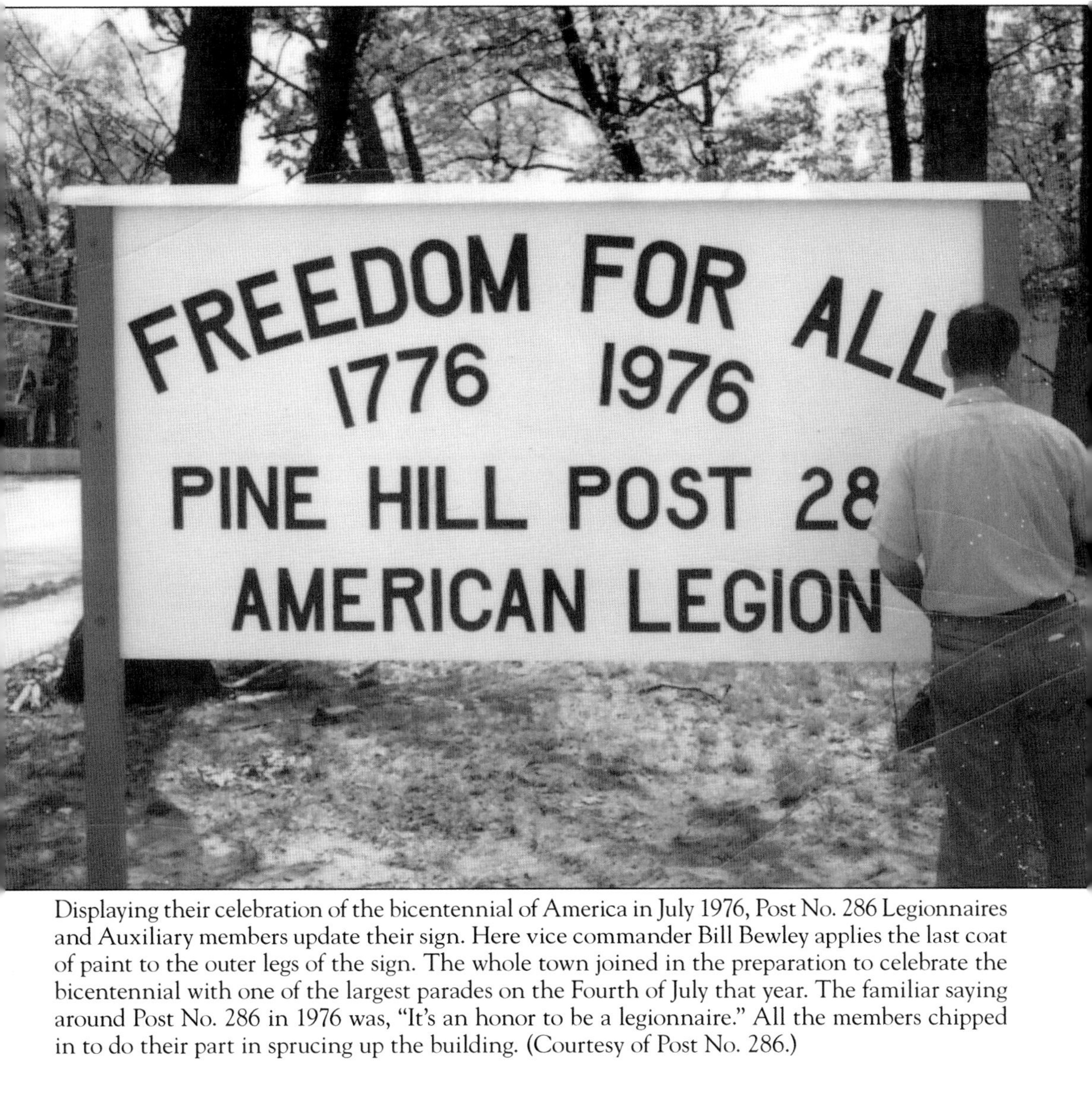

Displaying their celebration of the bicentennial of America in July 1976, Post No. 286 Legionnaires and Auxiliary members update their sign. Here vice commander Bill Bewley applies the last coat of paint to the outer legs of the sign. The whole town joined in the preparation to celebrate the bicentennial with one of the largest parades on the Fourth of July that year. The familiar saying around Post No. 286 in 1976 was, "It's an honor to be a legionnaire." All the members chipped in to do their part in sprucing up the building. (Courtesy of Post No. 286.)

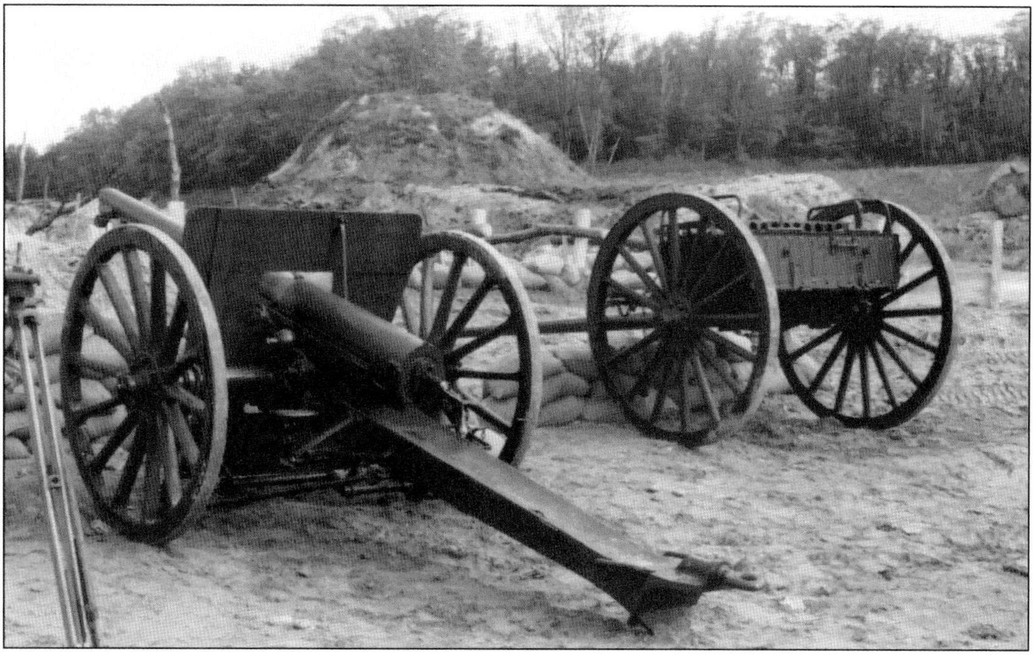

This 1898 French 75mm cannon, which was on display outside Post No. 286 since 1958, was donated to the Militia Museum of Sea Girt, New Jersey, in May 1984. This piece of history is still on display at the museum and is viewed by many members of the American Legion who attend the Legion College each year. (Courtesy of Post No. 286.)

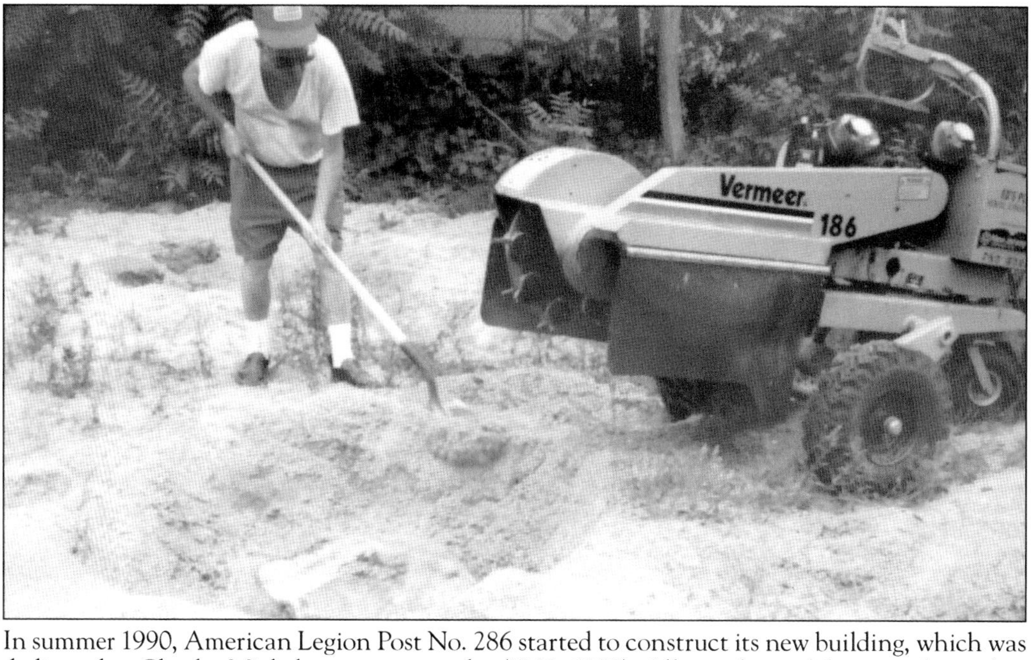

In summer 1990, American Legion Post No. 286 started to construct its new building, which was dedicated to Charles Mickel, past commander (1982–1983). All members of the post chipped in for the construction of the new building. The Ladies Auxiliary also chipped in with fund-raisers to help replenish the treasury. Bob McGlinchey does his part by running the underground wiring. (Courtesy of Post No. 286.)

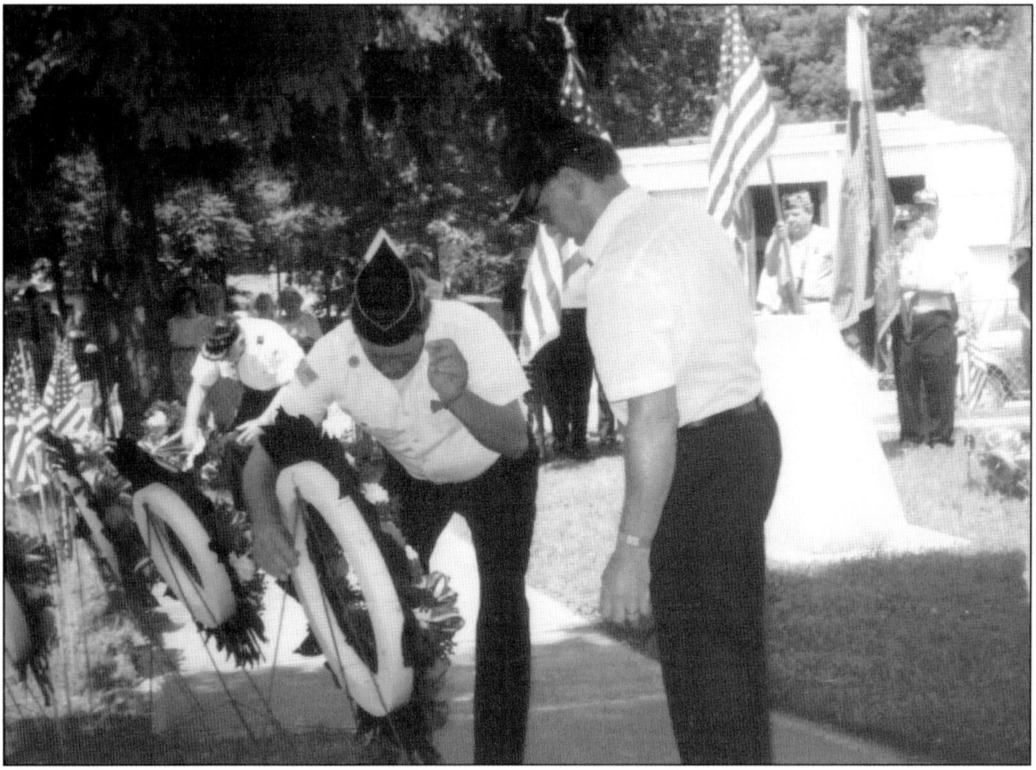

Mike Yaworski oversees the placement of the wreaths at the veterans memorial at the corner of Erial Road and Branch Avenue on Memorial Day in 1991. Each year, the American Legion and the Veterans of Foreign Wars (VFW) pay homage to their departed comrades lost in the line of duty. Wreaths are also placed by the mayor and council, the fire and police departments, the local school district, and the Boy Scouts. (Courtesy of Post No. 286.)

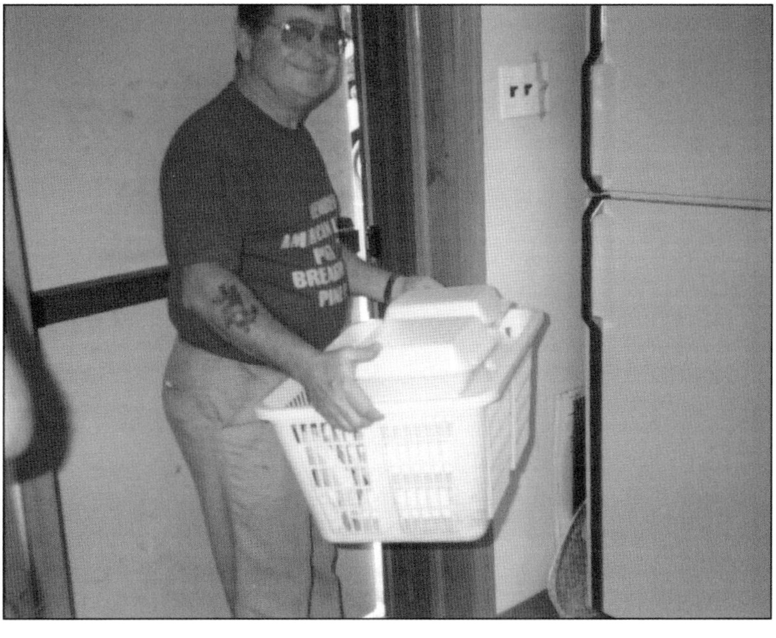

Here in 1992, Francis Bradley is loading up food for the veterans home for those veterans who are physically unable to travel. Each year, Post No. 286 holds a dinner for the veterans to give them a chance to get out and enjoy themselves. The Legionnaires cook a hot meal and distribute clothing and toiletries to the residents from the home. (Courtesy of Post No. 286.)

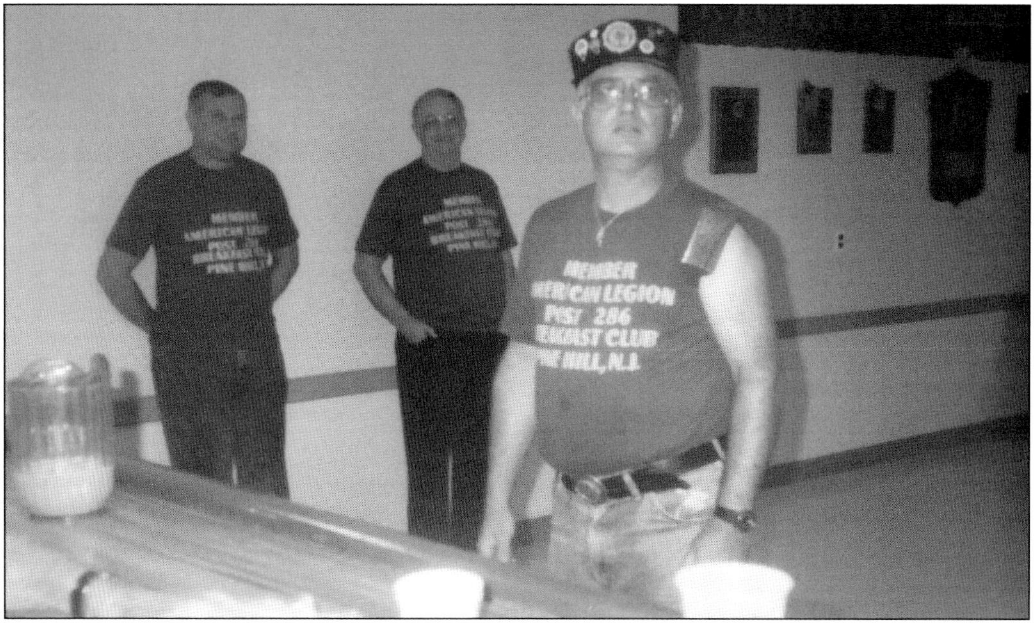

From left to right, Dave Flynn, Ed Domanski Sr., and Ed Domanski Jr. enjoy a social night in 1992 where members of the post gathered for some refreshments and fellowship. Social nights are a good time for the veterans to gather together to discuss the accomplishments of the year and tell old war stories. (Courtesy of Post No. 286.)

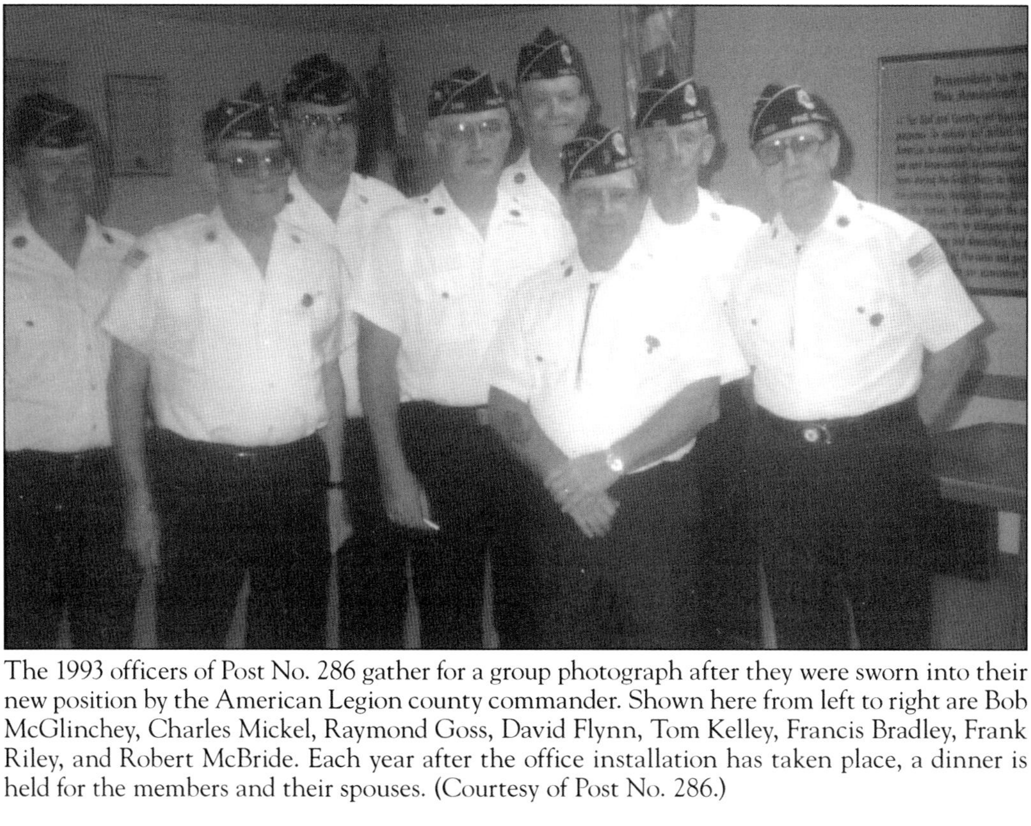

The 1993 officers of Post No. 286 gather for a group photograph after they were sworn into their new position by the American Legion county commander. Shown here from left to right are Bob McGlinchey, Charles Mickel, Raymond Goss, David Flynn, Tom Kelley, Francis Bradley, Frank Riley, and Robert McBride. Each year after the office installation has taken place, a dinner is held for the members and their spouses. (Courtesy of Post No. 286.)

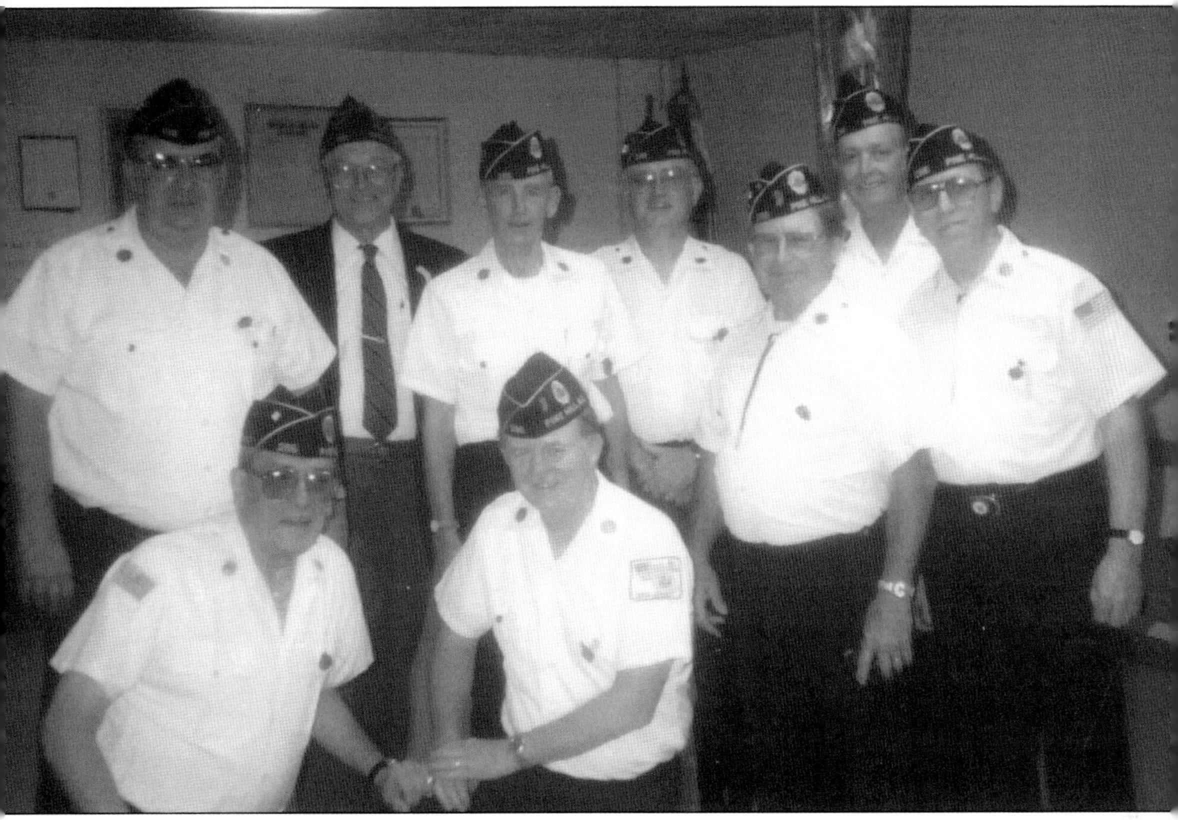

The county commander, William Breen, is wearing the tie and poses with the new officers in 1993. Commander Breen is also a resident of Pine Hill and a member of Post No. 286. Kneeling from left to right are Charles H. Mickel and Bob McGlinchey; (standing) Raymond J. Goss, William Breen, Frank Reily, David Flynn, Francis T. Bradley, Tom Kelly (the new Post No. 286 commander), and Bob McBride. Each year, the post elects new officers for the following year in April and have a formal dinner with distinguished visitors and entertainment. Pine Hill has a very active post where the main focus is community service. They visit the local schools several times a year as well as veterans and nursing homes. (Courtesy of Post No. 286.)

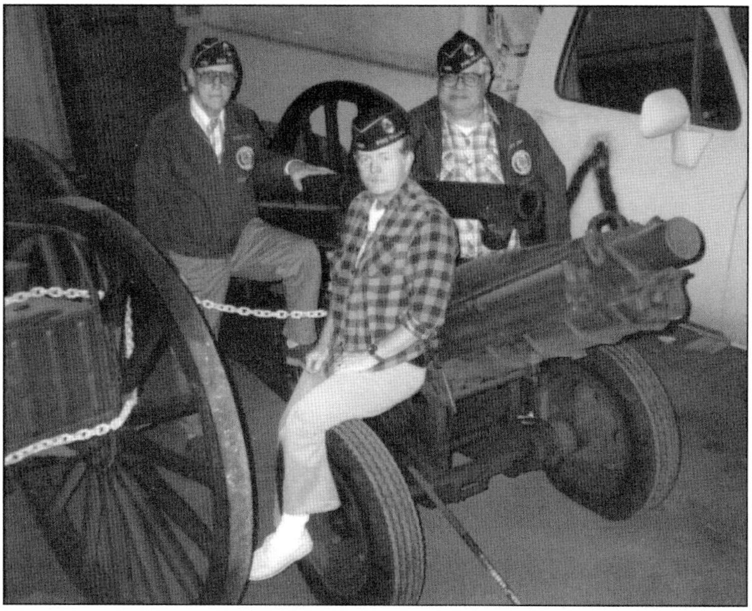

Members of Post No. 286 visited the military museum while attending the Legion College in 1993. The college is located in Sea Girt, New Jersey, at the National Guard Facility. Pine Hill members, from left to right, Bob McBride, Warren White, and Bob McGlinchey sit on a cannon that is displayed in front of the 1898 French 75mm that their post donated to the college in 1984. (Courtesy of Post No. 286.)

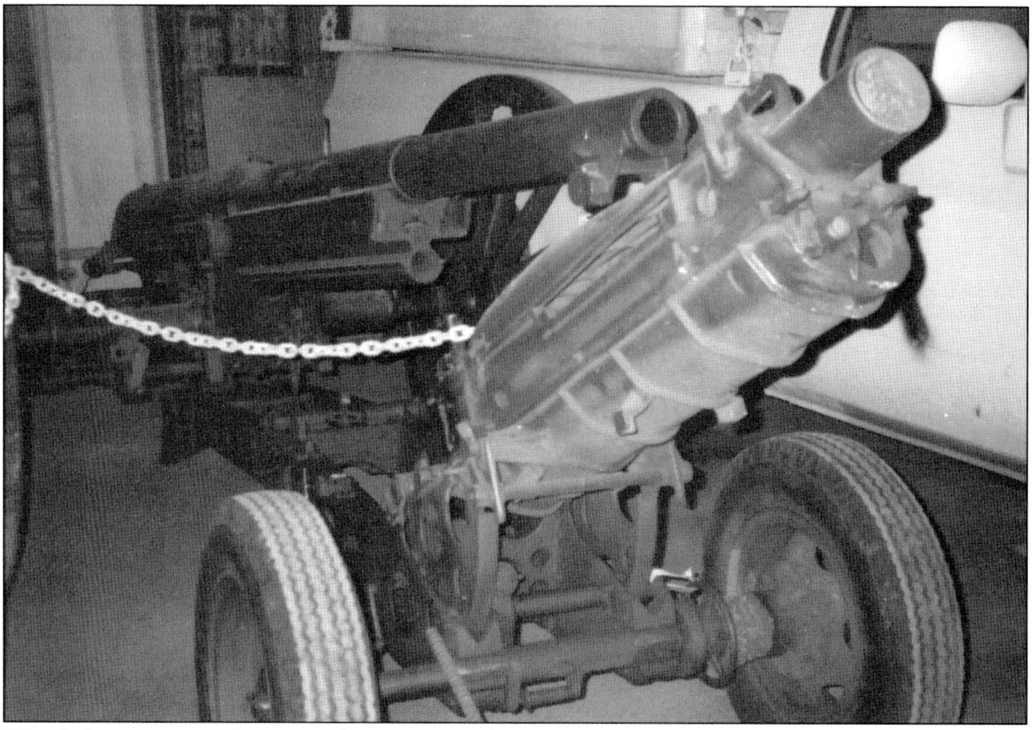

The dark cannon in the rear is the 1898 French 75mm cannon that the members of Post No. 286 donated. Whenever any members of Pine Hill attend the Legion College, they visit the cannon the first chance they get to make sure it is well taken care of. The members that have been around for a while make it a point to show the new members the cannon and fill them in on the history of where it came from. (Courtesy of Post No. 286.)

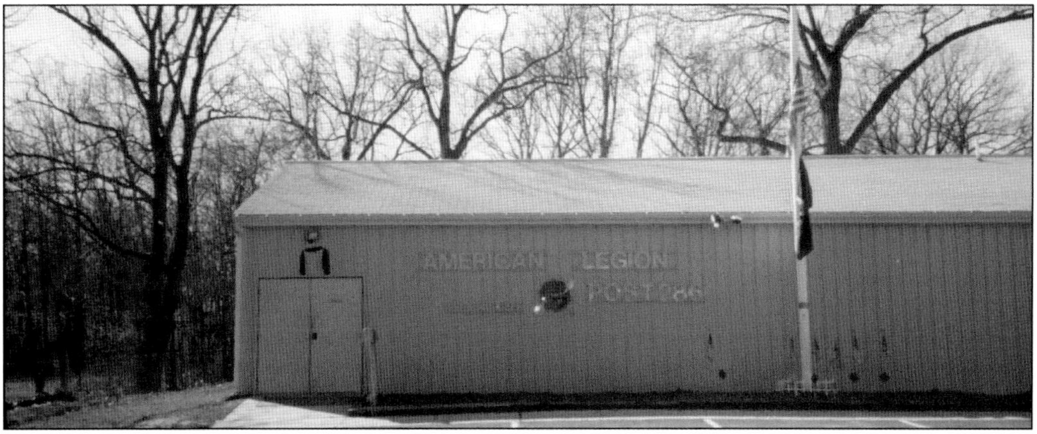

The new American Legion Post No. 286 stands completed prior to the dedication in 1998. During the next year, both the Legionnaires and Auxiliary members worked side by side to raise the funds to pay their obligations of the new building. Some of these fund-raisers continue today with cake and hoagie sales and a breakfast the first Sunday of the month.
(Courtesy of Post No. 286.)

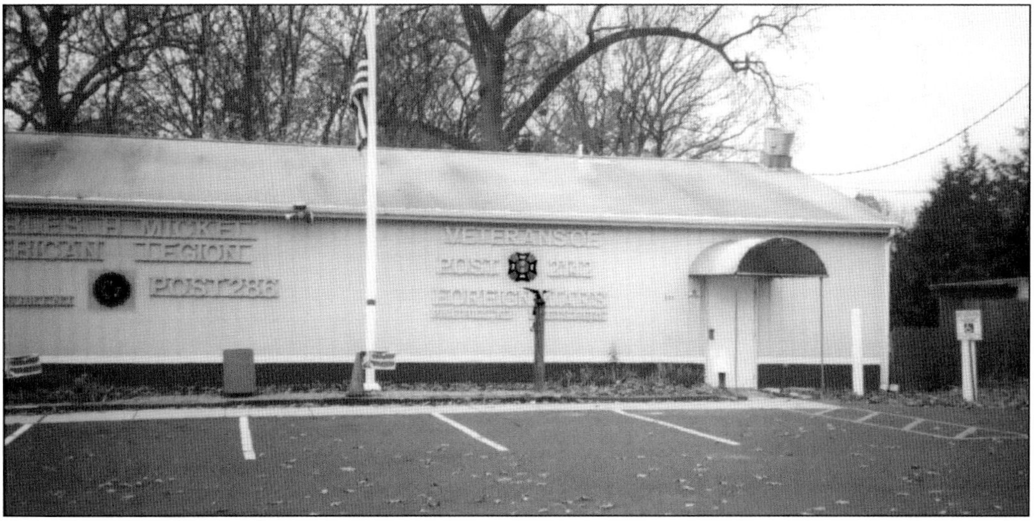

The American Legion and Veterans of Foreign Wars (VFW) now share the same building for their home in Pine Hill. This November 11 photograph shows the shared home of these two organizations. They may have separate names but they have the same goal, to serve the local community veterans who served in the military. (Courtesy of Les Gallagher Jr.)

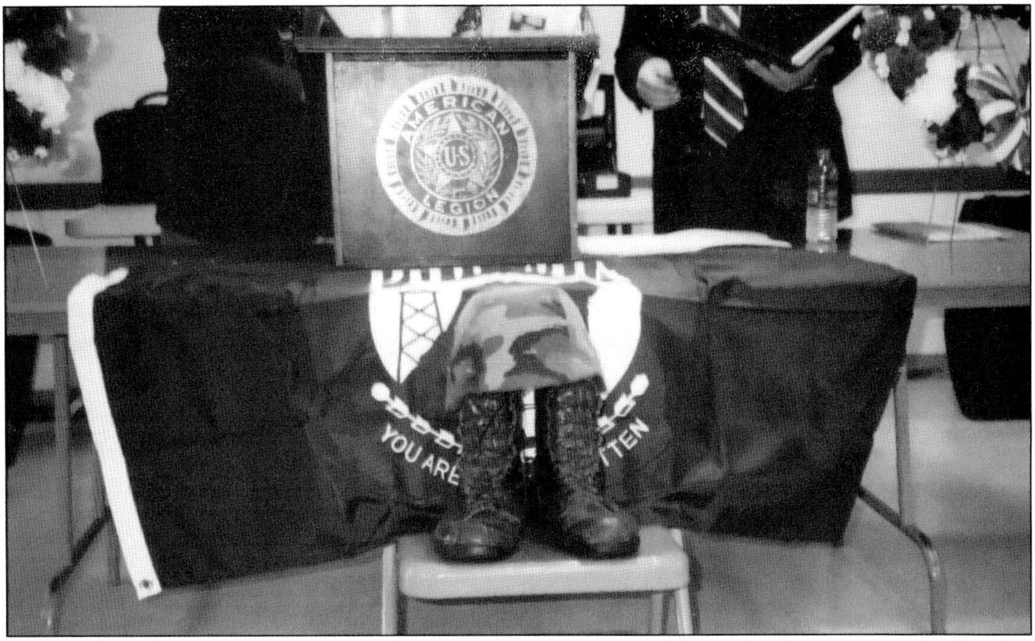

The American Legion remembers those who never returned home by keeping on display the POW/MIA flag with a pair of boots and a helmet. Every Veterans Day, the names of Pine Hill residents from all wars since World War I who never returned home are read. Here commander Joe Fisbeck along with Bud Bradley read the names of those Pine Hill residents who never returned home. (Courtesy of Les Gallagher Jr.)

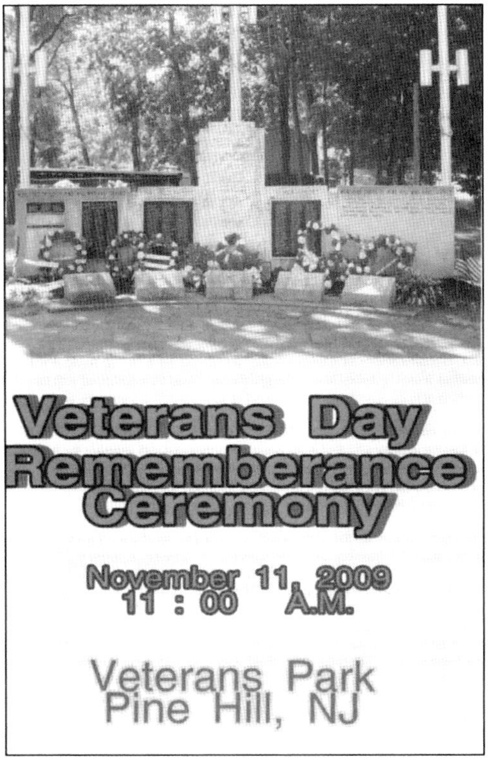

The dedication of the new veterans war memorial took place at 11:00 am on Veterans Day, November 11, 2009. The new memorial now has a stone honoring each branch of the U.S. military service. It also includes names of all residents of Pine Hill who left from here to serve their country in times of war/conflicts as members of the armed services. (Courtesy of Les Gallagher Jr.)

Five

RECREATION

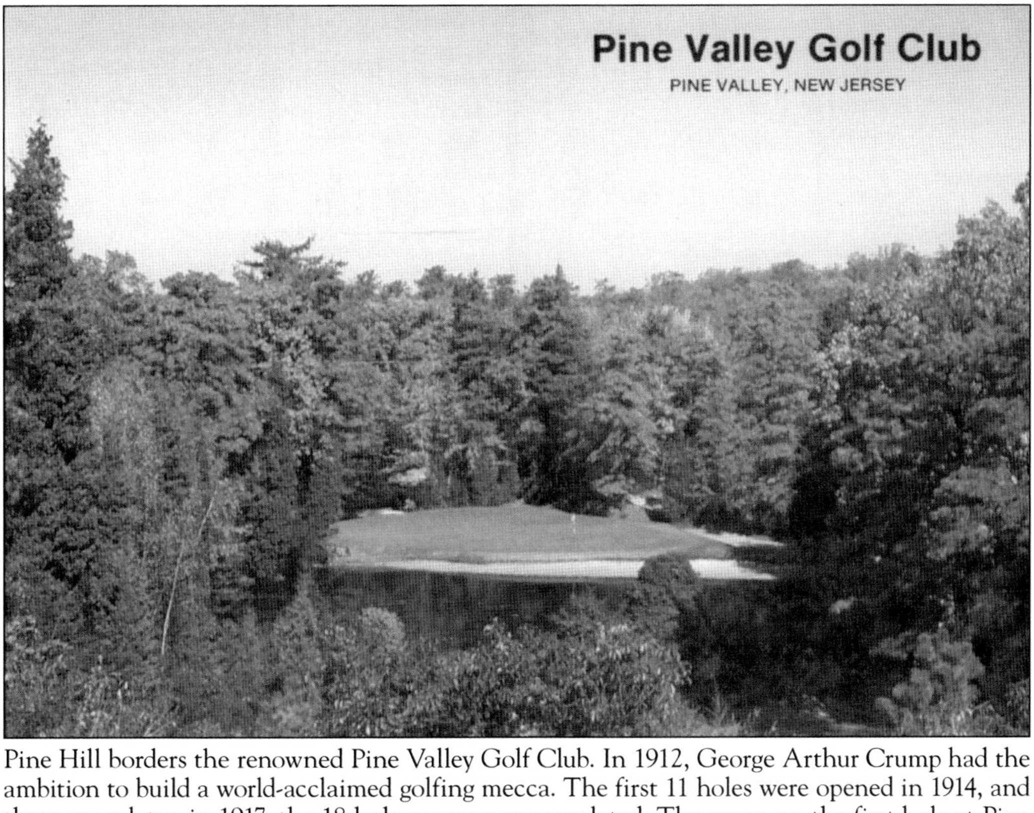

Pine Hill borders the renowned Pine Valley Golf Club. In 1912, George Arthur Crump had the ambition to build a world-acclaimed golfing mecca. The first 11 holes were opened in 1914, and three years later, in 1917, the 18-hole course was completed. The green on the first hole at Pine Valley is the second-highest point in South Jersey. Many Pine Hill residents found employment at the golf club. (Courtesy of John Elder.)

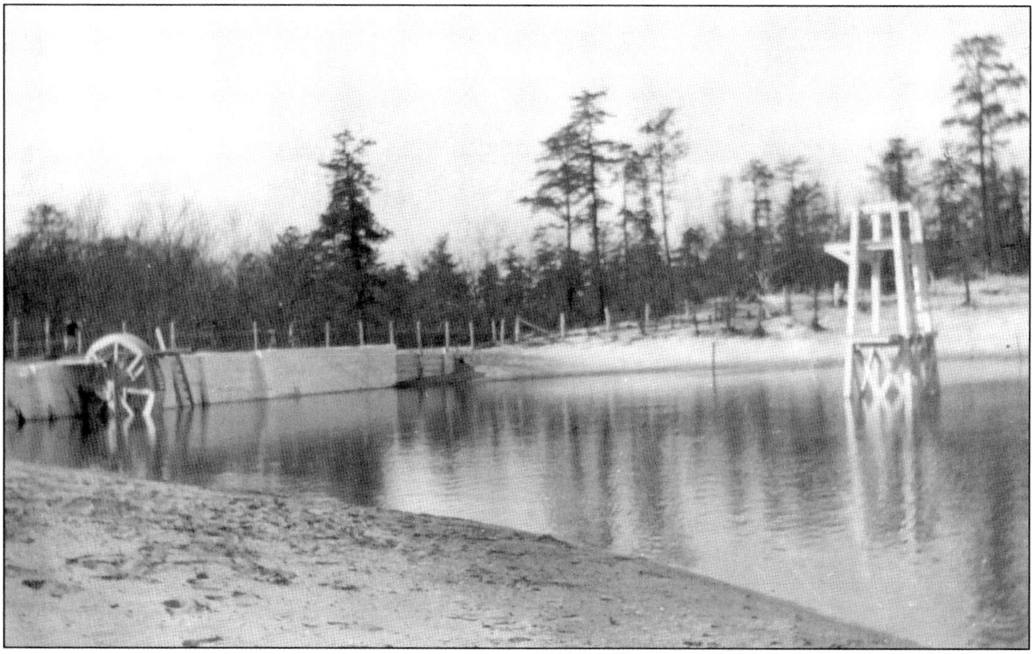

Steckys Lake was the hot spot in the early 1900s where most of the residents of Pine Hill would gather during the hot summer days. Here is what the lake looked like in 1928; it had a lifeguard chair and a pair of diving boards. The lake was fed by several underground springs that kept the water cool, and the large pine trees offered plenty of shade. (Courtesy of Ida Fisher.)

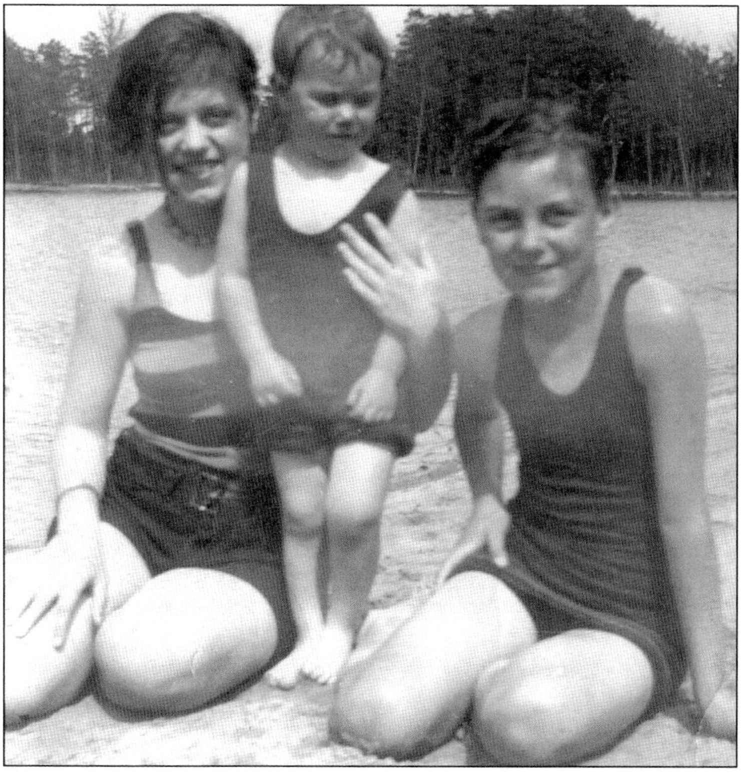

Ida poses with her older sisters Elly (left) and Ruth at the Pine Hill Park at Steckys Lake in the summer 1928. Ida said, "back then we had no air conditioning only a grating of fine wire to cover the windows to keep the bugs out and the air in." The lake was the best place to cool off and stay comfortable. (Courtesy of Ida Fisher.)

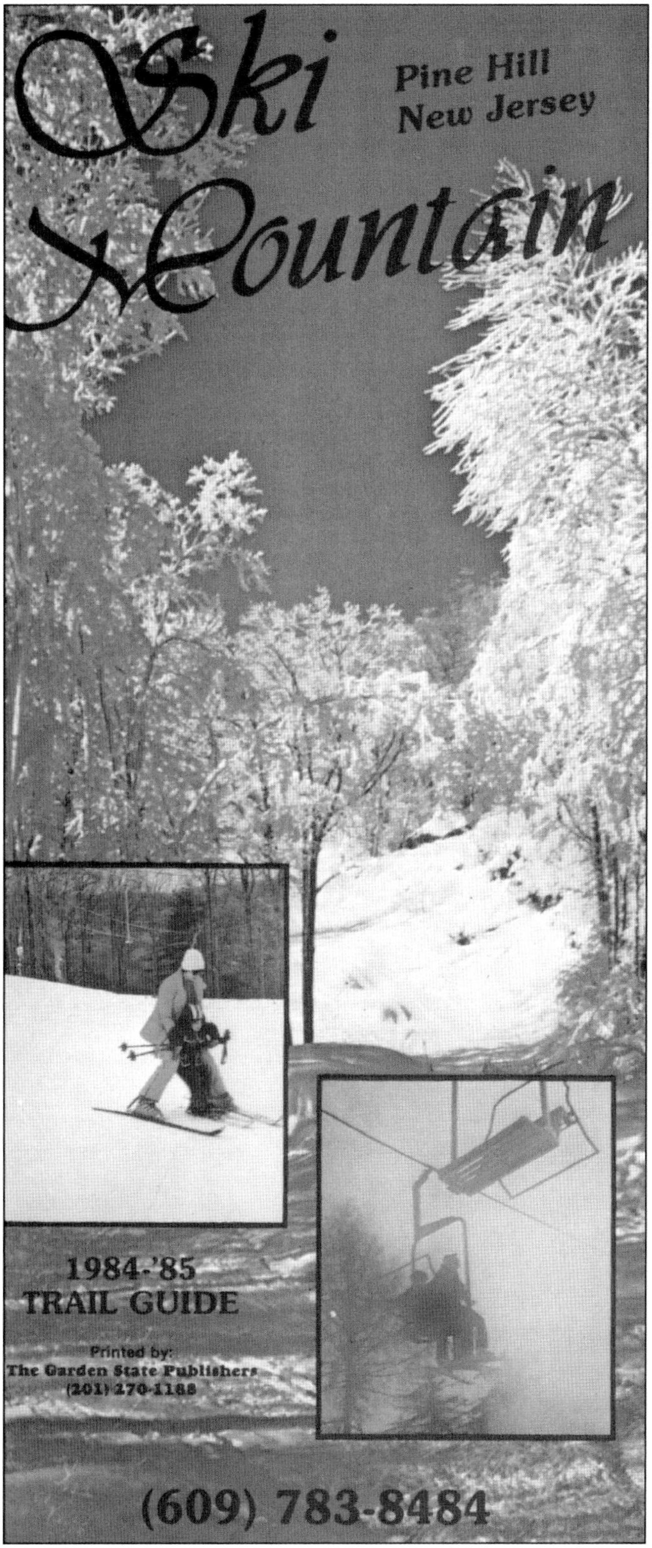

Ski Mountain ski area opened in the winter of 1964–1965. Ski Mountain is the highest point in South Jersey with a 214-foot elevation. The main slope had a 137-foot vertical. The ski area started with a beginner rope tow and a t-bar lift. Later a double pony lift was added, and the chair lift was installed in 1978 and opened in the winter of 1979. (Courtesy of Emil Del Conte.)

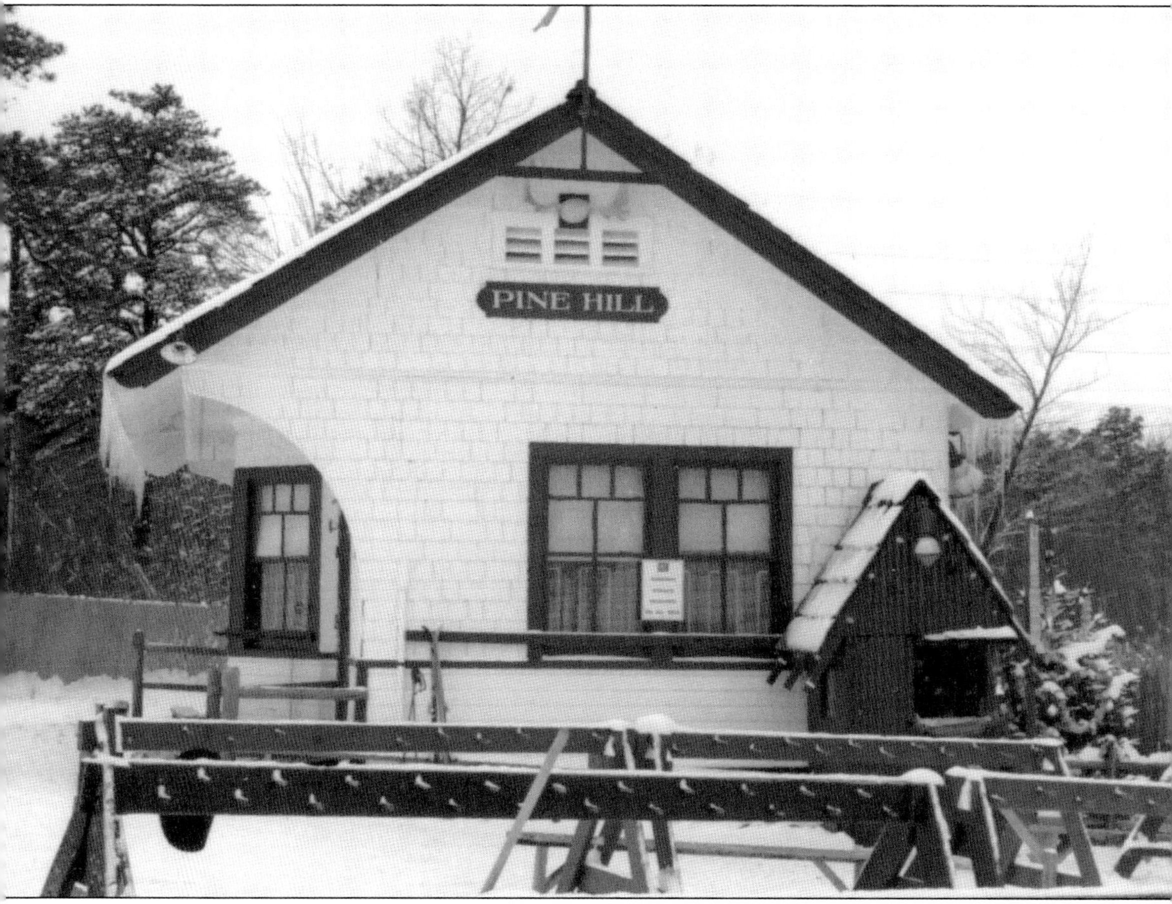

The first aid building at Ski Mountain was originally from the 94-year-old Clementon Station of the Pennsylvania Reading Railroad. Workmen transported the structure up the hill on a flatbed truck. The old railroad station served Ski Mountain well, housing the ski patrol and rental shop. (Courtesy of Emil Del Conte.)

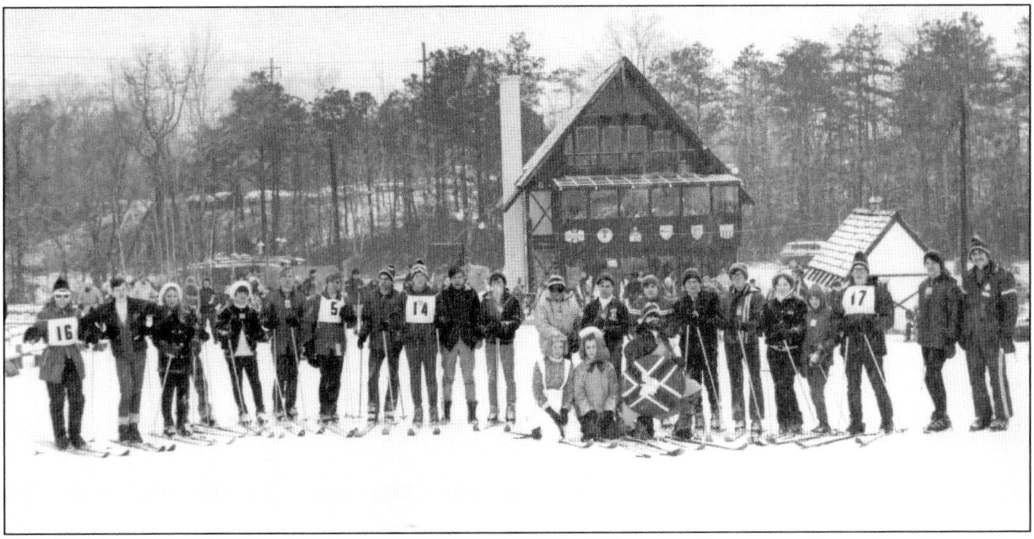

Racers gather on snowy race day at the mountain in 1967 with the original chalet lodge in the background. Race day was an annual event that attracted people from all over New Jersey and Philadelphia. Skiing in costumes on race day (like Raggedy Ann and Andy kneeling in the photograph) became a lasting tradition. (Courtesy of Emil Del Conte.)

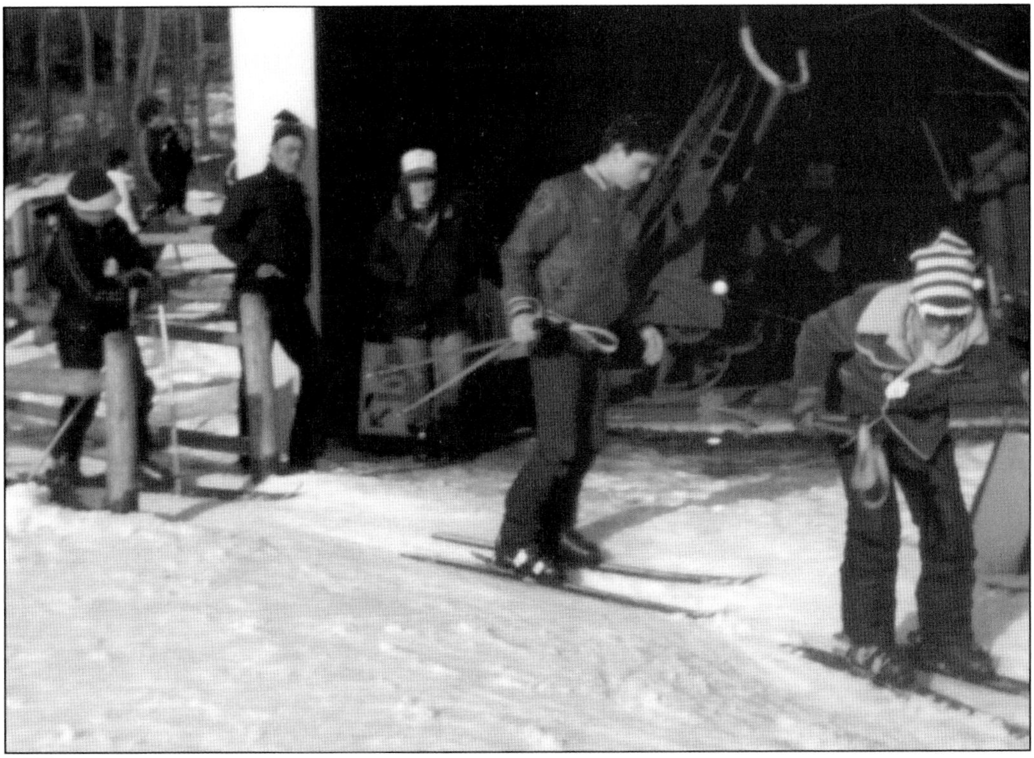

Skiers are loading the pony lift. This was a challenging lift for operator and skiers alike. If one skier fell, they usually knocked others off as well. The lift operator could be kept busy helping skiers right themselves and line their skis up in the snow track. Pictured beyond the skiers are lift operator Sherry and manager John Warner. (Courtesy of Judy Gallagher Lerner.)

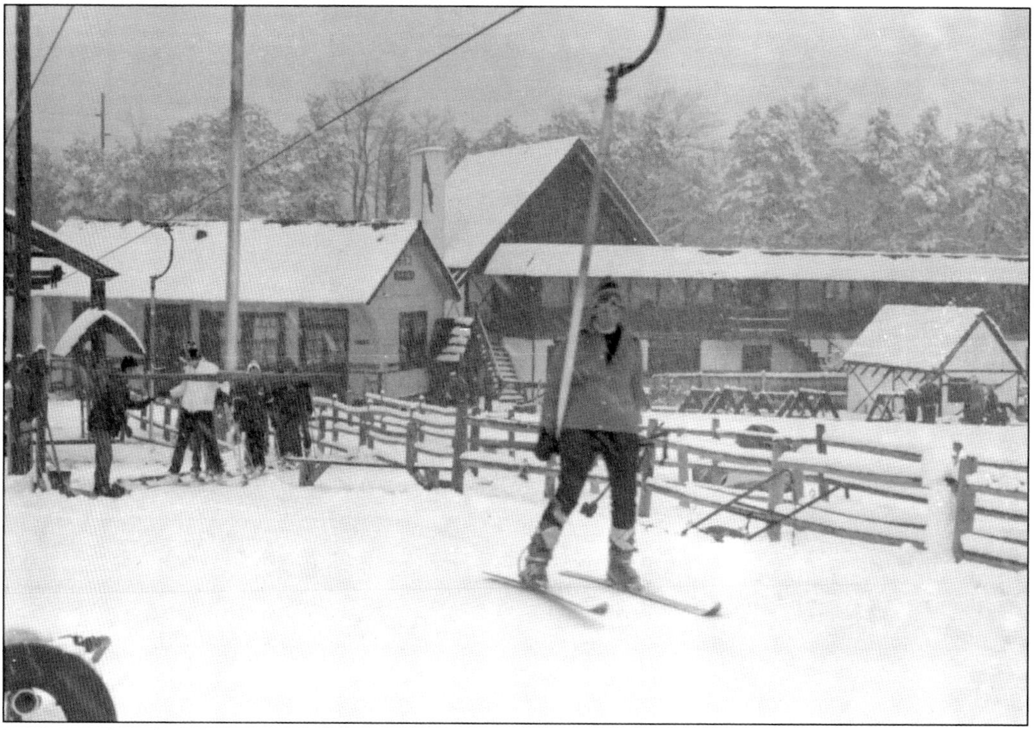

In 1973, the t-bar lift was a fast way to the top, but not for those skiers who tried to sit. Many would fall because the bar was on a spring inside the pole and was meant for leaning against. The t-bar is designed to push the skier up the hill, and if one tried to sit, the bar would spring out of the pole and ultimately knock anyone down. (Courtesy of Emil Del Conte.)

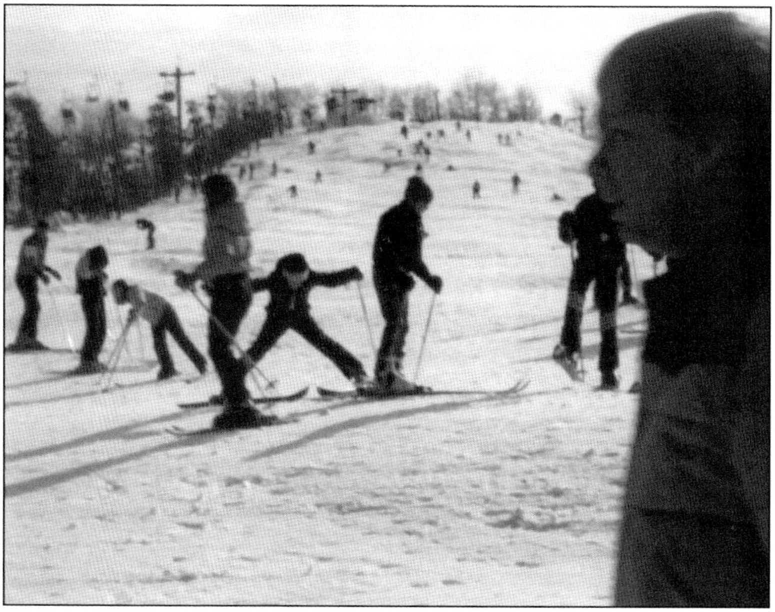

Ski Mountain was a family-oriented mountain, and many beginners made their debut on skis here. The snow-covered slope was developed with manmade snow using compressed air and water from the pond at the base of the hill. Skiers learning to ski at the base of the main slope would sometimes lose their skis in the pond. (Courtesy of Judy Gallagher Lerner.)

If weather cooperated, Ski Mountain tried to open by Thanksgiving, and the season would usually end around St. Patrick's Day. A snowstorm came in March after the mountain had closed for the season, and the ski lift mechanic had to put the pony-lift handles back on to reopen. (Courtesy of Judy Gallagher Lerner.)

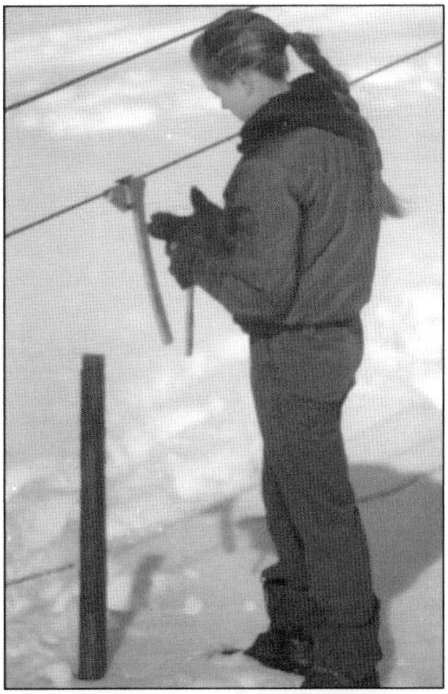

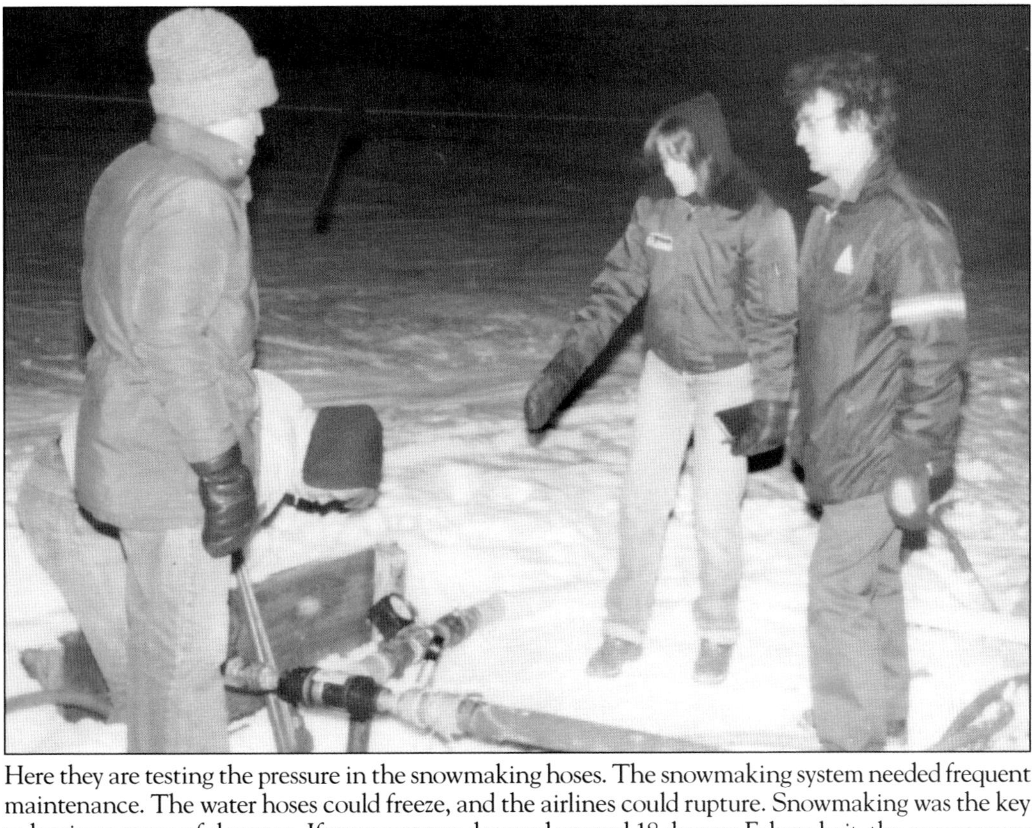

Here they are testing the pressure in the snowmaking hoses. The snowmaking system needed frequent maintenance. The water hoses could freeze, and the airlines could rupture. Snowmaking was the key to having a successful season. If temperatures dropped around 18 degrees Fahrenheit, the compressors would have to make snow. Pictured from left to right are owner Emil Del Conte, manager John Warner, assistant manager Judy Gallagher, and Ken Larsen. (Courtesy of Judy Gallagher Lerner.)

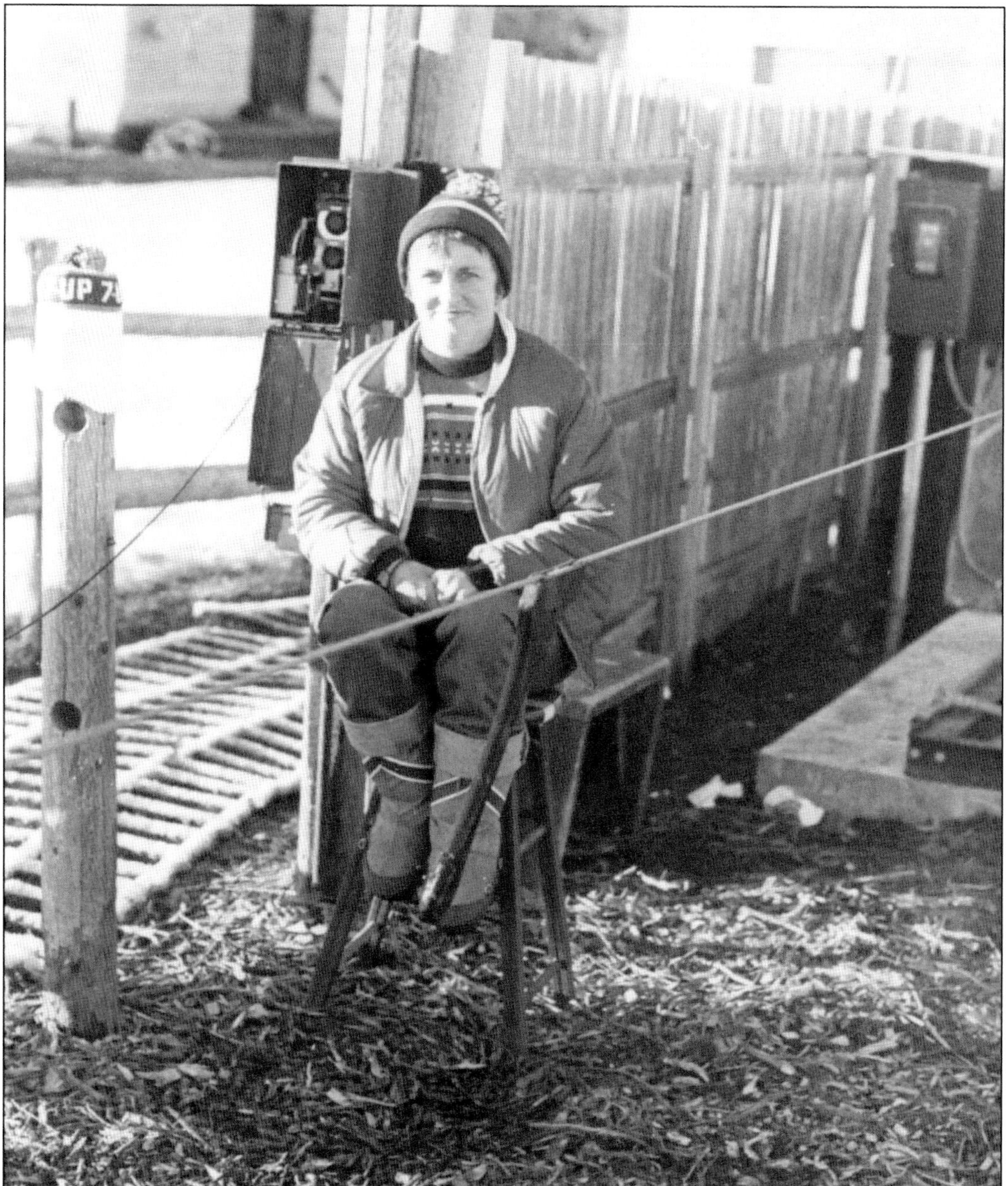

Ski Mountain lift operator Ronnie Black is pictured at the beginner rope tow. At the end of the season, when snow was getting scarce, wire mats with a grass covering would allow skiers to glide up the to the lift line. The emergency brake is the thin cord to the right of the lift operator. If a beginner fell, the operator could quickly stop the lift by pulling the emergency cord. (Courtesy of Judy Gallagher Lerner.)

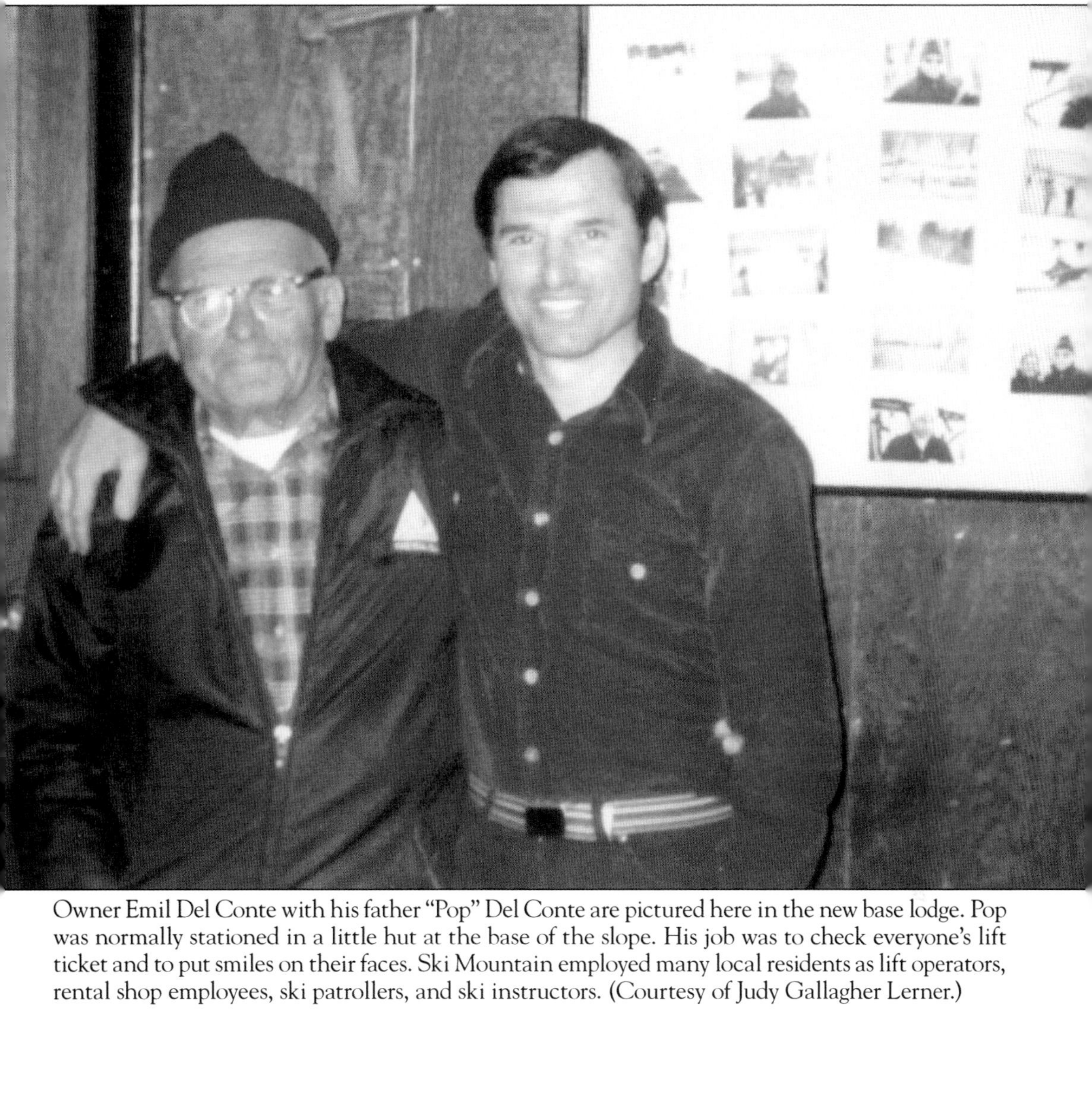

Owner Emil Del Conte with his father "Pop" Del Conte are pictured here in the new base lodge. Pop was normally stationed in a little hut at the base of the slope. His job was to check everyone's lift ticket and to put smiles on their faces. Ski Mountain employed many local residents as lift operators, rental shop employees, ski patrollers, and ski instructors. (Courtesy of Judy Gallagher Lerner.)

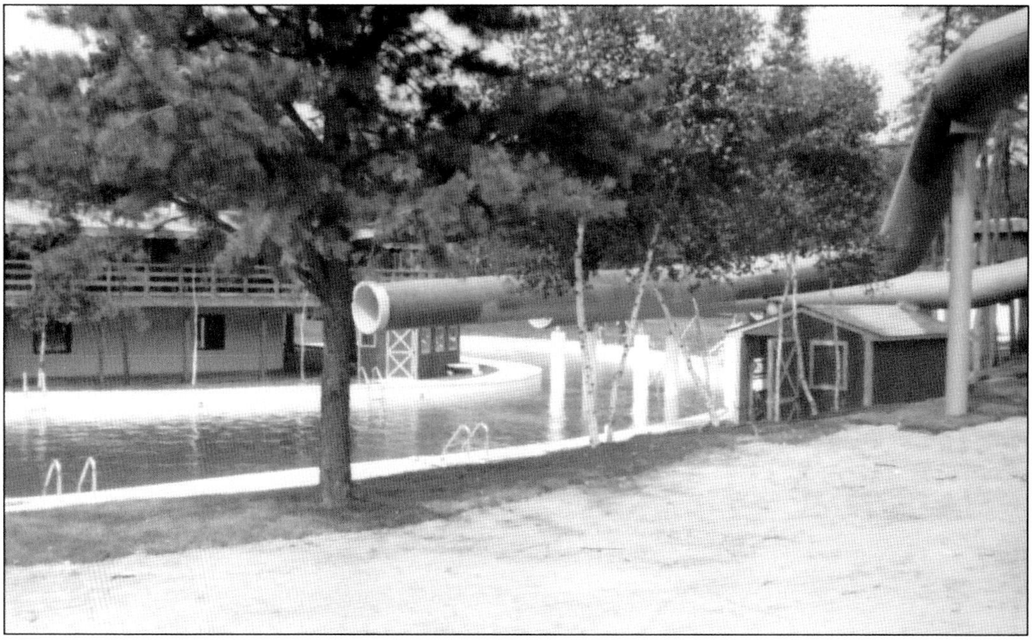

Ski Mountain underwent a massive transformation to become Action Mountain for summer recreation in June 1984. Featuring over 15 different attractions with new and exciting rides, the waterpark became popular with groups and companies, which had daily outings from May through September and weekends through November. A pool was added to the base of the mountain where the water slide would drop visitors with a splash. (Courtesy of Emil Del Conte.)

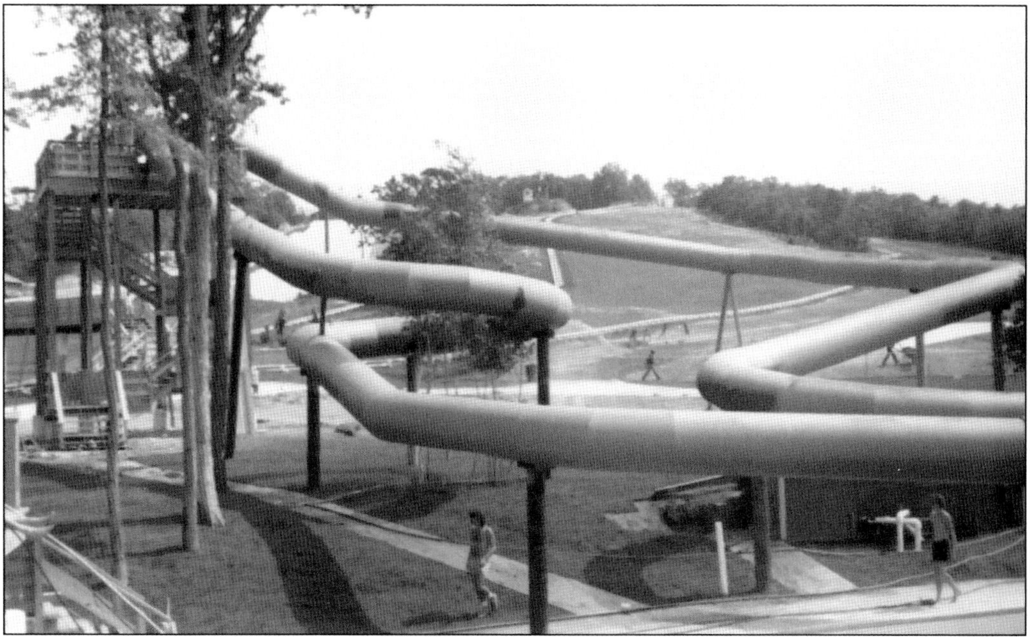

Workers are busy getting the new Action Park ready to open. The new owners also own Vernon Valley Great Gorge Ski Area. Slides and water lines traverse the mountain that was snow covered just a few months earlier. Once again, the mountain becomes a good source of employment for local residents. (Courtesy of Emil Del Conte.)

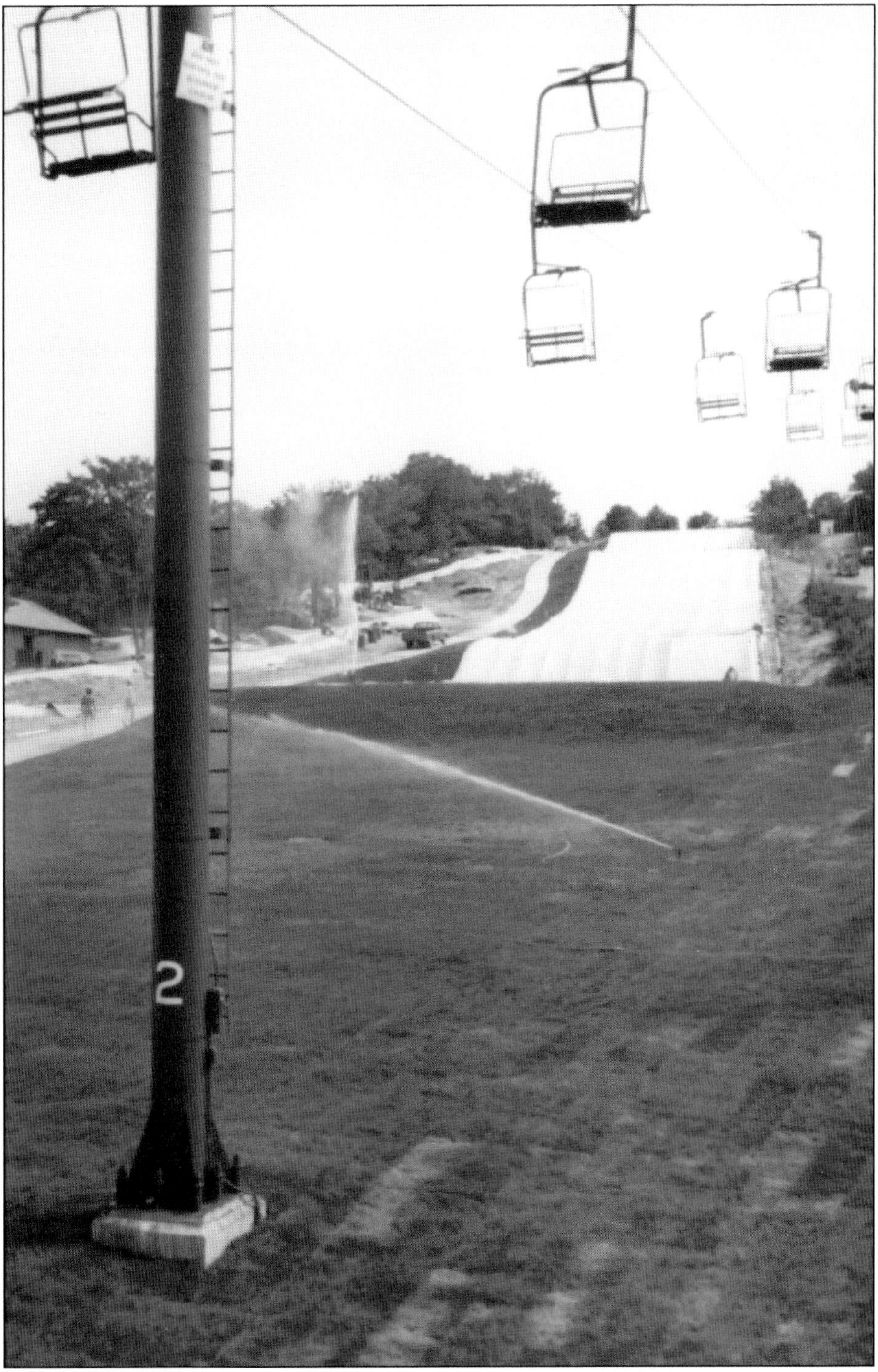

This photograph looks up from the base of the hill and shows the giant slide being prepared for opening day of Action Mountain, June 1984. A great deal of sod was installed, and sprinklers worked hard to keep it from drying out. The chair lift was used to take visitors to the top of the giant slide and the rapids. (Courtesy of Emil Del Conte.)

Action
Ski Mountain

P. O. Box 111
Pine Hill, N.J 08021
(609) 783-8564

Dear Neighbor,

We are now offering an exciting benefit, which we feel you are sure to appreciate.

It's our Community Club Card family discount program! A new discount card program designed exclusively for the residents of Pine Hill.

With just one Community Club Card you receive a generous 50% savings on every visit, anytime for the entire family at Action/Ski Mountain. Action/Ski Mountain is a family oriented park featuring an array of the most spectacular rides and skiing facilities. Action Mountain will kick off it's season sometime in June. Don't miss the fun filled days you can experience at Action/Ski Mountain.

If you have any questions please give us a call at 783-8564.

Sincerely,

Dale E. Kelley

Dale E. Kelley
General Manager

*REMINDER: No food or beverage is permitted in the park.
No jewelry or cut-off jeans permitted on the rides.

Looking to attract customers, general manager Dale Kelly sent out a flyer announcing the opening of the new Action/Ski Mountain. It included a special offer only to local Pine Hill residents. Residents of Pine Hill had the opportunity to save 50 percent on every visit to the park with the new community club discount card. (Courtesy of Natalie Maguire.)

Community Club Card
Action Mountain/Ski Mountain

____
Family Name

This card entitles you, your family and friends to a special ticket discount at Action Mountain & Ski Mountain.

Limit 10 purchases per card per day.

50% Savings

On a clear summer day, one can view the Philadelphia skyline from the top of Action Mountain, located on Branch Avenue. Tubes were used to ride the roaring rapids all the way down the mountain. Many local children spent hours having summer fun here. (Courtesy of Emil Del Conte.)

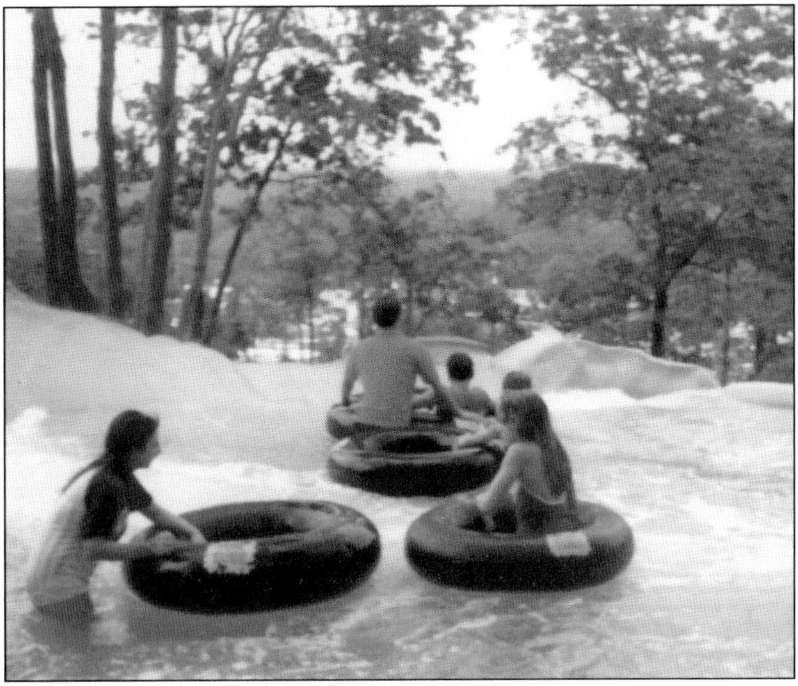

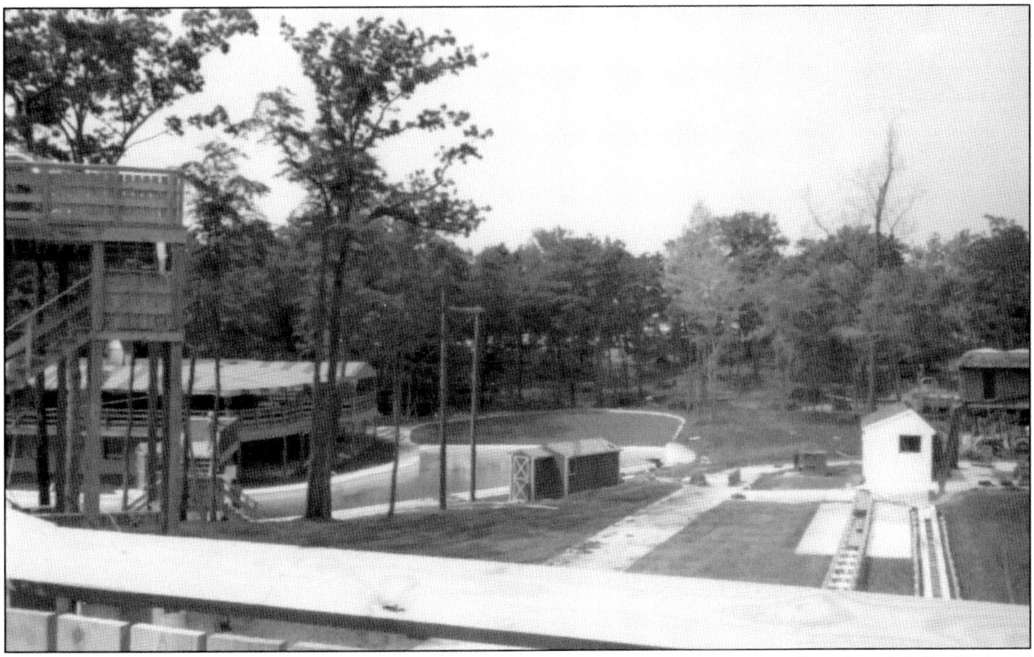

Looking down from the top of Action Mountain in 1984, one can see the chairlift bullwheel and building on the right and the new pool and slides on the left. Action Mountain was a new self-participation park that kept children and adults active during the summer. (Courtesy of Emil Del Conte.)

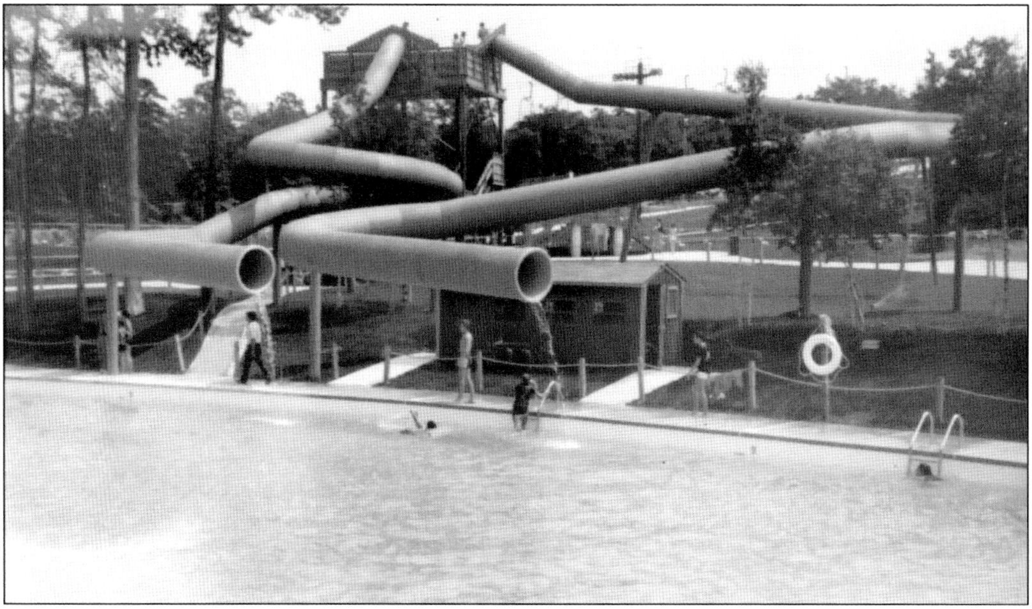

The double-tube water slides provided friends with hours of fun racing to be dumped into the pool below. Although this was at the base of the mountain, park visitors had quite a climb to reach the top. At the opposite end, the pool could also be used for swimming. (Courtesy of Emil Del Conte.)

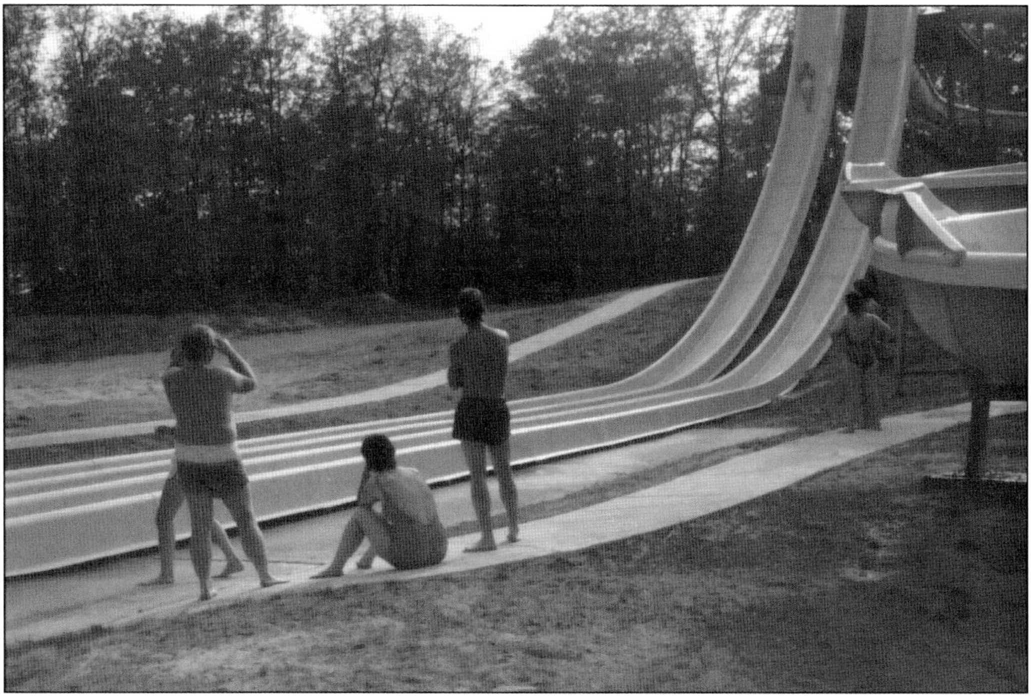

This photograph shows people resting and taking pictures of friends and family as they come down the open-cliff water slide, which has a 60-foot drop. Local children could walk to the waterpark where they paid $18 for the season package to use the park, all of the slides, and rides. (Courtesy of Emil Del Conte.)

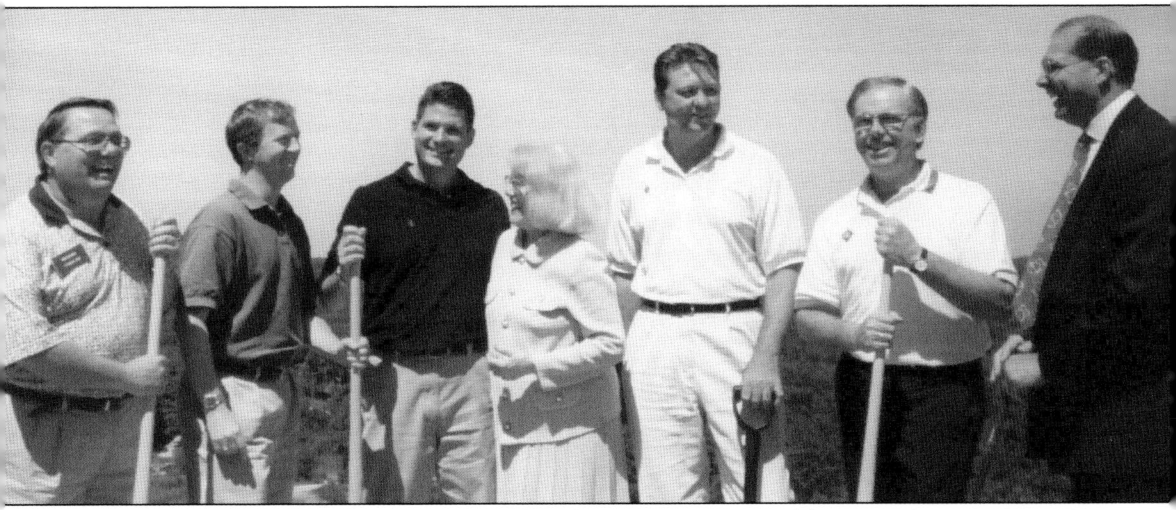

The ground breaking of the new Pine Hill Golf Course is pictured here on August 10, 1999. Designed by legendary golf architect Tom Fazio and built by Eric Bergstol, the exceptional golf course was developed on the site where Ski Mountain once stood (500 West Branch Avenue). Pictured from left to right are Tom Hasset, John Adler, Lou Greenwald, Mary Previte, Eric Bergstol, Tom Fazio, and Ora L. Wooster. (Courtesy of Natalie Maguire.)

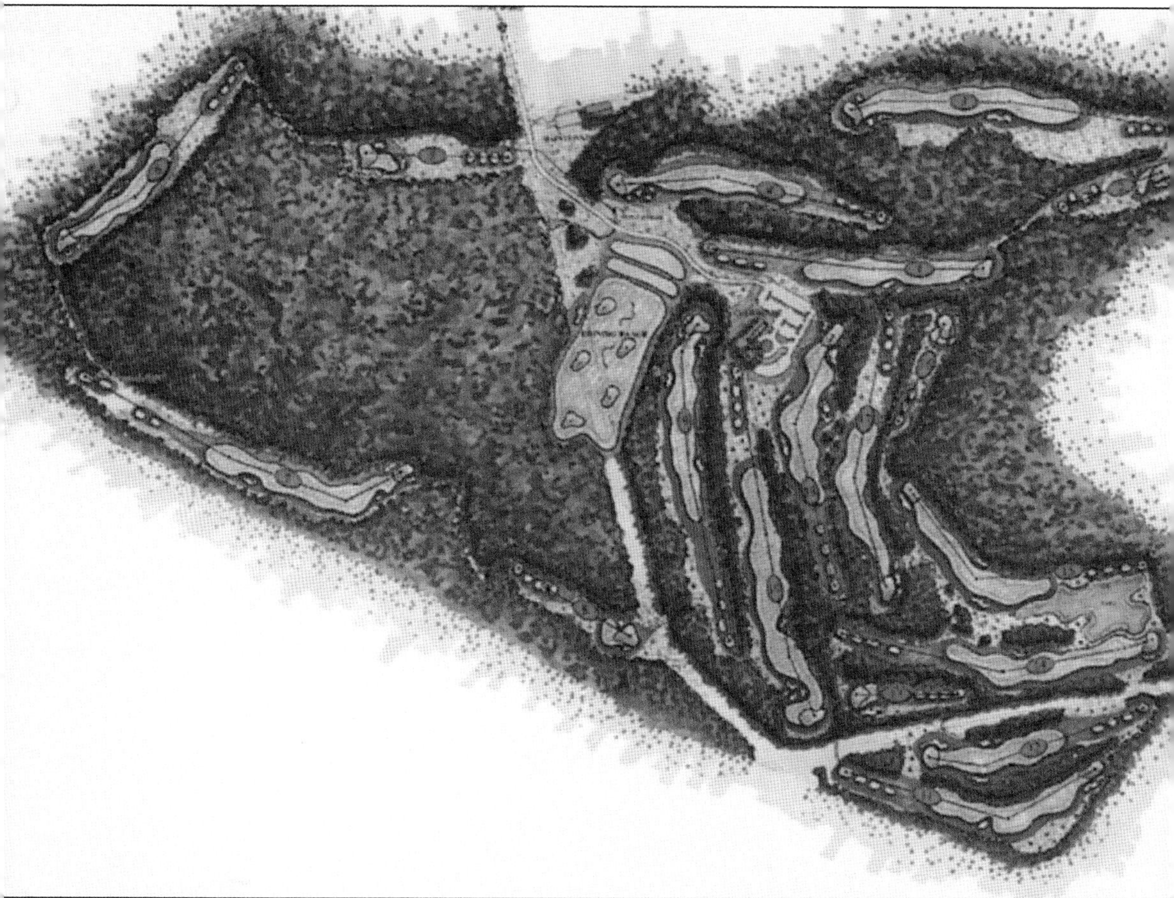

The 18-hole Pine Hill Golf Club opened in 2000. At 6,900 yards and par 70, the course is challenging and breathtaking. Each hole seems to be in its own private world, hidden by the tree-lined fairways. The 43,000-square-foot clubhouse is perched on the highest point in southern New Jersey, where it offers the stunning view of the Philadelphia skyline. (Courtesy of Eric Bergstol.)

Six

People and Places Around Town

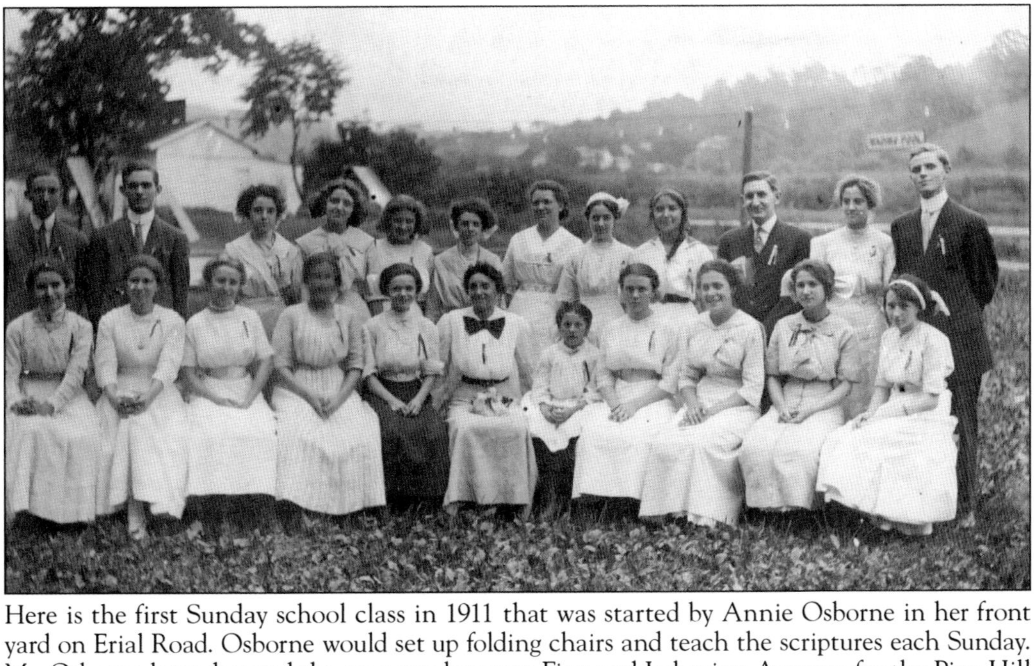

Here is the first Sunday school class in 1911 that was started by Annie Osborne in her front yard on Erial Road. Osborne would set up folding chairs and teach the scriptures each Sunday. Mr. Osborne later donated the property between First and Lakeview Avenues for the Pine Hill Methodist Episcopal Church to be built. (Courtesy of Dr. Al Davies.)

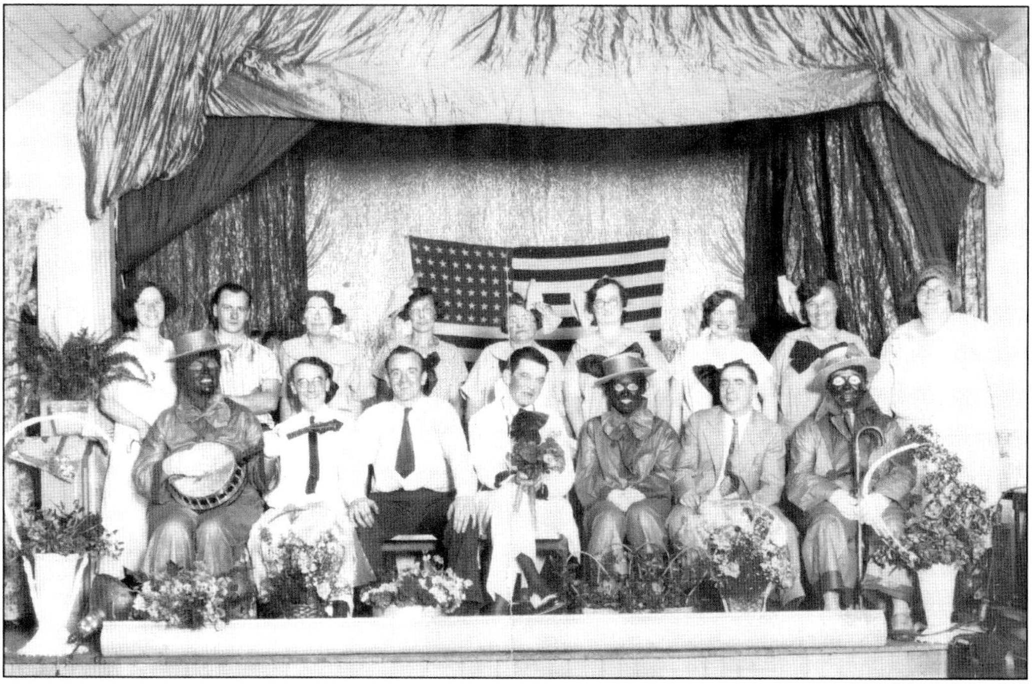

In 1915, the local townspeople put on their first minstrel show at the No. 1 Fire Company. Pictured in the first row are the following: E. Woehr, J. McGuirl, Mayor J. Stetson, E. Fisher, A. Gauden, E. Stroup, and unidentified; (second row) E. Campbell, M. Bennet, E. Appenzeller, F. Lang, E. Woehr, M. Stout, Y. Walls, M. Gregory, and unidentified. (Courtesy of Ida Fisher.)

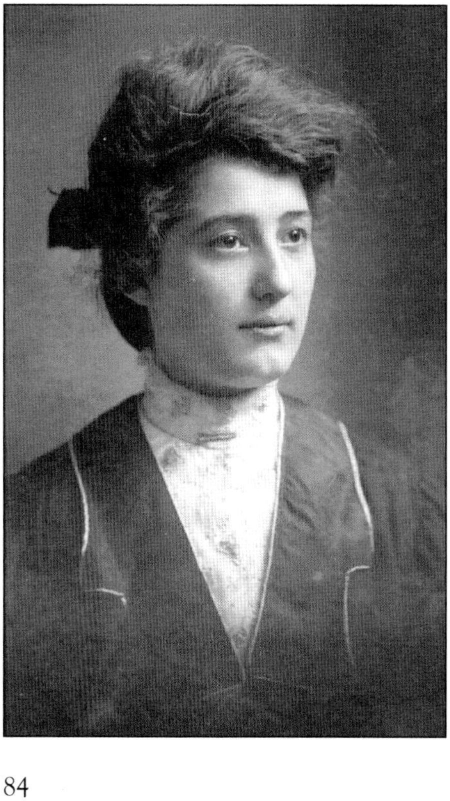

Here is a portrait of Eliza Brooks in 1910. Her family was one of the first early full-time residents of Clementon Heights, which became Pine Hill in 1929. The majority of the residents were summer residents who came to enjoy the therapeutic sand, natural springwater, and fresh pine smell. (Courtesy of Mary Gallagher.)

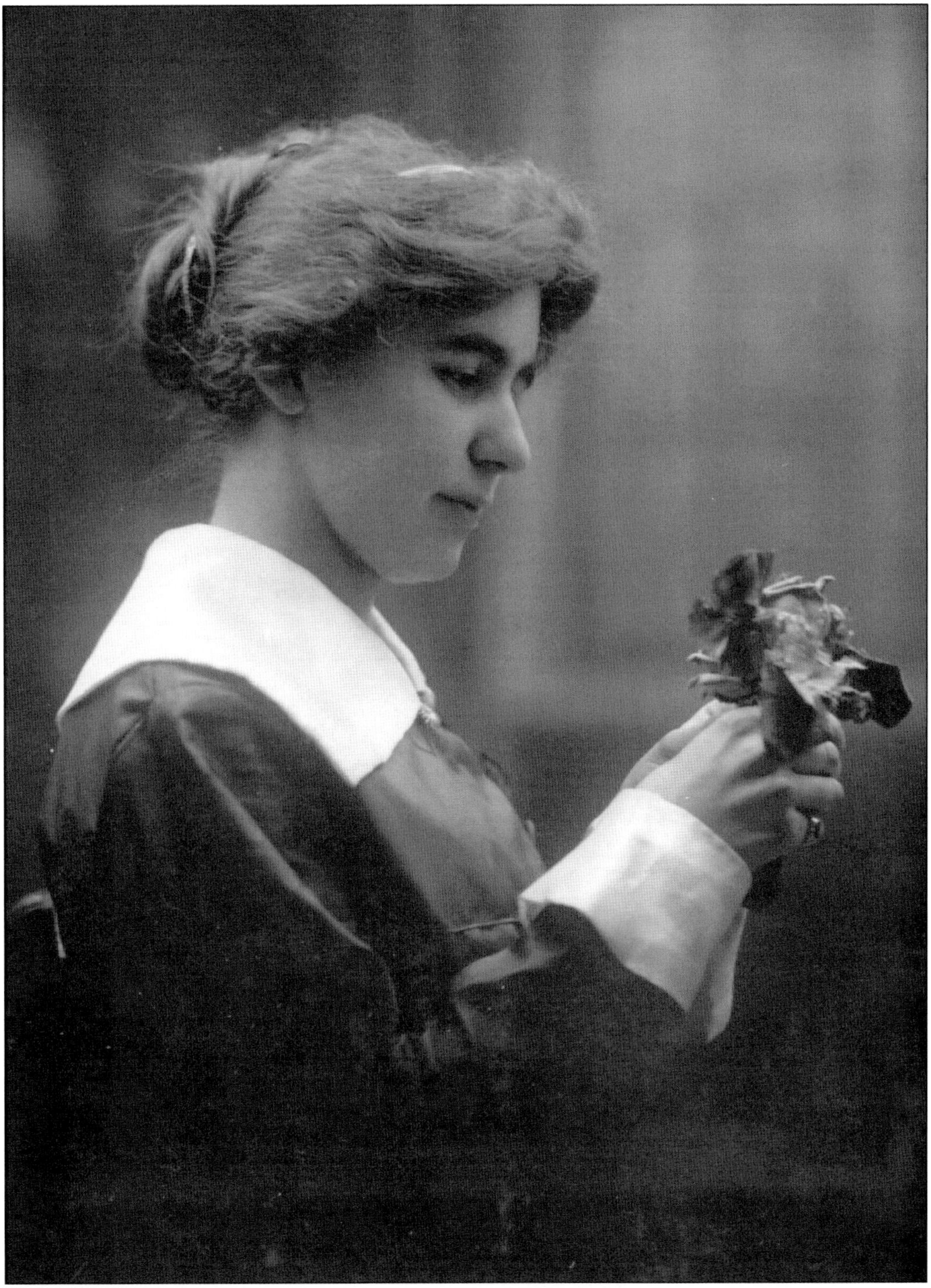

Another of the early full-time settlers were the Meinhardts who lived on Third Avenue. In this photograph is Mable Meinhardt holding some of the flowers she grew in her backyard. The white sand made it hard to grow grass, but many families had small gardens where they grew fruit and vegetables and flowers; Mable preferred the flowers. (Courtesy of Mary Gallagher.)

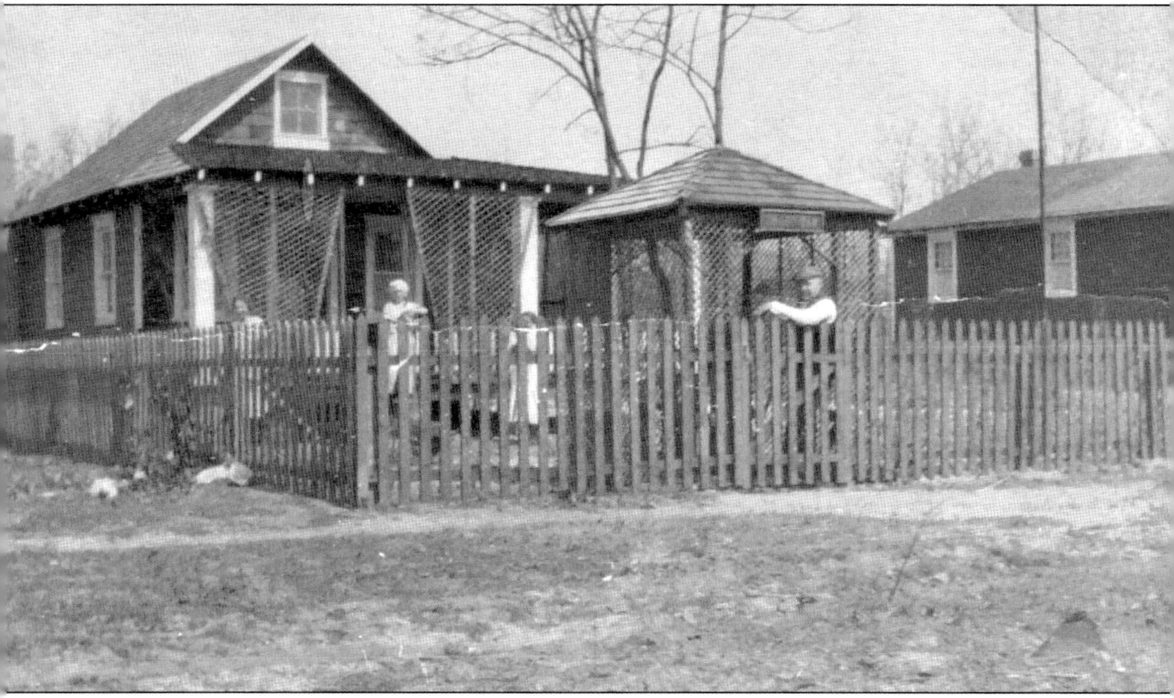

Mr. Fieger stands at the gate of his home on Eighth Avenue, as Mrs. Fieger stands on the front stoop in 1920. The homes in Pine Hill were very small in the 1920s. They were mainly wood structures with only two rooms, and they had no electricity or indoor plumbing. The Fiegers would fetch their water from the hand pump out in the yard and use kerosene lamps for light at night. They did not own a car, so they would walk everywhere. (Courtesy of Ida Fieger.)

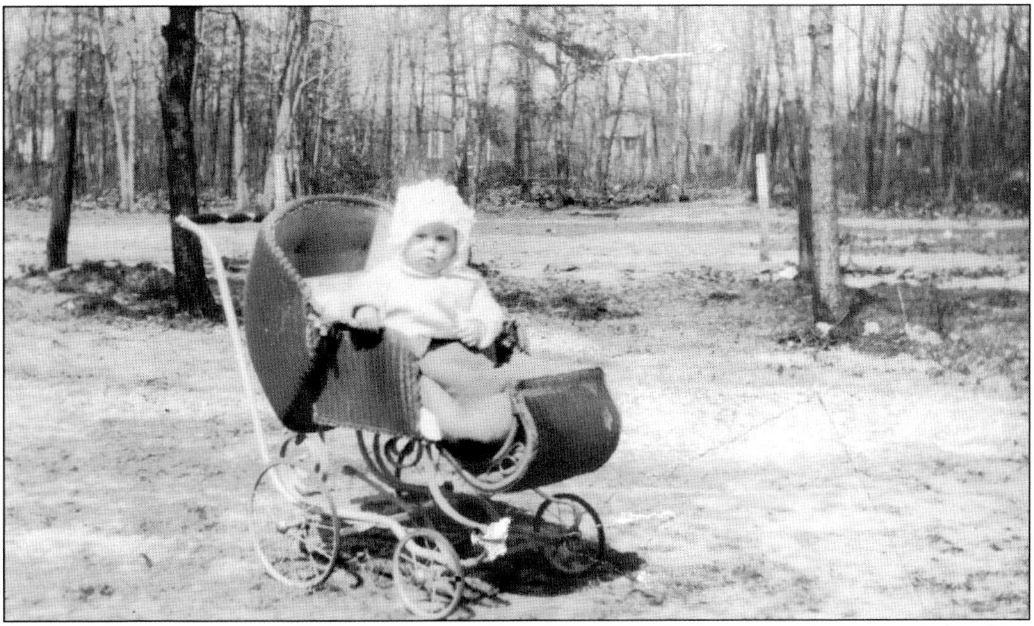

Here Ida Fisher sits in her carriage ready to go somewhere in 1926. Ida and her family lived on Seventh Avenue, and her rides in that carriage were very bumpy due to the fact that there were no paved roads or sidewalks at that time. All the roads in town were dirt. (Courtesy of Ida Fieger.)

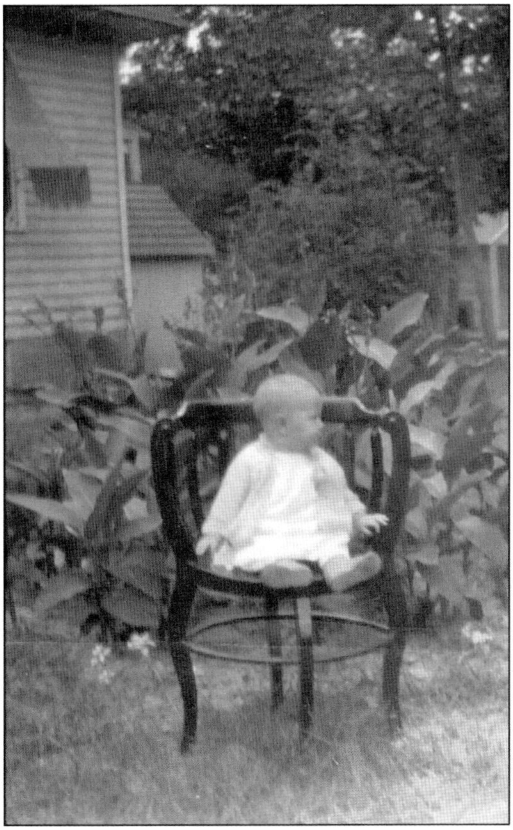

The Fishers moved to Pine Hill from Philadelphia in the early 1920s. Ida was born in 1926 at home on Seventh Avenue when doctors still made house calls and babies were delivered at home. Here Ida sits in her favorite chair that her mother brought from Philadelphia. She said she loved that chair because it made her feel so big and grown up. (Courtesy of Ida Fieger.)

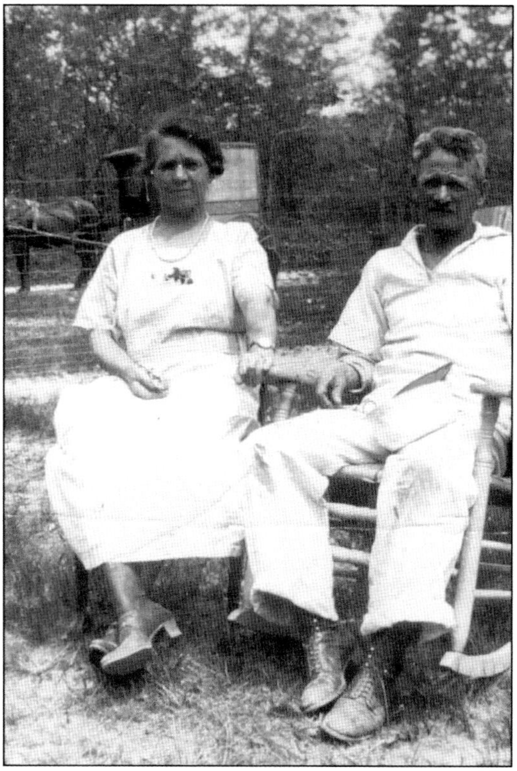

Mr. and Mrs. George Creely sit in the front yard on the corner of Seventh and Kayser Avenues in 1928. As they enjoy a cool summer evening, the milk wagon is in the background making its rounds. Milk was delivered several days a week so people would have fresh milk. They did not have an indoor ice box. (Courtesy of Ida Fieger.)

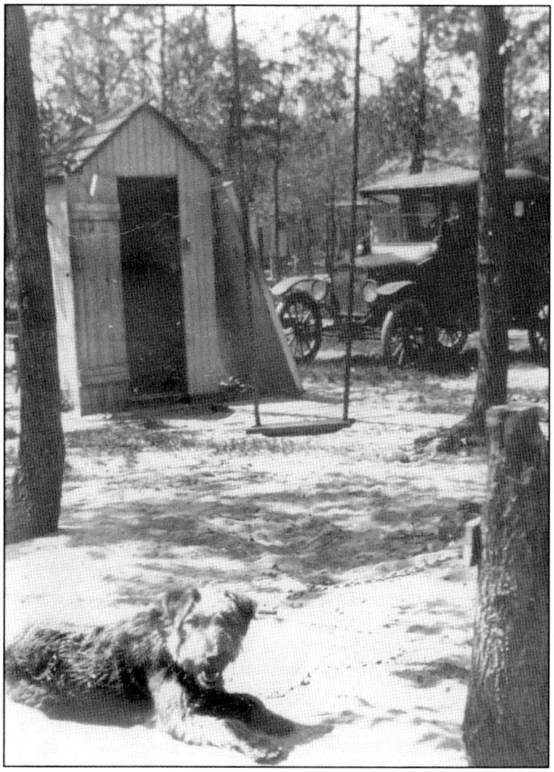

In 1930, Ida's dog sits guarding the family out house and Mr. Fishers' Model-T car. Ida would say, "if you've never taken that trip to the old outhouse in all kinds of weather you haven't lived." Mr. Fisher would get his parts for the Model T from Wilford Forrest Sr. at the Model-T Parts Store. (Courtesy of Ida Fieger.)

Here is a copy of the November 3, 1931, election from the Borough of Pine Hill. Edward D. Johnson was elected mayor with 396 votes defeating George Edinger, who received 110 votes. William McManus at 374 votes, and William Royd at 378 votes were elected as members of council defeating Agnes M. Weber at 155 votes and William T. Dougherty at 147 votes. (Courtesy of Mary Gallagher.)

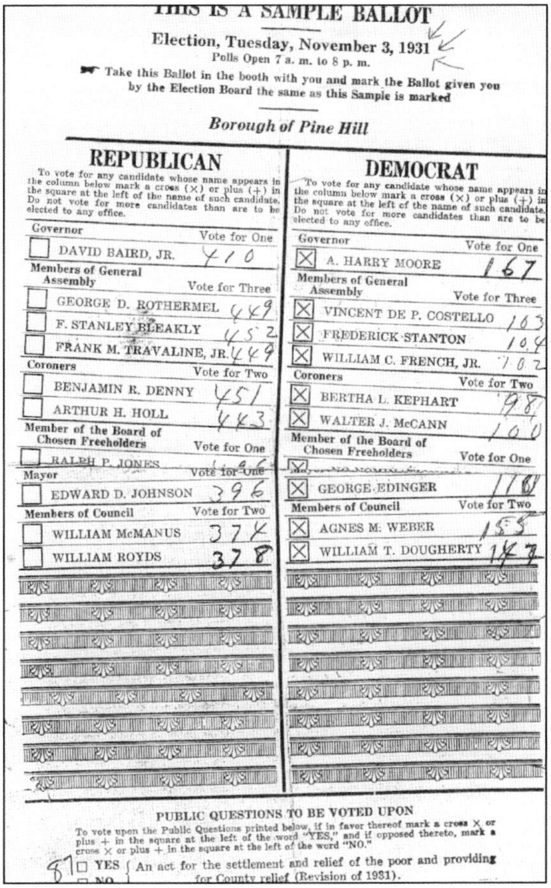
THIS IS A SAMPLE BALLOT

Election, Tuesday, November 3, 1931

Polls Open 7 a. m. to 8 p. m.

Take this Ballot in the booth with you and mark the Ballot given you by the Election Board the same as this Sample is marked

Borough of Pine Hill

REPUBLICAN

To vote for any candidate whose name appears in the column below mark a cross (×) or plus (+) in the square at the left of the name of such candidate. Do not vote for more candidates than are to be elected to any office.

Office	Candidate	Votes
Governor (Vote for One)	DAVID BAIRD, JR.	410
Members of General Assembly (Vote for Three)	GEORGE D. ROTHERMEL	449
	F. STANLEY BLEAKLY	452
	FRANK M. TRAVALINE, JR.	449
Coroners (Vote for Two)	BENJAMIN R. DENNY	451
	ARTHUR H. HOLL	443
Member of the Board of Chosen Freeholders (Vote for One)	RALPH P. JONES	[illegible]
Mayor (Vote for One)	EDWARD D. JOHNSON	396
Members of Council (Vote for Two)	WILLIAM McMANUS	374
	WILLIAM ROYDS	378

DEMOCRAT

To vote for any candidate whose name appears in the column below mark a cross (×) or plus (+) in the square at the left of the name of such candidate. Do not vote for more candidates than are to be elected to any office.

Office	Candidate	Votes
Governor (Vote for One)	A. HARRY MOORE	167
Members of General Assembly (Vote for Three)	VINCENT DE P. COSTELLO	103
	FREDERICK STANTON	104
	WILLIAM C. FRENCH, JR.	102
Coroners (Vote for Two)	BERTHA L. KEPHART	98
	WALTER J. McCANN	100
Member of the Board of Chosen Freeholders (Vote for One)	[illegible]	
Mayor	GEORGE EDINGER	110
Members of Council (Vote for Two)	AGNES M. WEBER	155
	WILLIAM T. DOUGHERTY	147

PUBLIC QUESTIONS TO BE VOTED UPON

To vote upon the Public Questions printed below, if in favor thereof mark a cross × or plus + in the square at the left of the word "YES," and if opposed thereto, mark a cross × or plus + in the square at the left of the word "NO."

87 ☐ YES ☐ NO { An act for the settlement and relief of the poor and providing for County relief (Revision of 1931).

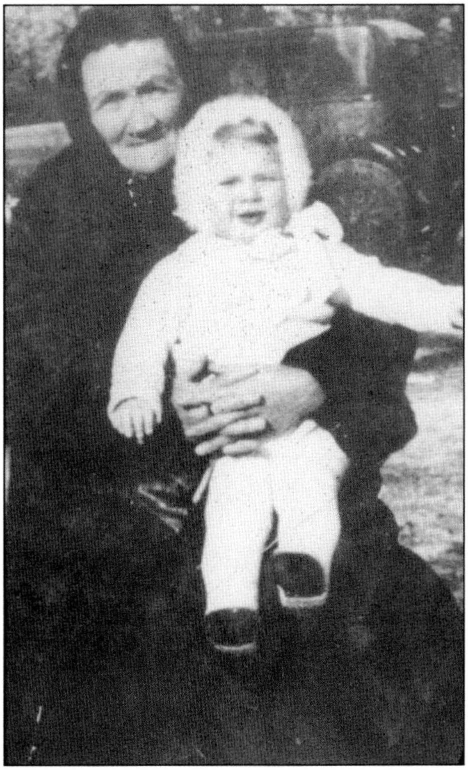

Rosalie Henshke sits on her grandmother Frances Bolinski's lap in the front yard of grandparents William and Emma Henshke's house on West Woodburn Avenue in 1933. Grandpa Henshke owned three houses on West Woodburn; one was a summer home where Rosalie lived with her parents and two sisters Maxine and Natalie. (Courtesy of Rosalie Henshke Hunt.)

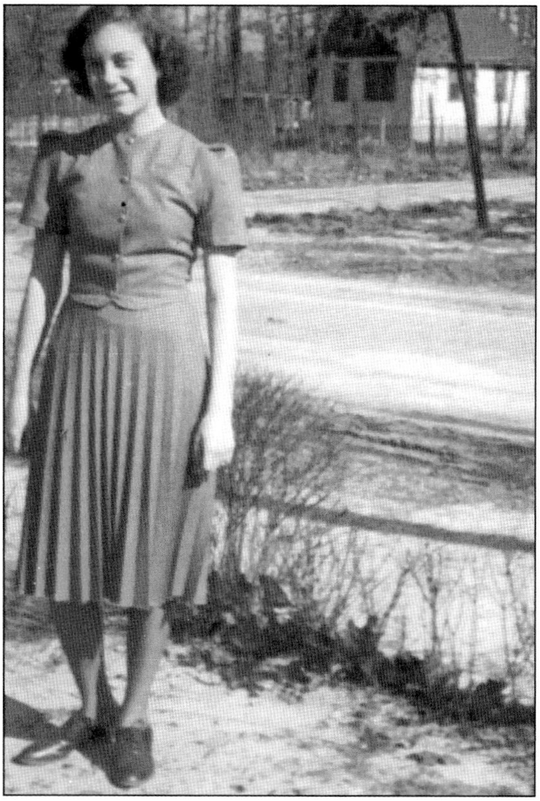

Ida Fisher poses here in her Sunday best in May 1935 standing in her front yard on Seventh Avenue and Keyser Street. In the background is one of the summer cottages here in town. Most of these were two-room buildings that later became permanent homes when owners added heat and more rooms. (Courtesy of Ida Fisher Fieger.)

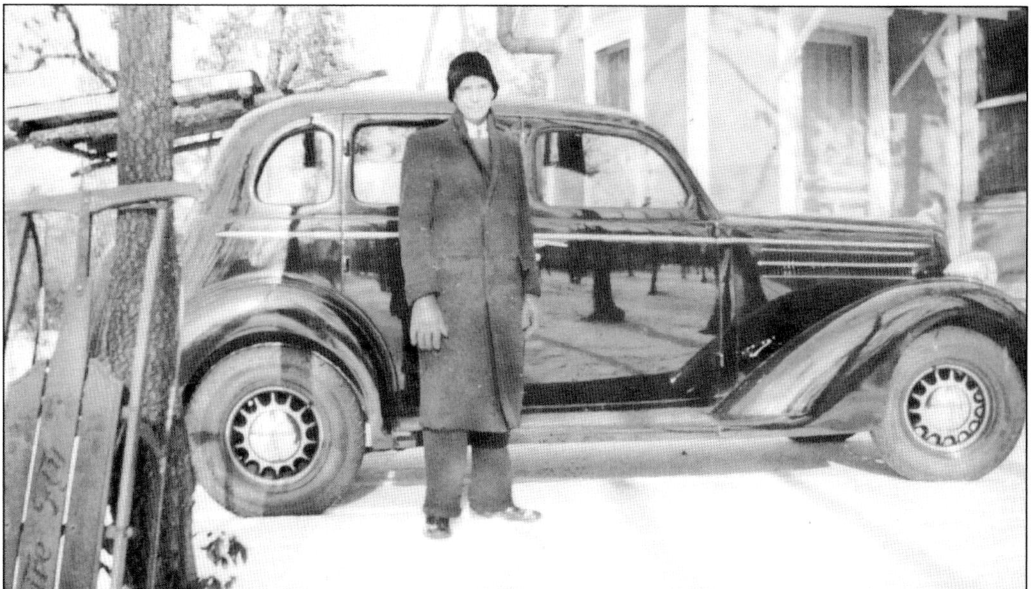

On February 1, 1936, Mr. Meinhard stands in front of his home on Third Avenue after returning home from sledding with his family. The Fire Fly sled is leaning against the tree. He loved the outdoors as much as he loved his new car, as seen by the shine he kept on the car even in bad weather. (Courtesy of Mary Gallagher.)

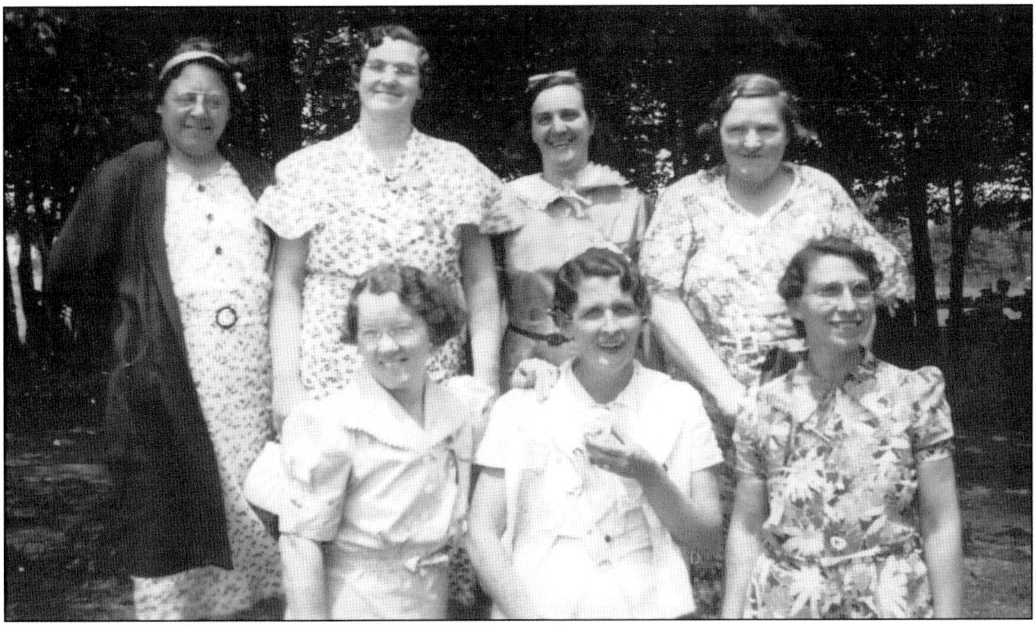

The Pine Hill PTA at their end of year picnic in 1936. Every year the ladies of the PTA would gather at Pine Hill Park and Stecky's Lake for a picnic excursion with a meal that they would eat on a blanket. Pictured here are, from left to right, (first row) Christine Scott, Mrs. Crosby, and Mrs. Horner; (second row) Florence Fisher, Mrs. Ladislaw, Mrs. Harding, and Mrs. Delaney. (Courtesy of Ida Fieger.)

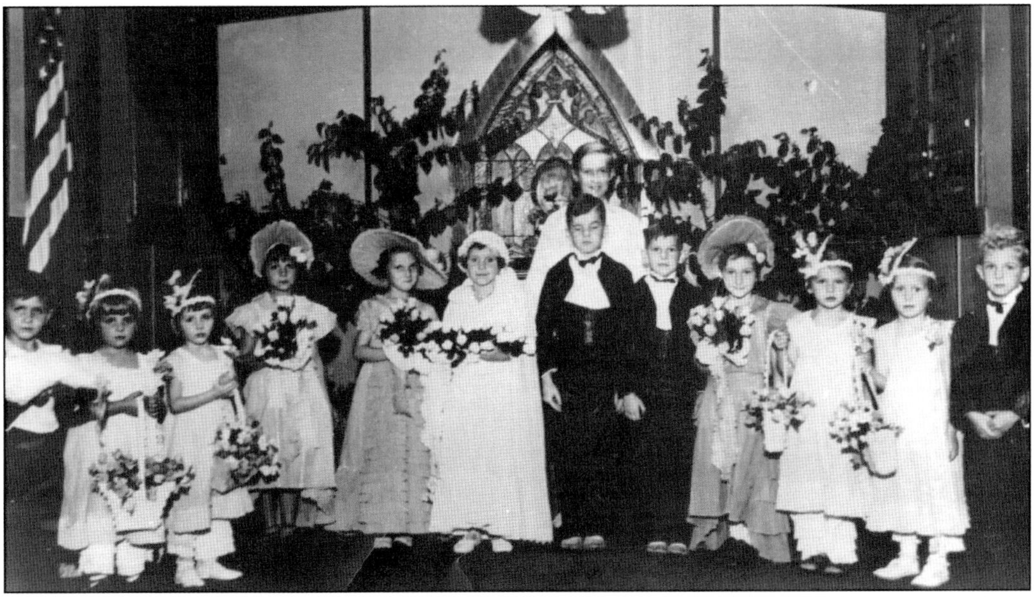

The United Methodist Church put on a production of *Tom Thumb's Wedding* in 1936. The costumes were made of crepe paper that year. The members of the cast were Alfred Davies (as the minister) and the wedding party, from left to right, Donald Campbell, Lois Snuffin, Patsy Campbell, Ruth Snuffin, Clara Davis, Marry Hofacker (the bride), Hary Spangler (the groom), Chester Spangler, Virginia Zwaegler, Mildred Wilson, Georgiana Hofacker, and Bert Miller. (Courtesy of Mary Gallagher.)

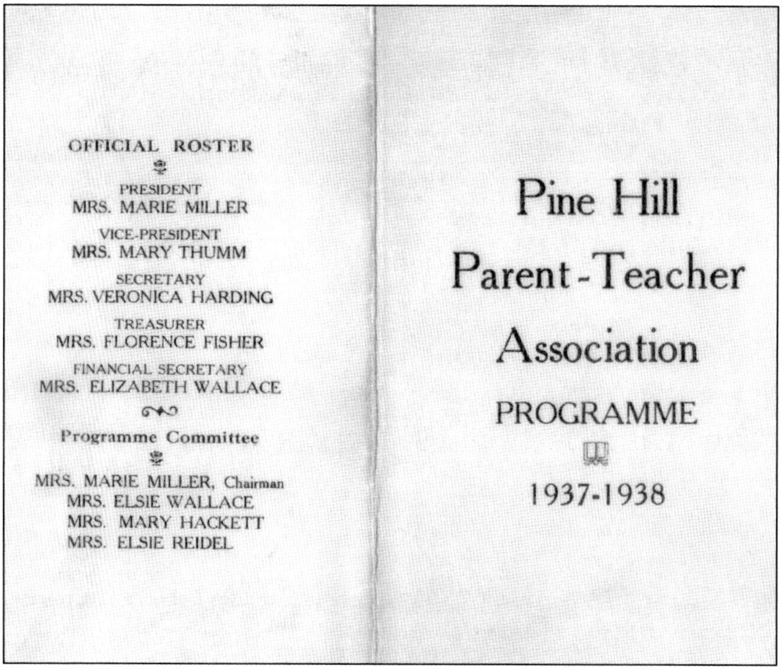

OFFICIAL ROSTER

PRESIDENT
MRS. MARIE MILLER

VICE-PRESIDENT
MRS. MARY THUMM

SECRETARY
MRS. VERONICA HARDING

TREASURER
MRS. FLORENCE FISHER

FINANCIAL SECRETARY
MRS. ELIZABETH WALLACE

Programme Committee

MRS. MARIE MILLER, Chairman
MRS. ELSIE WALLACE
MRS. MARY HACKETT
MRS. ELSIE REIDEL

Pine Hill
Parent-Teacher
Association
PROGRAMME
1937-1938

This photograph shows the program of the Pine Hill PTA for the 1937–1938 school year. Shown on the roster are the officers for that school year as well as the committee responsible for putting the program schedule together showing that year's meetings. (Courtesy of Mary Gallagher.)

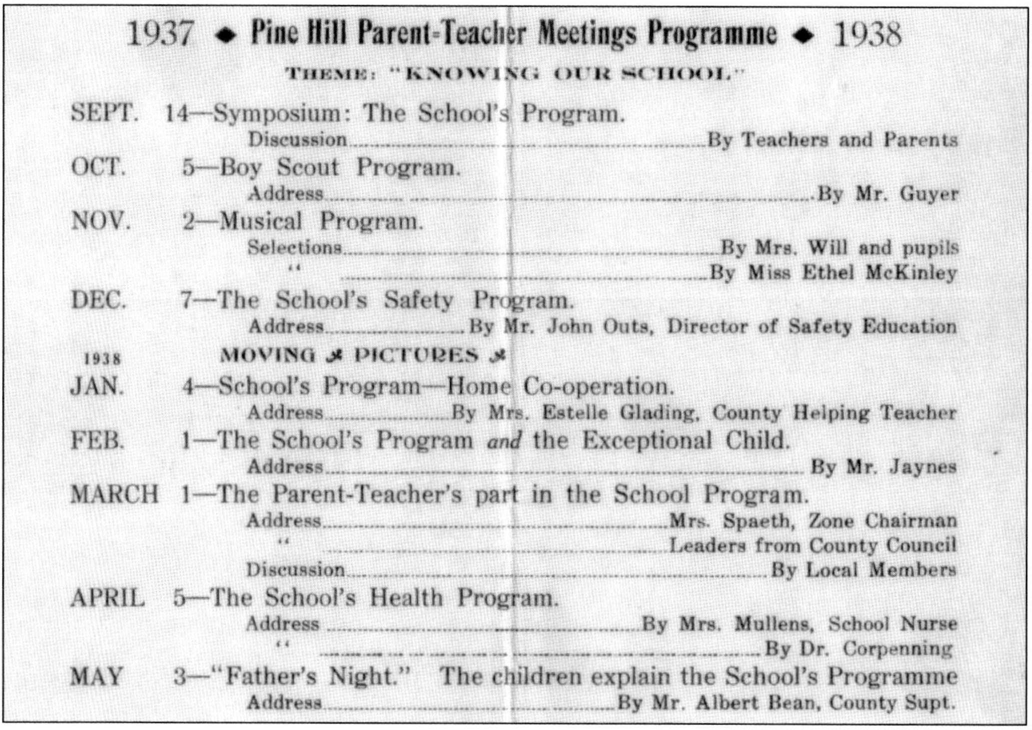

1937 ◆ Pine Hill Parent-Teacher Meetings Programme ◆ 1938

THEME: "KNOWING OUR SCHOOL"

SEPT. 14—Symposium: The School's Program.
Discussion.......By Teachers and Parents

OCT. 5—Boy Scout Program.
Address.......By Mr. Guyer

NOV. 2—Musical Program.
Selections.......By Mrs. Will and pupils
" ....By Miss Ethel McKinley

DEC. 7—The School's Safety Program.
Address.......By Mr. John Outs, Director of Safety Education

1938 MOVING PICTURES

JAN. 4—School's Program—Home Co-operation.
Address.......By Mrs. Estelle Glading, County Helping Teacher

FEB. 1—The School's Program *and* the Exceptional Child.
Address.......By Mr. Jaynes

MARCH 1—The Parent-Teacher's part in the School Program.
Address.......Mrs. Spaeth, Zone Chairman
" ....Leaders from County Council
Discussion.......By Local Members

APRIL 5—The School's Health Program.
Address.......By Mrs. Mullens, School Nurse
" ....By Dr. Corpenning

MAY 3—"Father's Night." The children explain the School's Programme
Address.......By Mr. Albert Bean, County Supt.

The theme of the 1937–1938 school year for the PTA meetings was "knowing our school." The meetings for the whole year were planned in advance, and each meeting had a special theme that covered programs offered at the school and guest speakers. The last speaker in May was Albert Bean, the county superintendent, who was so well liked that the town named a school after him. (Courtesy of Mary Gallagher.)

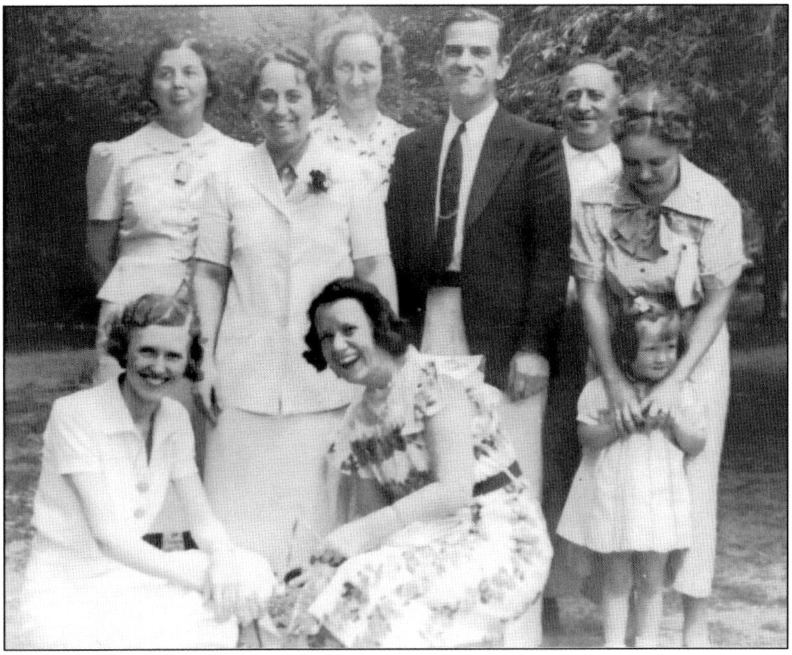

The teachers of the first school in Pine Hill gather at Stecky's Lake Park for their end of year picnic in 1938. The school was located on Sixth Avenue and was named Clementon Heights. There was no bus transportation for the students in the 1930s, so they all had to walk no matter how far they lived from the school. (Courtesy of Ida Fieger.)

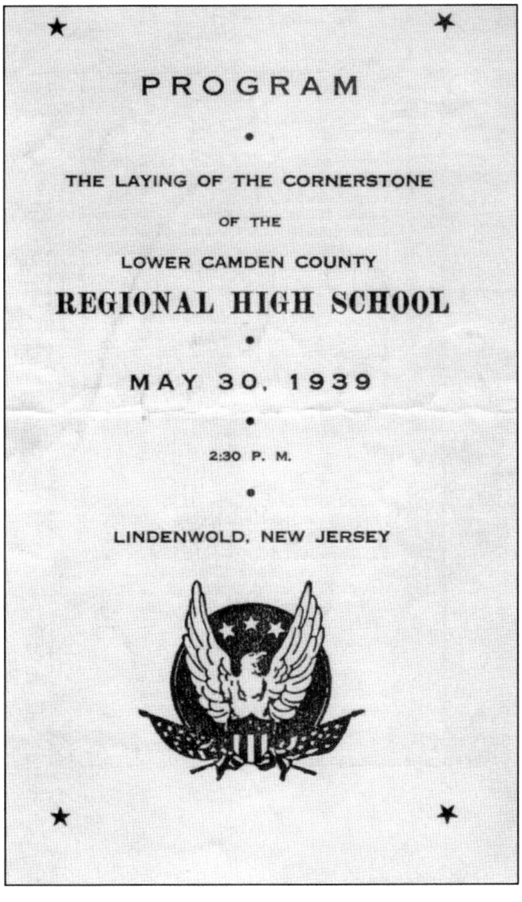

PROGRAM

THE LAYING OF THE CORNERSTONE

OF THE

LOWER CAMDEN COUNTY

REGIONAL HIGH SCHOOL

MAY 30, 1939

2:30 P. M.

LINDENWOLD, NEW JERSEY

On May 30, 1939, the Pine Hill community, along with six other local communities, gathered for the cornerstone to be laid for their new high school. The students of Pine Hill would now be able to attend school beyond the eighth grade. Pine Hill resident Charles F. Skerrett set the cornerstone in place of the Lower Camden County Regional High School. (Courtesy of Ida Fisher.)

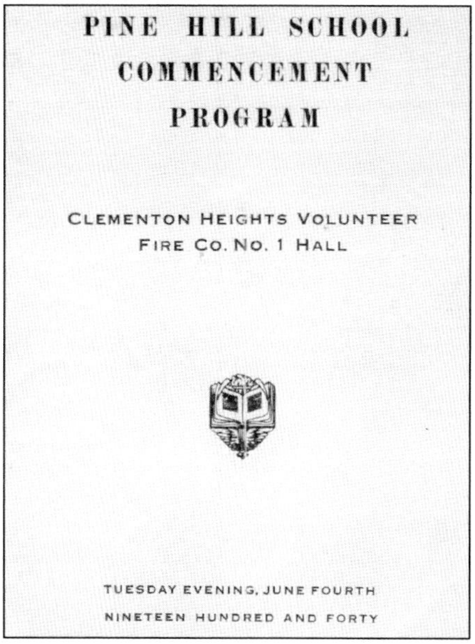

PINE HILL SCHOOL
COMMENCEMENT
PROGRAM

CLEMENTON HEIGHTS VOLUNTEER
FIRE CO. NO. 1 HALL

TUESDAY EVENING, JUNE FOURTH
NINETEEN HUNDRED AND FORTY

The program for eighth grade graduation of 1940 from the Pine Hill School is shown at left. The graduation took place at the local fire company on June 4 at 8:00 pm. Ida Fisher, who was the vice president of the class of 1940, was more than happy to share with us that the school had 30 graduates that year. (Courtesy of Ida Fisher.)

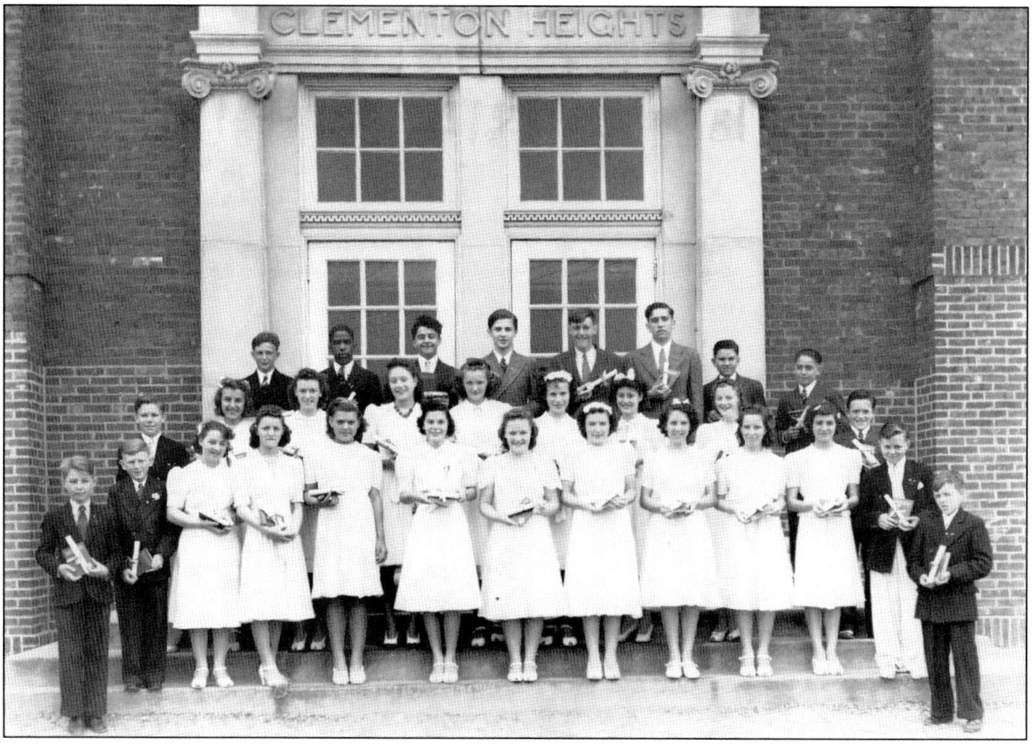

The entire eighth grade class of Pine Hill in 1940 is pictured here. The girls are, in alphabetical order, Betty Atkins, Leona Blake, Edna Bock, Bernadine Campbell, Bessie Crosby, Doris Davis, Edith Davis, Mae Delany, Alice Devlin, Ida Fisher, Irene Harding, Sara Hullings, Marie Kergides, Virginia Mitchell, Lois Mullin, and Elsie Wallace. The boys are Edward, Berkey, Edward Damerau, Billy Davies, Billy Floating, Andrew Hagelin, Charles Hinson, James Jackson, Havard Ludwick, Wallace Oehrl, Earl Rocker, Raymond Worrell, James Young, Donald Springer, and Herman Strater. (Courtesy of Ida Fisher.)

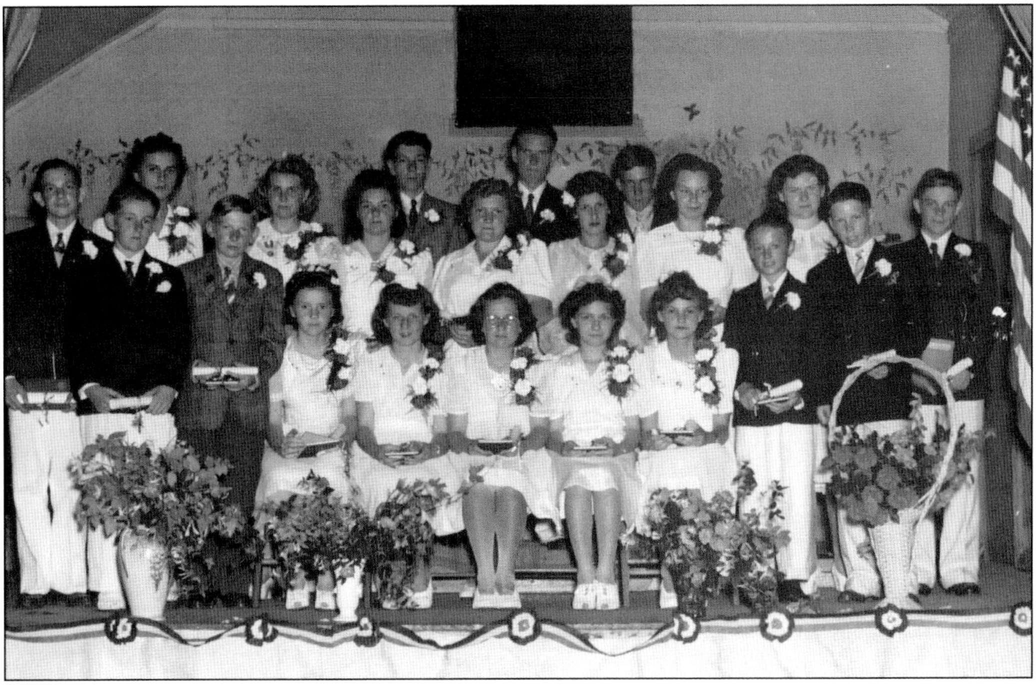

In 1940, some of the members from the eighth grade graduating class posed for a picture. The young ladies were Ida Fisher, Lois Mullin, Marie Kergides, Alice Devlin, Edna Bock, Elsie Wallace, Virginia Mitchell, Sara Hullings, Mae Delany, Doris Davis, Leonia Blake, and Betty Atkins. The young men were Charles Hinson, Andrew Hagelin, Edward Berkey, William Floating, James Young, and Raymond Worrell. (Courtesy of Ida Fisher Fieger.)

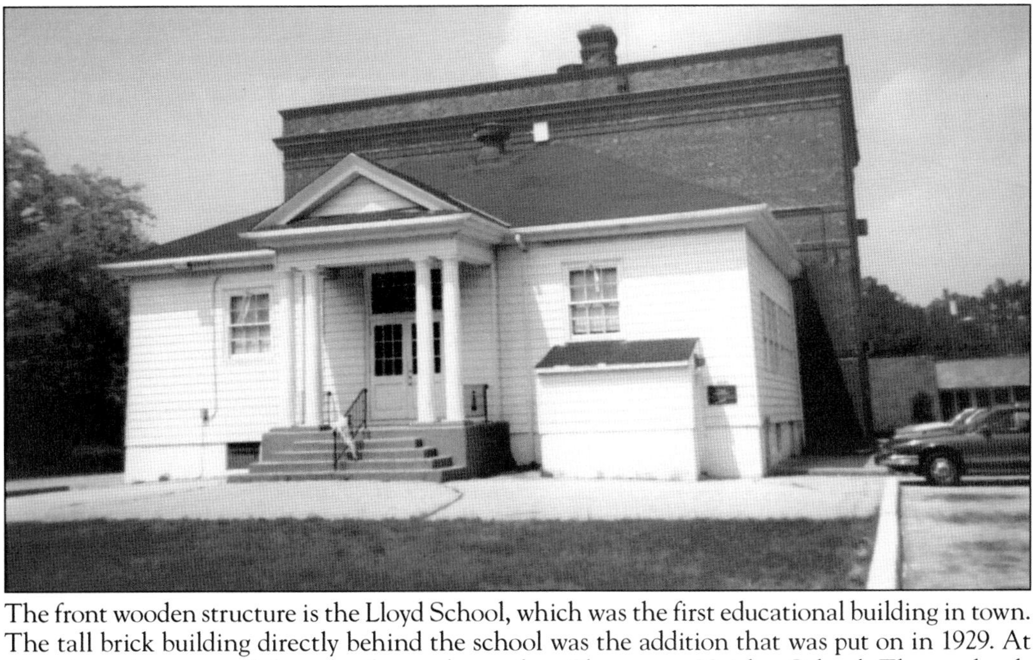

The front wooden structure is the Lloyd School, which was the first educational building in town. The tall brick building directly behind the school was the addition that was put on in 1929. At that time, the name of the school was changed to Clementon Heights School. These schools only taught up until eighth grade. (Courtesy of Peggy Steelman.)

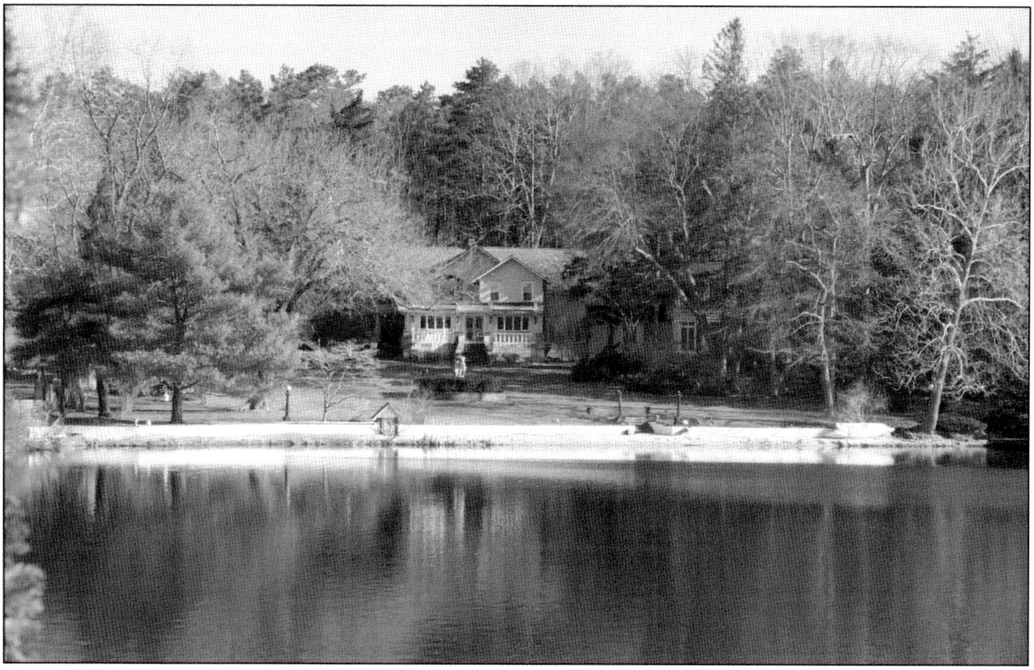

Here is the Blanchard's Mansion; it is located in a secluded area of Pine Hill. During the 1920s, the notorious gangster Al Capone would stay here when things were too hot for him in Chicago. The older town folks would say moonshine is not only found in the hills of Kentucky but also in the hills of Pine Hill. Benjamin Blanchard, who owned the house, was credited with perfecting the first radar during the World War II era. (Courtesy of Les Gallagher Jr.)

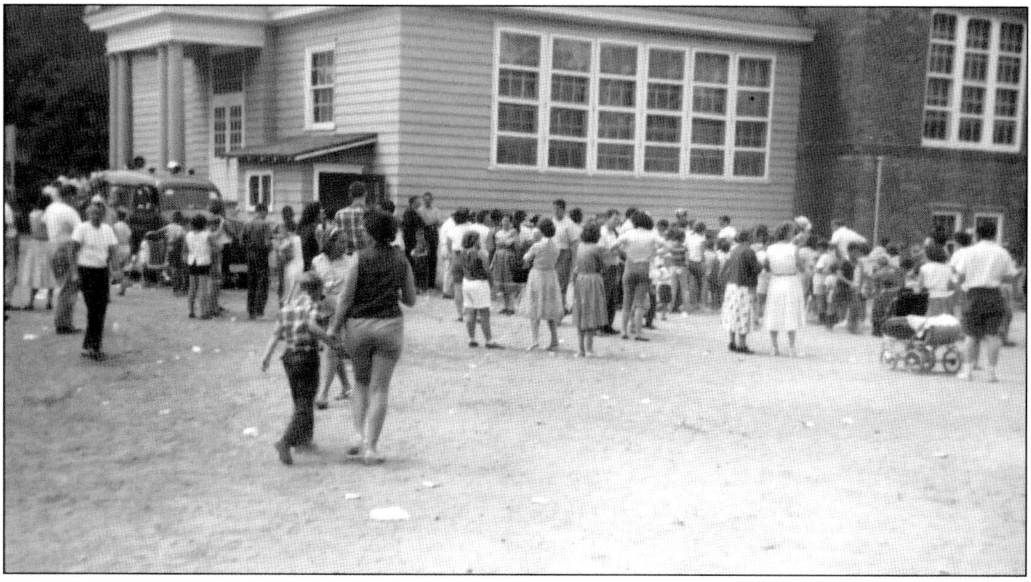

On July 4, 1940, the people from town were gathering on the school grounds for hot dogs and soda after the parade. Next to the school is the Civil Defense Van that was used to make the announcements over the PA system for the parade. It would also go up and down the street before a blackout and tell people to pull their shades down. (Courtesy of Bill Dukes.)

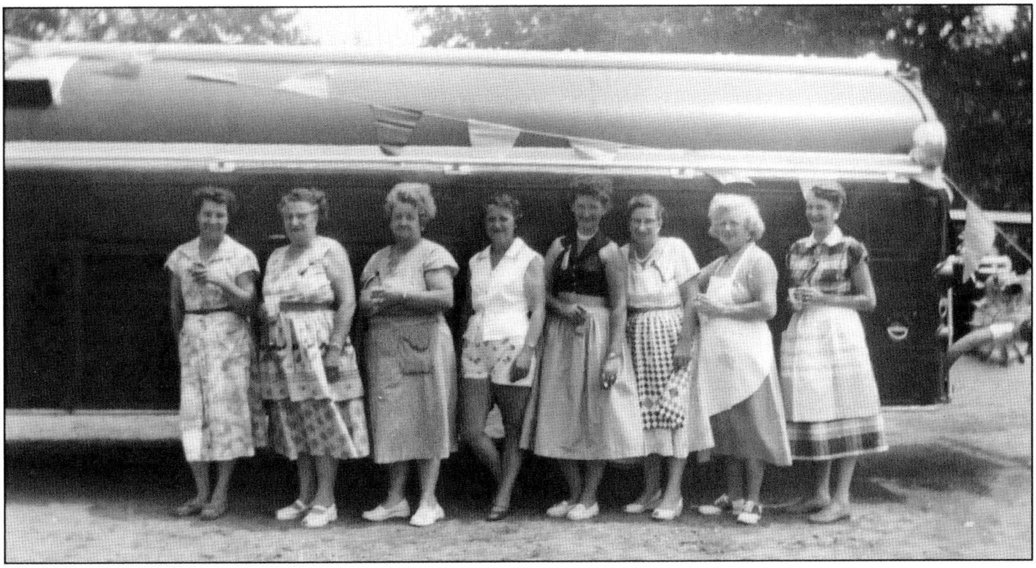

In 1942, the Ladies Auxiliary of Eagle Fire Company stopped for a break from the festivities near the tanker truck. They were busy getting everything ready for the firemen's carnival, which was a major fund maker for the fire company each year. The ladies would pitch in by helping to set up run games and serve refreshments. (Courtesy of Bill Dukes.)

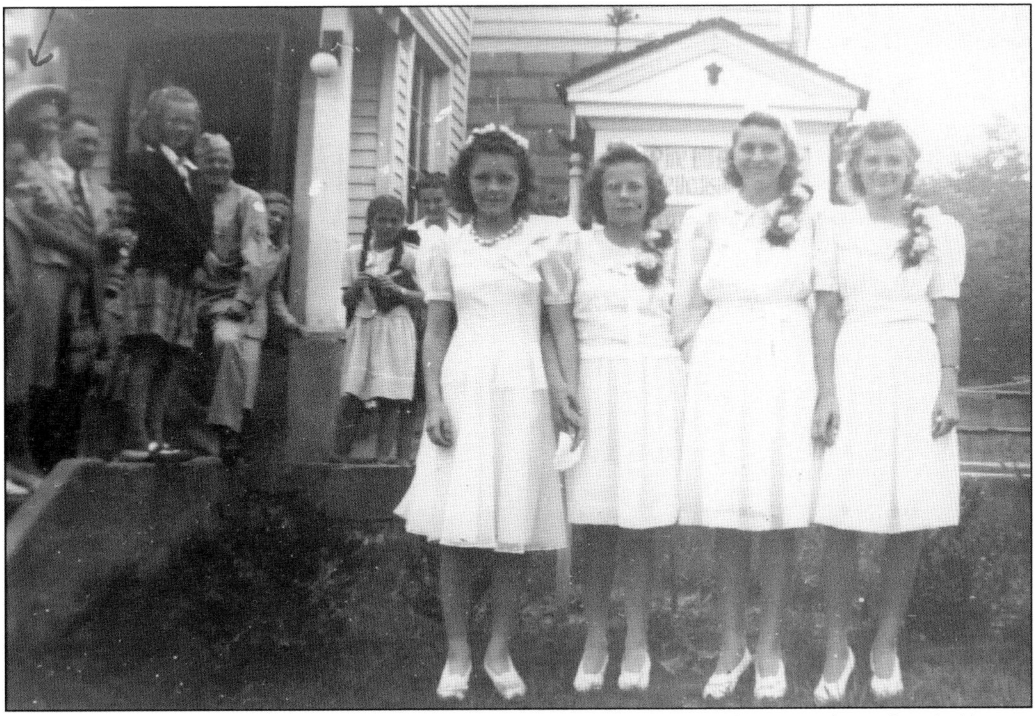

In June 1943, Mary Hofocker, Barbara Eaberwien, Ellen Keefier, and Jeane Rhainehardt (shown from left to right) were standing in front of the Memorial United Methodist Church at the triangle of Erial Road, First Avenue, and Lakeview Avenue after their eighth grade graduation. The church was moved in 1956, and the lot was renamed the Freedom Triangle. (Courtesy of Mary Gallagher.)

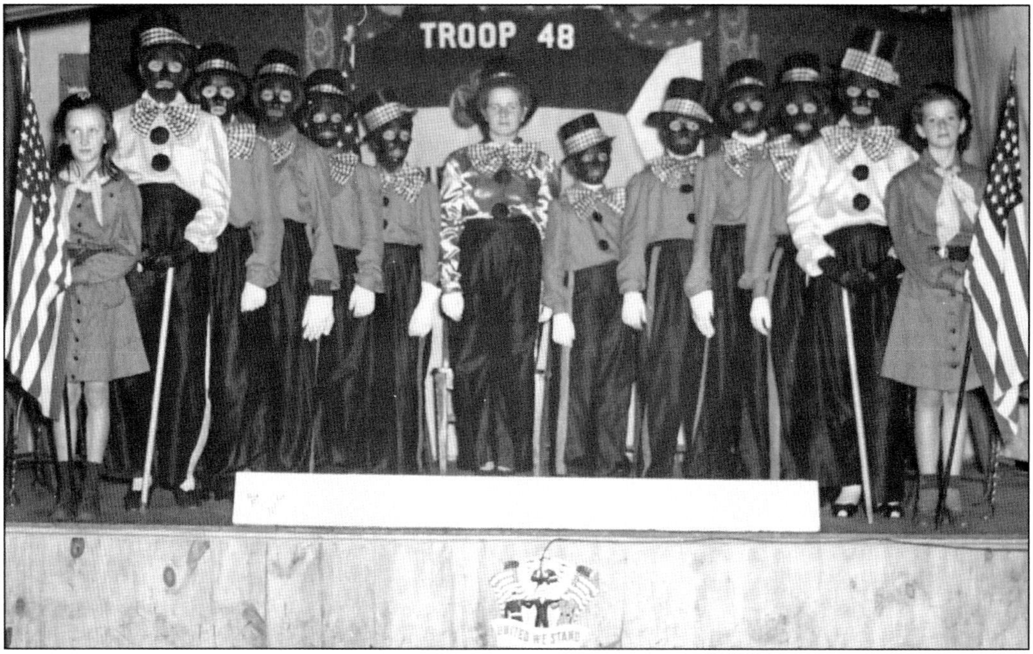

In 1943, Girl Scout Troup No. 48 had several methods of fund-raising, but the most prevalent were the vaudeville-type shows. They also held dinners at the local fire station to help in their fund-raising efforts, which were well attended by the local community. Donations were also solicited from local residents, and in return, a small metallic fire mark to display at the front door was presented to the home owner. (Courtesy of Ellen Kiefer Kerby.)

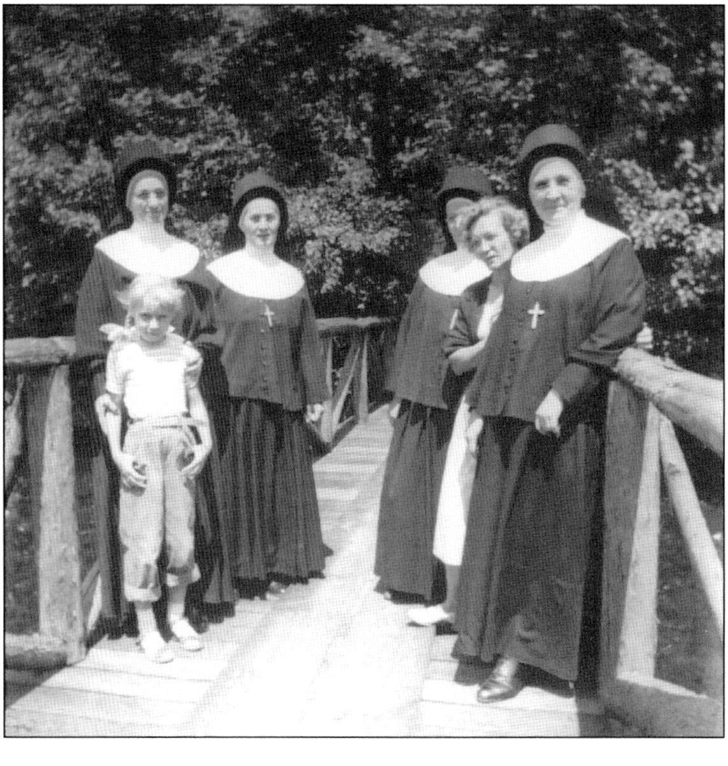

Natalie Henshke (front, left) is standing on the bridge at the fifteenth tee of Pine Valley Golf Club in 1947. She and her mother, Rose Henshke, took the Nuns of the Holy Family of Nazareth on a tour of the golf club where Mr. Henshke was a caddy. They stopped on the bridge so they could see the turtles on the nearby rocks. (Courtesy of Natalie Maguire.)

This 1947 Pontiac was the first car Mr. Leslie P. Gallagher owned after World War II, when he was living on Thirteenth Avenue. He bought it new and was very proud of it. Not many people in town had cars at that time. Most of the people took a taxi or would walk up the hill. At this time, most of the people were only summer residents who lived in Philadelphia during the rest of the year. (Courtesy of Les Gallagher Jr.)

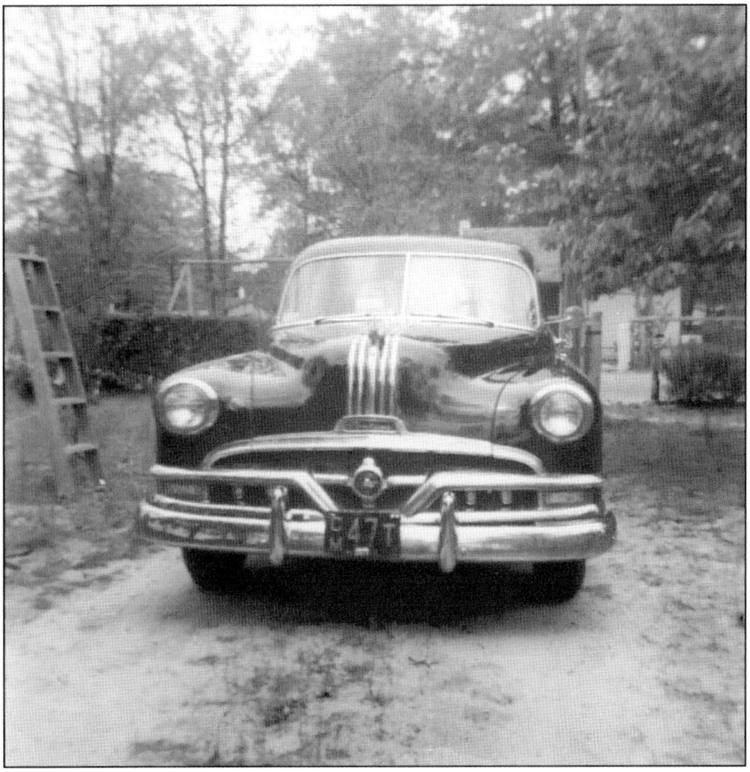

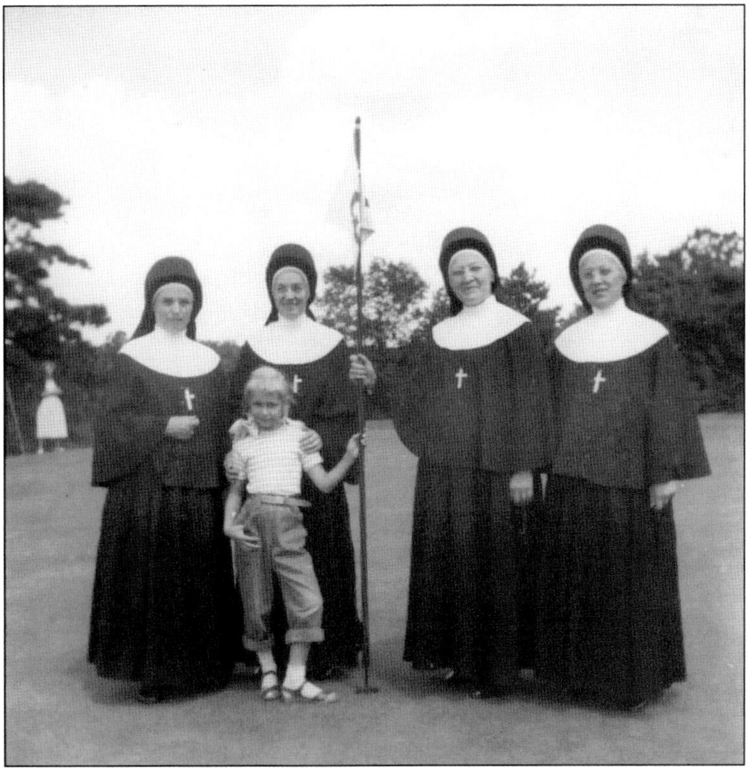

In the summer of 1949, John Arthur Brown, president of the Pine Valley Golf Club, invited the Holy Family of Nazareth nuns to tour his golf course. Max Henshke of Pine Hill was responsible for this visit. He was a caddy at the course where he had the occasion to play himself and shoot in the low 70s. Pictured here are Sisters deLourdes, Antonia, Aldona, and Iluminata with Natalie Henshke Maguire standing in front. (Courtesy of Natalie Maguire.)

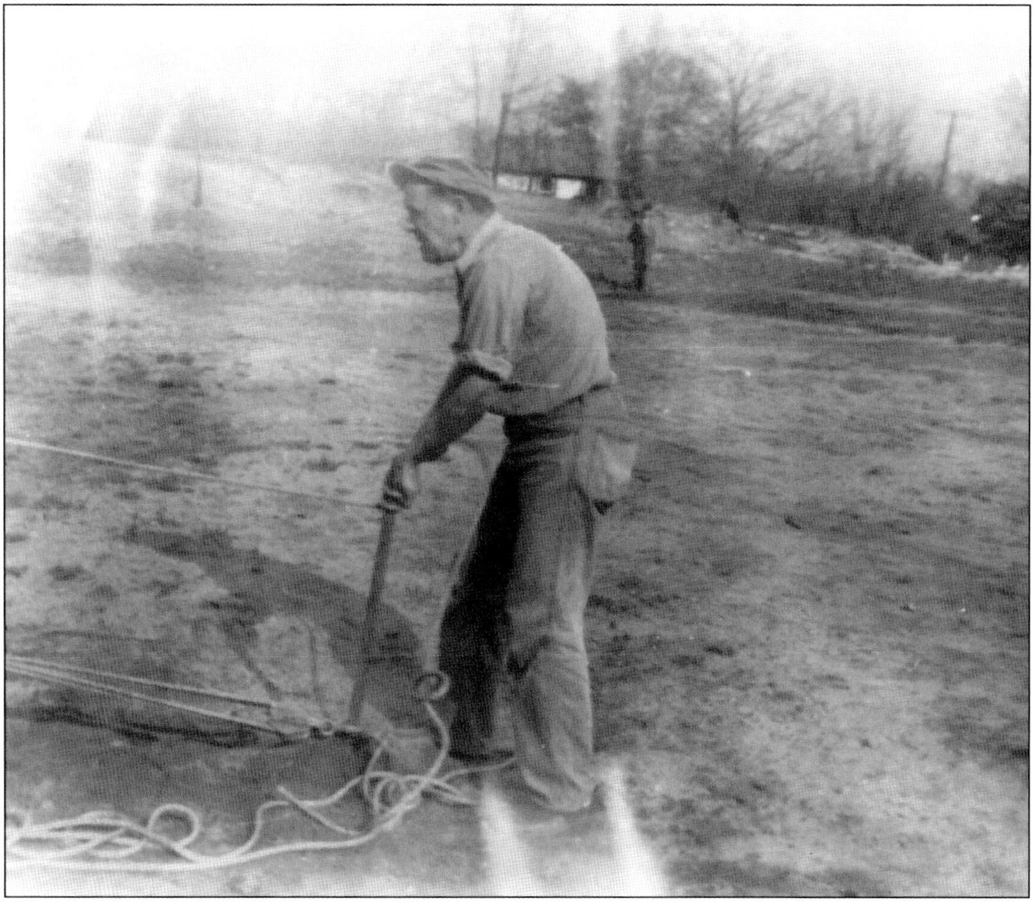

Mr. Hofacker is getting his garden ready for the 1948 planting. Here he is putting up a new fence around the area, and then he will be planting the garden. The soil was so sandy that it was not always easy having a garden, but the tomatoes loved the sand and grew in abundance. (Courtesy of Mary Gallagher.)

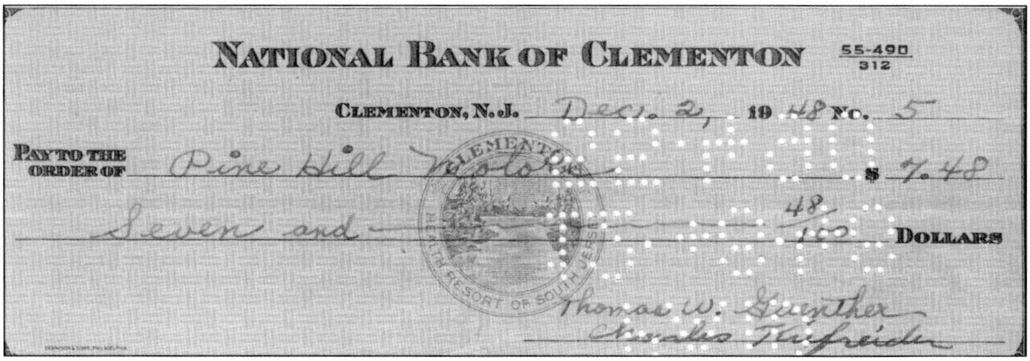

A check from the Eagle Fire Department of Pine Hill was paid to the order of Pine Hill Motors in December 1948 in the amount of $7.48. The check was to pay for parts purchased for the maintenance of company vehicles. The check was signed by Thomas W. Guenther (treasurer) and Charles Kiefreider (secretary). (Courtesy of Bill Dukes.)

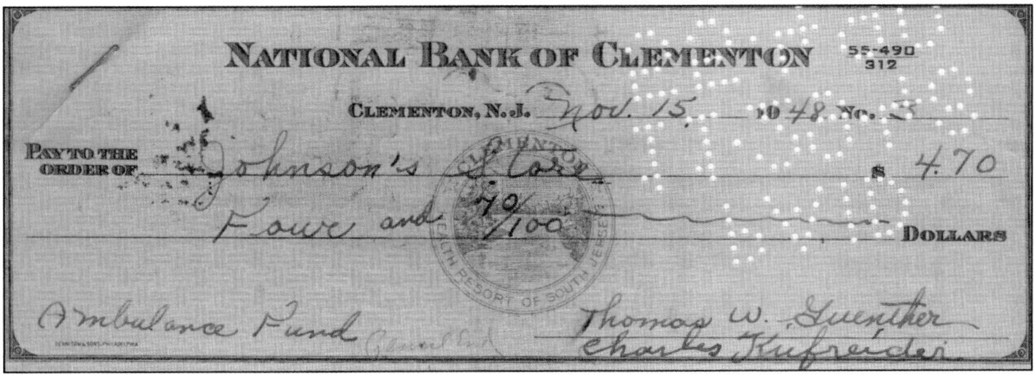

This photograph shows a check paid to the order of Johnson's Store out of the ambulance fund for the purchase of materials used on the ambulance in November 1948. The first aid squad was under the Eagle Fire Department, so their funds came out of the general fund. Thomas W. Guenther, as treasurer, had to authorize any funds spent for all functions of the fire company. (Courtesy of Harriet Johnson.)

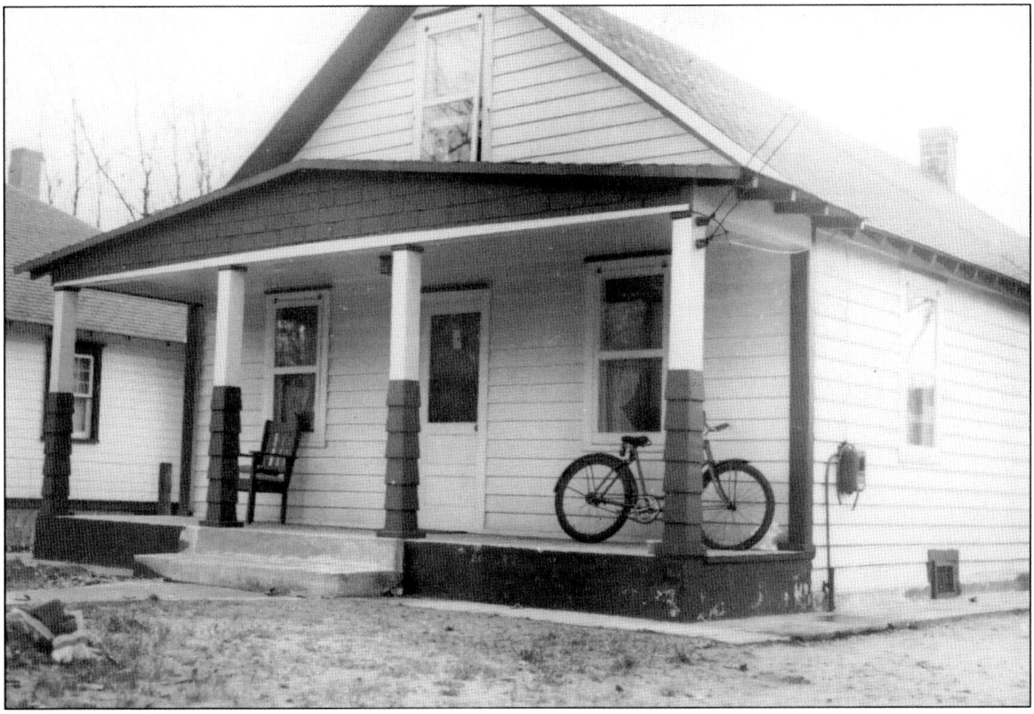

Here is the Kerby house on East Eighth Avenue in 1948. The bike that can be seen on the front porch was a main mode of transportation, since everyone did not own a car. A bike was good to get around as long as one did not have to go up the hill coming into town, because it was too steep. (Courtesy of Ellen Kerby.)

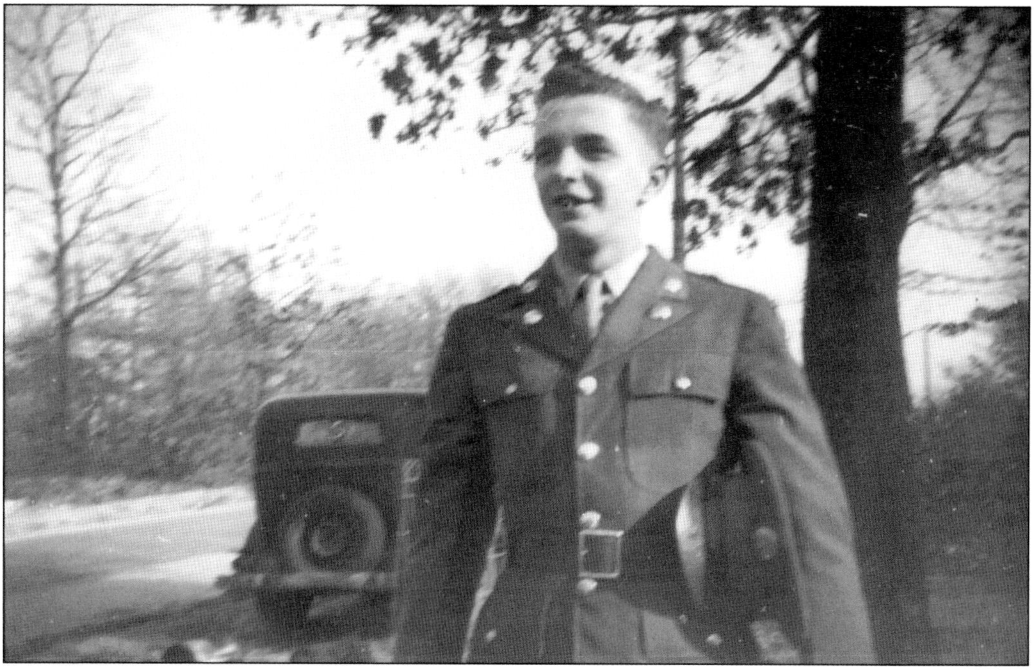

In 1950, George Gallagher was home on leave after completing basic training and medical training school. His basic training took place at Fort Sam Houston in Texas, and medical school was in Denver, Colorado. He was home for 14 days before returning to Texas for final training after which he was shipped to Germany and the war. (Courtesy of Les Gallagher Jr.)

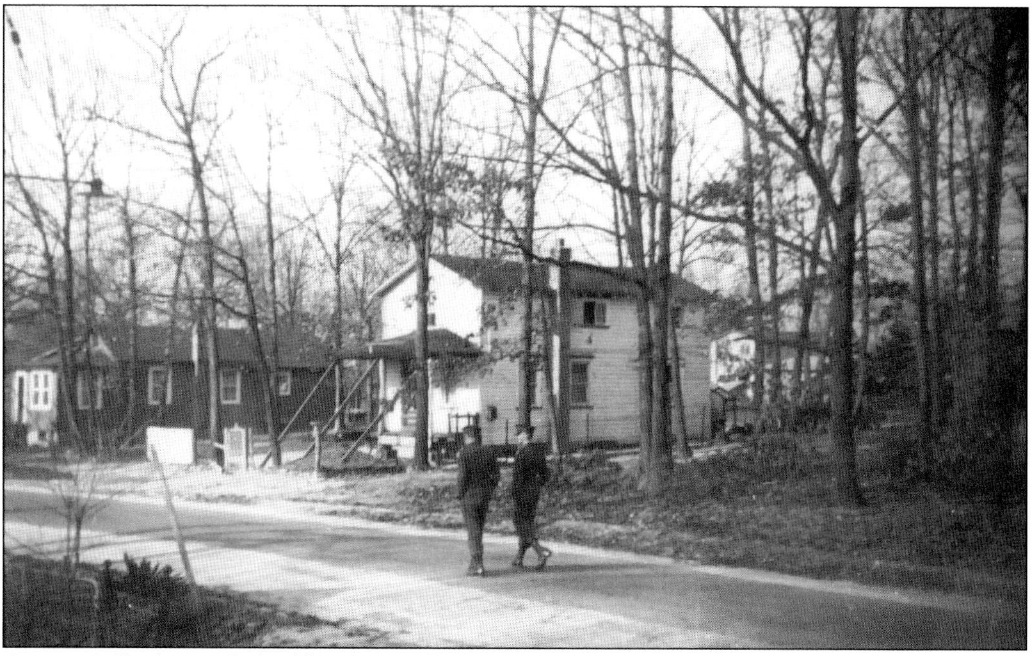

George Gallagher and a buddy take a walk down Clearview Avenue in their military uniforms in 1950. Home on leave, these young men were looking around for some of their friends before they shipped off to war and an uncertain time in their lives. (Courtesy of Les Gallagher Jr.)

Verna and Robert Appenzeller have their wedding pictures taken at her parents' house on Erial Road in June 1950. Seidell's Store can be seen in the background; it was a combination ice cream parlor and general store. In the 1920s, a double-decker ice cream cost 5¢. (Courtesy of Tom McCouch.)

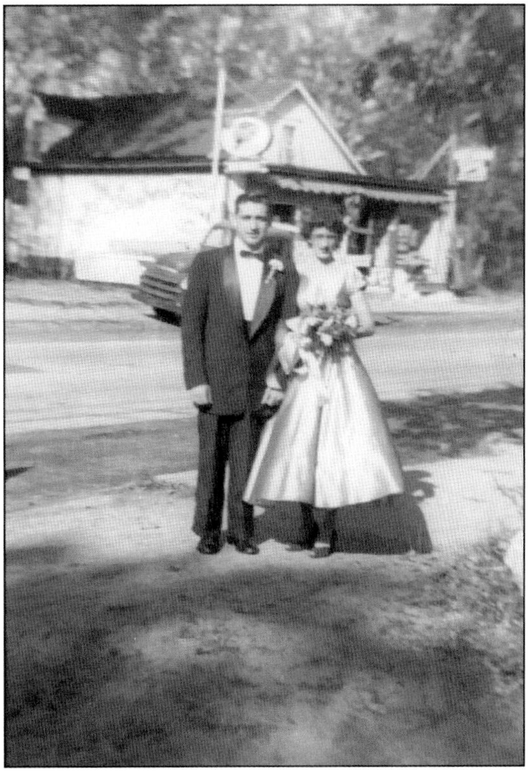

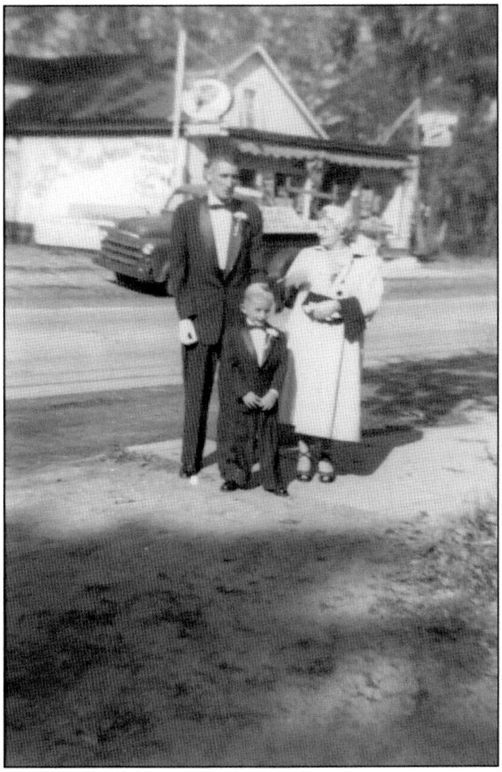

Verna's parents pose with the ring bearer on their wedding day in June 1950 outside their home on Erial Road. They lived across the street from Seidell's Store, which, in the 1920s, had a speakeasy at the back with near beer and beer. (Courtesy of Tom McCouch.)

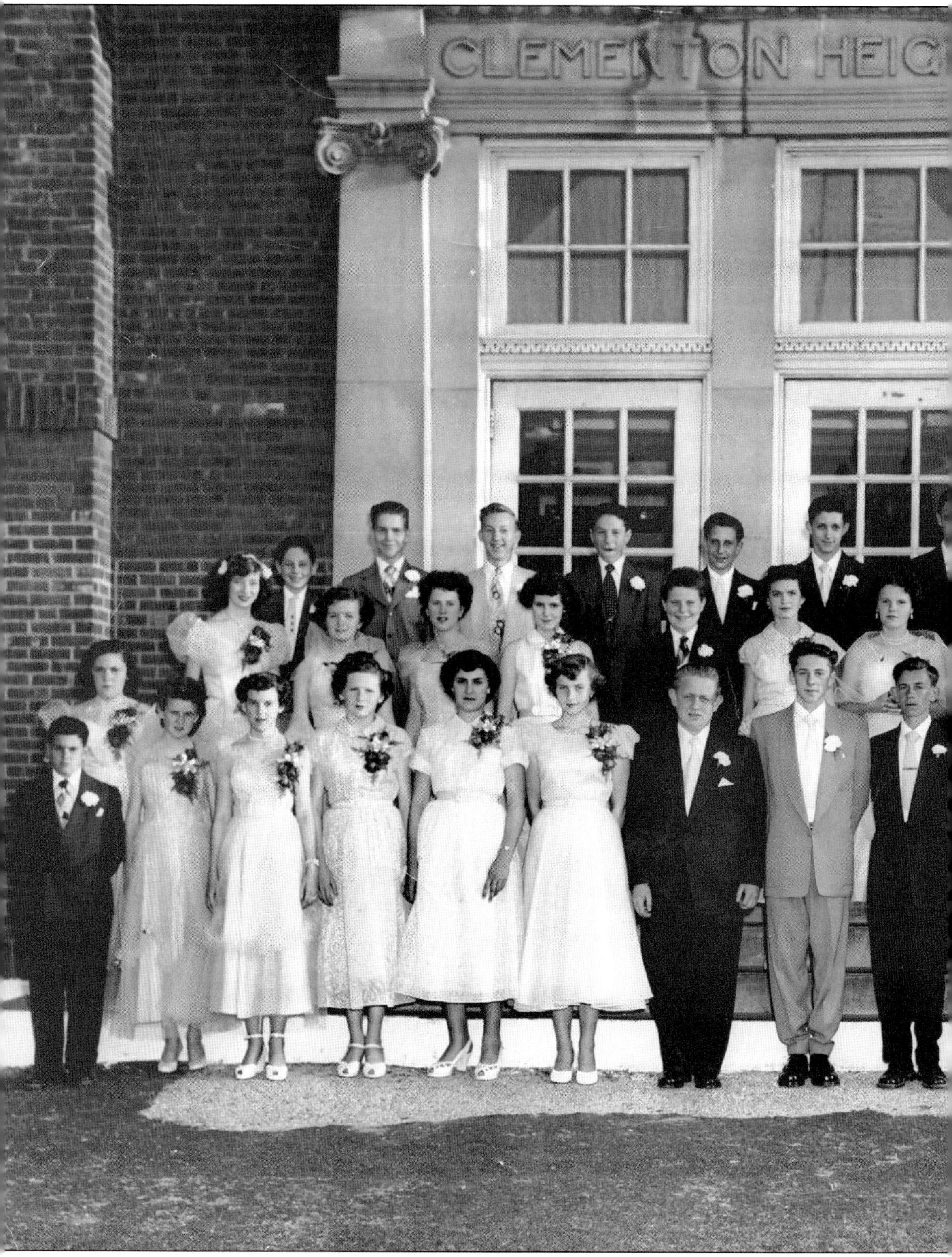
CLEMENTON HEIG

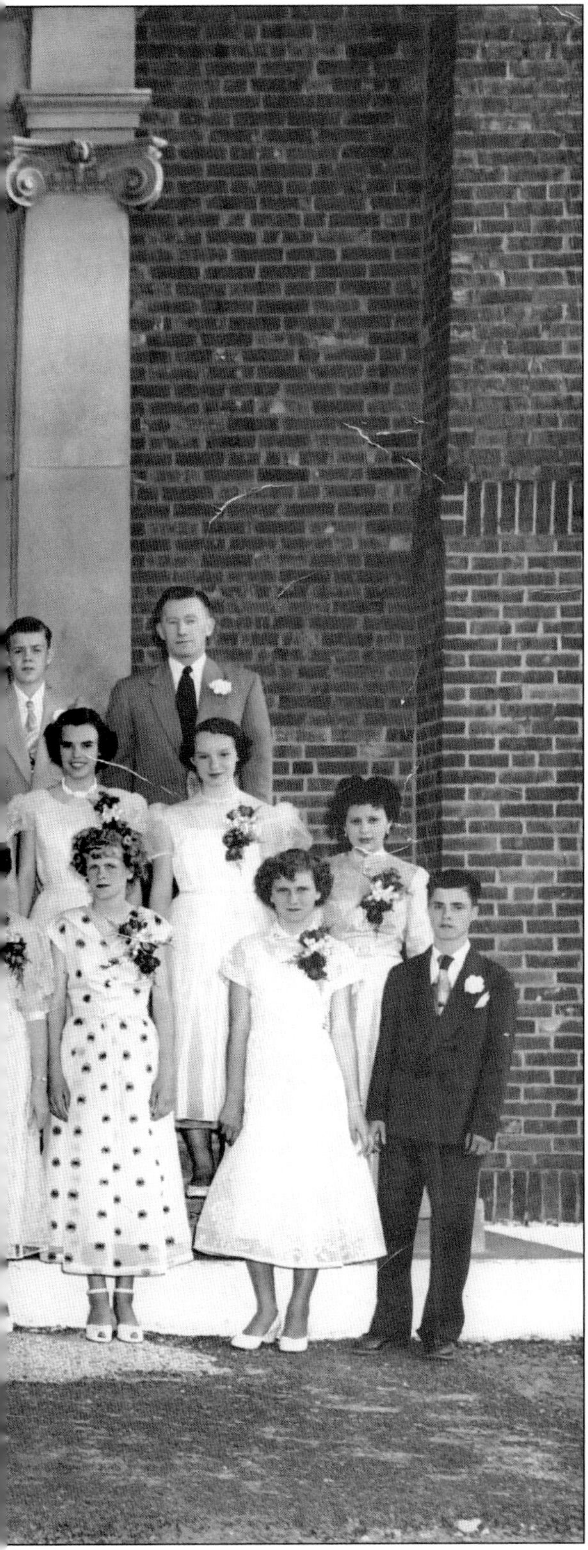

This photograph shows the eighth grade class of 1952. In the first row are, from left to right, Edward Hembold, Dolores Worrell, Joan Morgan, Sarah Wolbert, Florence Chinchillo, Veda Mathis, Alexander Cole, William Harner, Earl Shone, Frances White, Ethel, Patrica Regan, and John Scroader; (second row) Anna Peden, Glenola Osborne, Elizabeth McGurk, Elizabeth Jane Smith, Beatrice Hudson, George Bowman, Joyce Blakeley, Jeannette Wandel, Dorthy Bock, Shirley Williams, Marie McCullen, and Dorothy Barbour; (third row) John Jones, Elton Wilde, Robert Stelzner, Edward Doyle, Harry Lutz, Leslie Gallagher, Norman Hamilton, Kenneth Scheller, and James McElhenny. (Courtesy of Veda Drummond.)

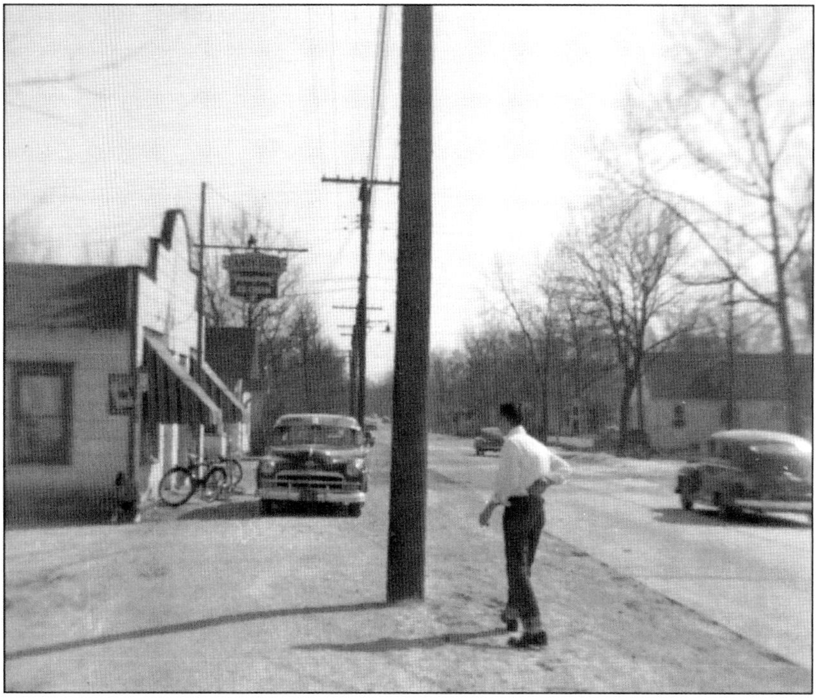

Joe McElroy walks up to Pratts Candy Store on Sixth Avenue and Erial Road in 1952. Joe said that there were not many cars on the road then. They would gather out front of the store and count the cars going by. If they were lucky, four cars might pass in three hours and maybe a pickup truck. (Courtesy of Peg Lesher.)

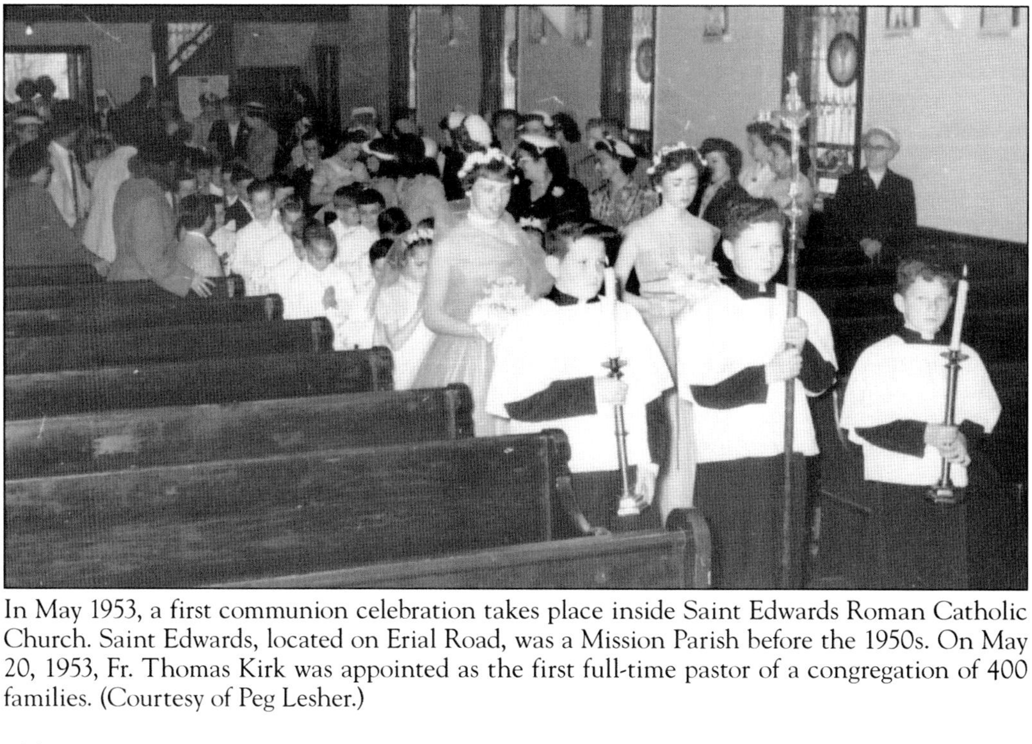

In May 1953, a first communion celebration takes place inside Saint Edwards Roman Catholic Church. Saint Edwards, located on Erial Road, was a Mission Parish before the 1950s. On May 20, 1953, Fr. Thomas Kirk was appointed as the first full-time pastor of a congregation of 400 families. (Courtesy of Peg Lesher.)

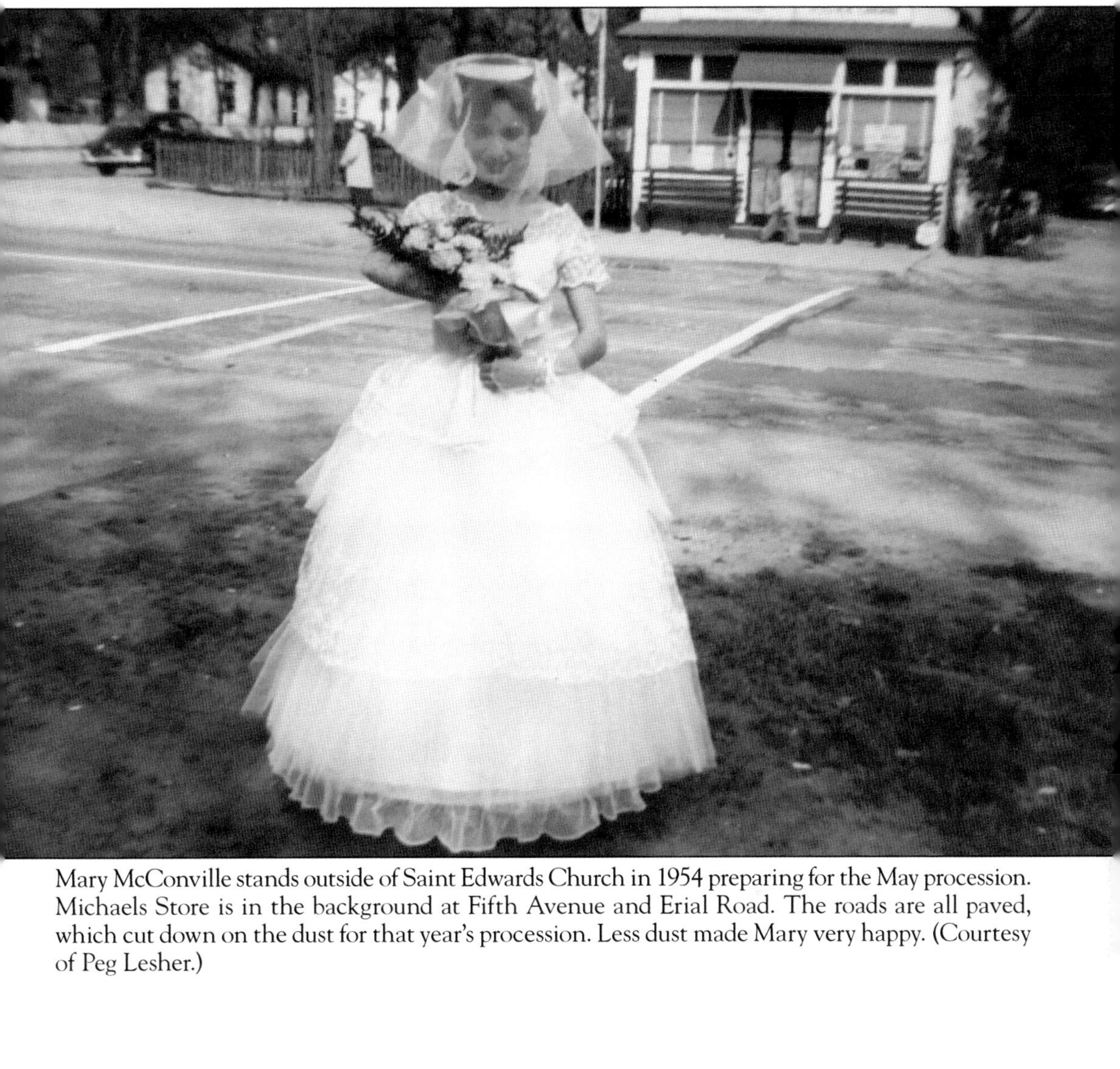

Mary McConville stands outside of Saint Edwards Church in 1954 preparing for the May procession. Michaels Store is in the background at Fifth Avenue and Erial Road. The roads are all paved, which cut down on the dust for that year's procession. Less dust made Mary very happy. (Courtesy of Peg Lesher.)

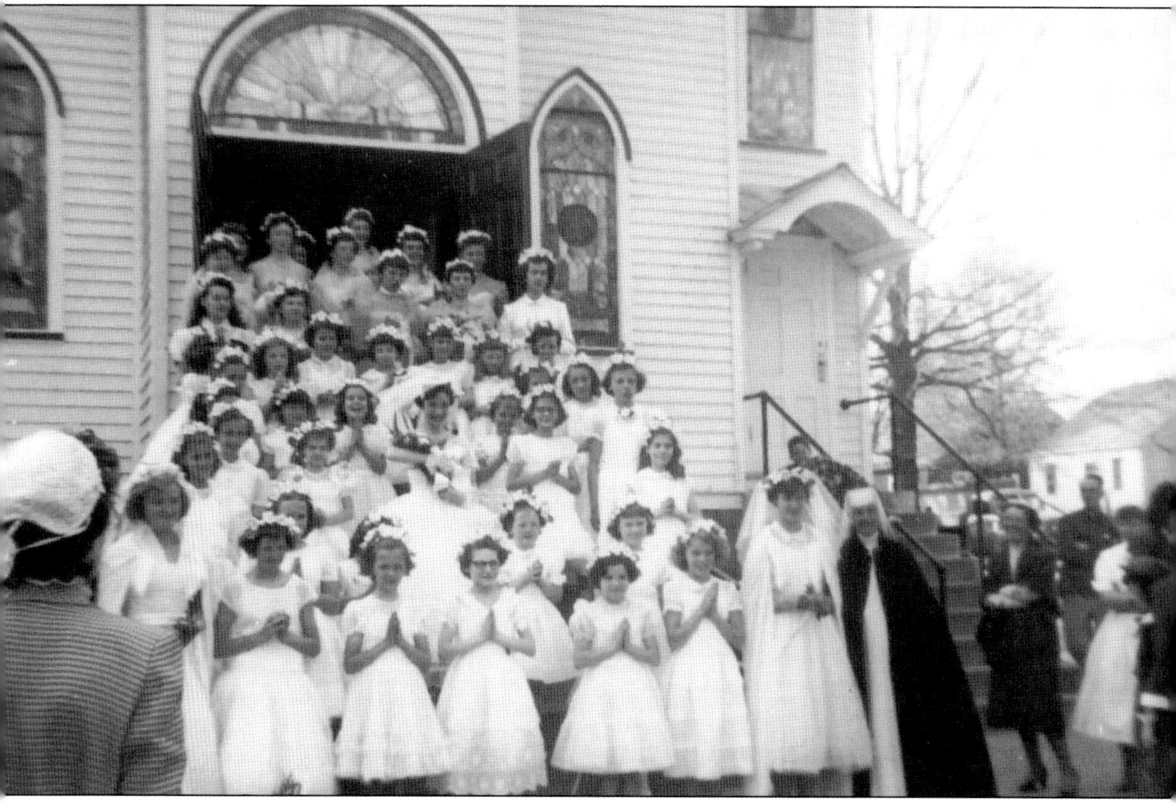

Here stand the children of Saint Edwards Church preparing for the May procession 1954. The church was located at 500 Erial Road on the corner of Fifth Avenue. They are all dressed in white and stand ready to pay honor to the Blessed Mary and crown her with flowers. (Courtesy of Peg Lesher.)

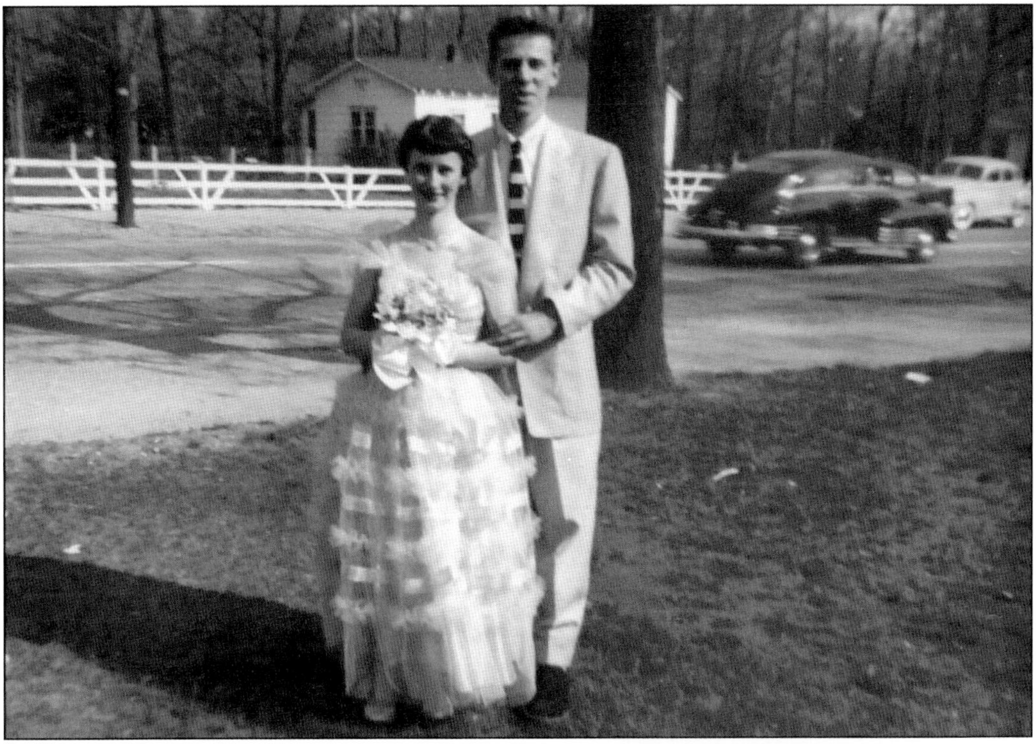

Billy Horner and Veronica Kaighn are shown above after the May procession in 1954. There was a big turn out that year for the procession, and the weather was great—plenty of sun and no rain. Horner and Kaighn later married and made Pine Hill their home for a lifetime. (Courtesy of Peg Lesher.)

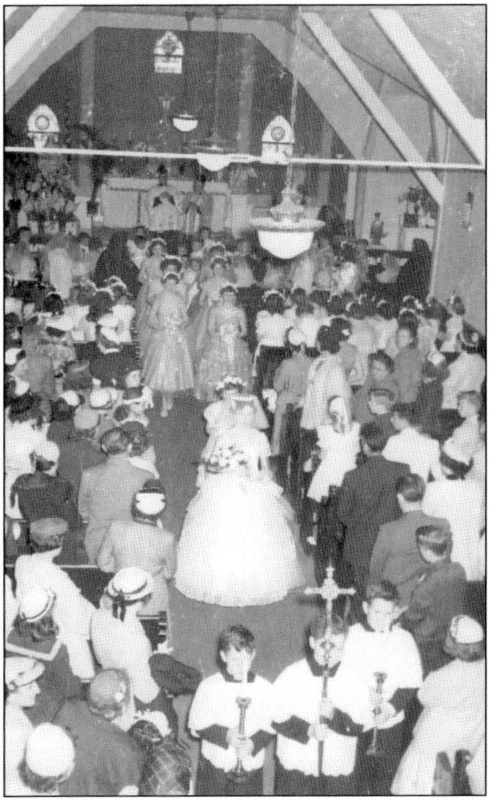

At right is Mary McConville leading the May procession out the front door of Saint Edwards Church in 1955. Following Mary is Ann Binky, Rosemary Schock, Bonnie McElroy, and Peg Lesher. The whole congregation would then follow and join in the ceremony, which ended outside at the statue of Mary where the flowers were placed. (Courtesy of Peg Flesher.)

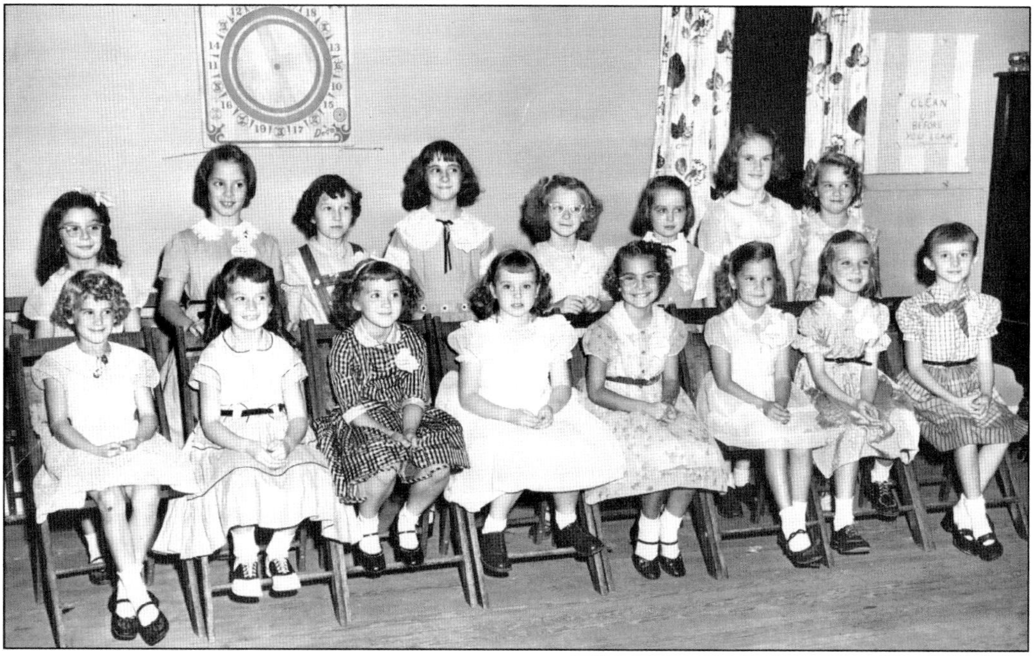

The local Girl Scout troop is photographed at the Pine Hill Fire Hall No. 1 by a professional studio in 1955. This was a highlight for the year; they would meet at the fire hall to work on their badges and learn how to serve their community. (Courtesy of Beckey Blakeley.)

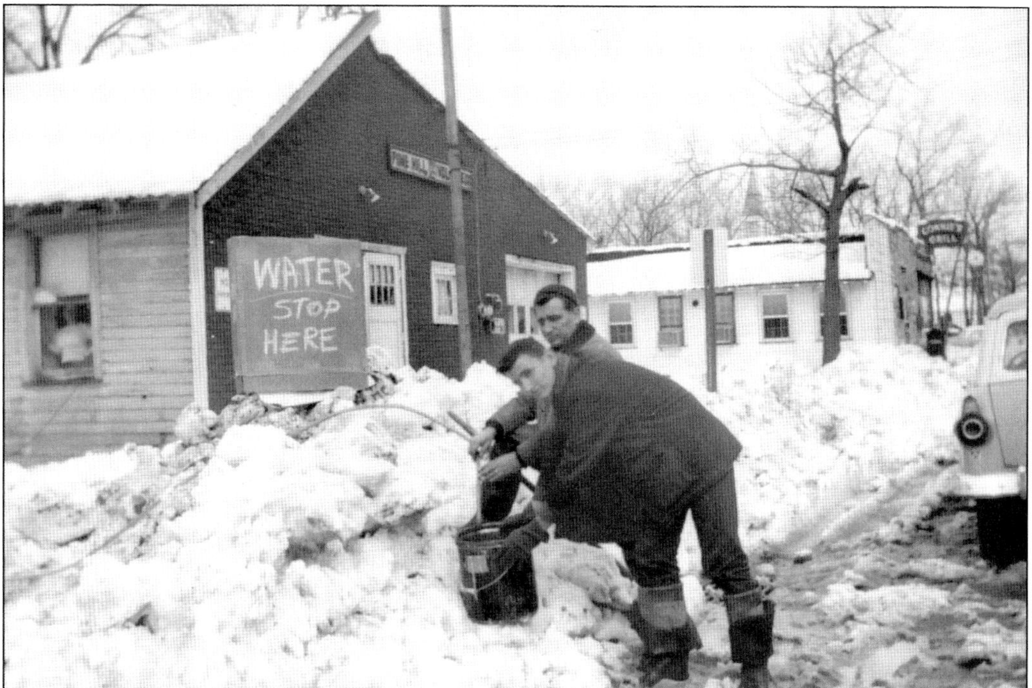

In 1958, a big snow and ice storm hit Pine Hill. No one could get water from their wells, and all the underground springs were frozen over. The local fire company set up a water stop where the people in town could get water for their daily needs. (Courtesy of Bill Dukes.)

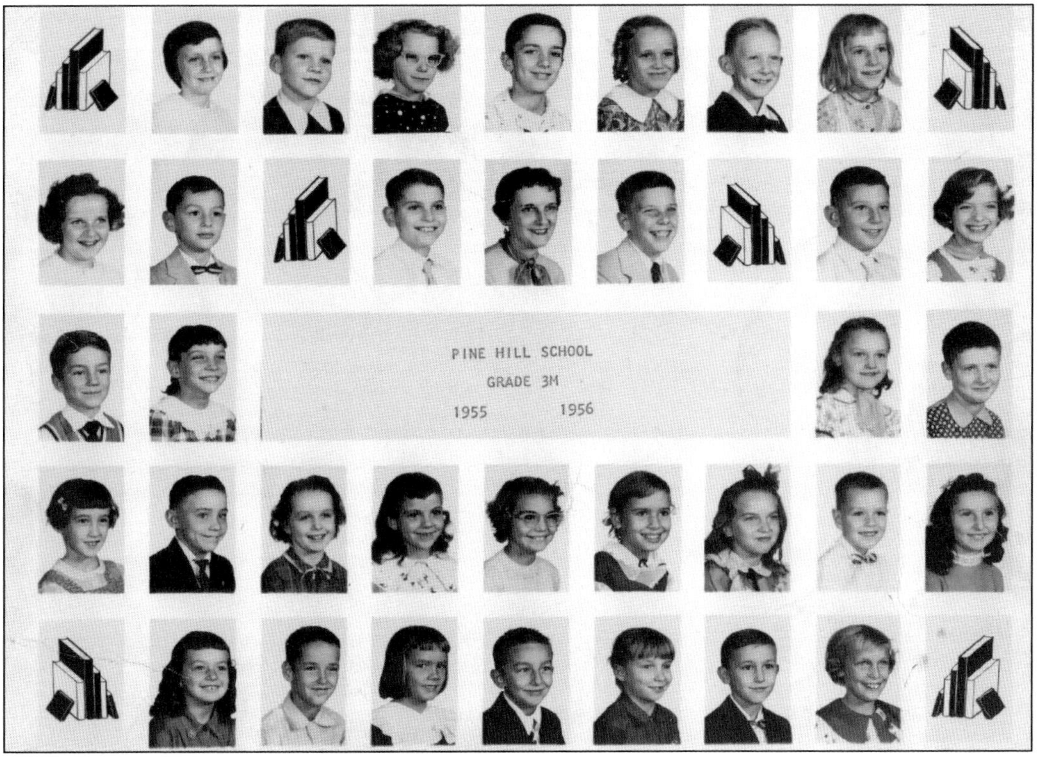

In the third grade class at the Dr. Albert Bean School in 1956, the teacher was Mrs. Mackelheny. Some of the class members were Sissy Bleatler, K. Bleatler, Becky Blakeley, Joan Delaney, Gary Larsen, Betsey White, Bob Proctor, Bobby Beerns, Darlene Armstrong, Al Crosby, Barbara Harris, Toni Hughes, Lee Hudson, and Connie Schaffer. (Courtesy of Beckey Blakeley.)

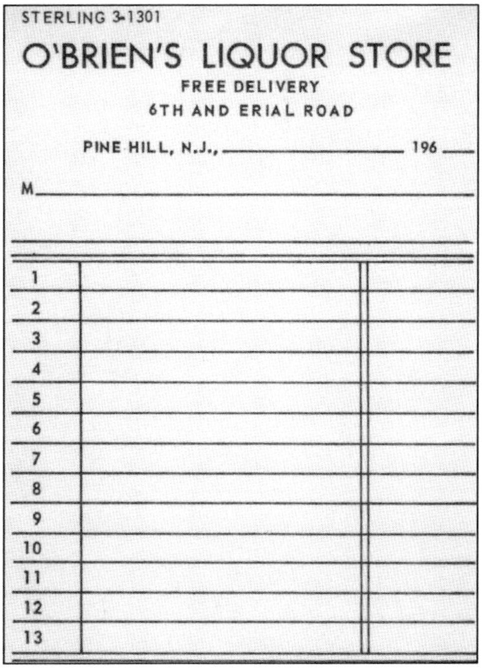

STERLING 3-1301

O'BRIEN'S LIQUOR STORE

FREE DELIVERY

6TH AND ERIAL ROAD

PINE HILL, N.J., ______ 196__

M______

1		
2		
3		
4		
5		
6		
7		
8		
9		
10		
11		
12		
13		

This delivery ticket was used by O'Brien's Liquor Store in the 1960s. Patrons would stop in or call to place an order of whatever beverage they wanted. When the order was completed, the clerk would then hand it to the customer or prepare it for delivery. (Courtesy of Natalie Maguire.)

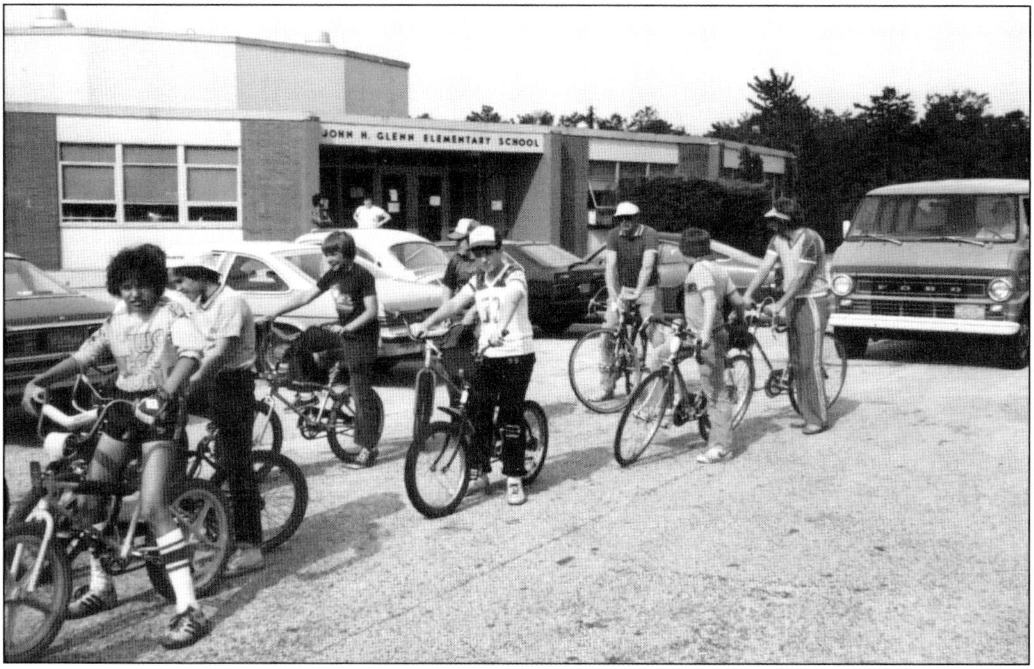

In the late 1960s, the two elementary schools in town started a bike-a-thon for the sixth grade classes. It was a rite of passage to leave town for the next step in education. All the students would pull out their bikes and get them ready for the big day, and if someone did not have one they borrowed one. In 1970, they all stand waiting for the trip to begin. (Courtesy of Peggy Steelman.)

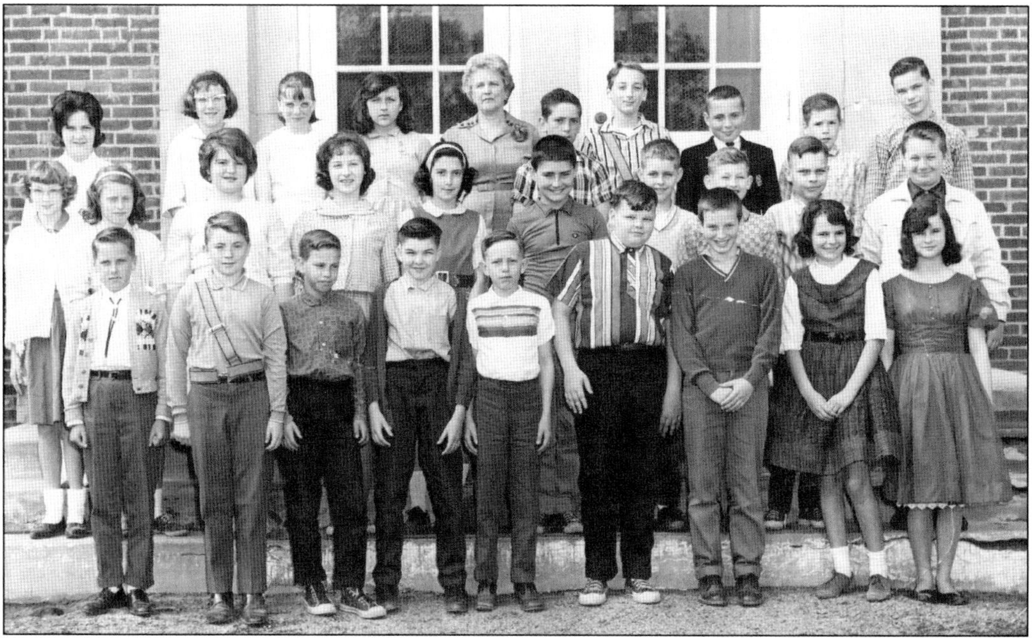

The sixth grade class of 1962 gathers at the front of the Dr. Albert Bean School on Third Avenue. By the 1960s, the schools in Pine Hill only taught students until the sixth grade. They would then attend Overbrook Regional High School in Lindenwold for the remainder of their education. (Courtesy of Mable Thumm.)

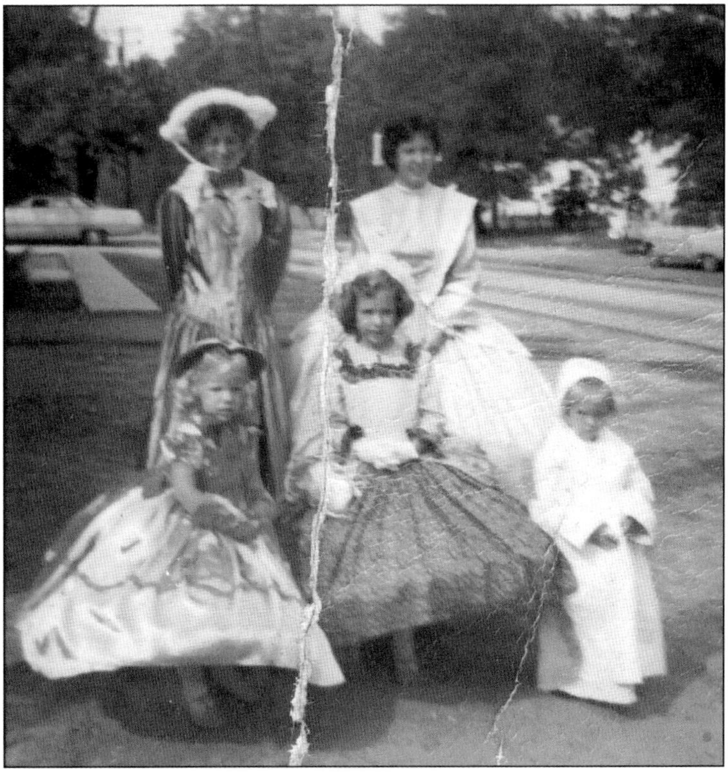

Ronnie Gallagher (left) and Ruth McCullen stand behind their daughters as they prepare for the 1964 July 4 parade. That year, the theme was American history, covering the pilgrims landing to the colonial days. Sherry McCullen (left) and Sue McCullen are fashioning their 1700 gowns that their mother handmade; Judy Gallagher (right) shows her Pilgrim fashion that her father hand sewed. (Courtesy of Ruth McCullen.)

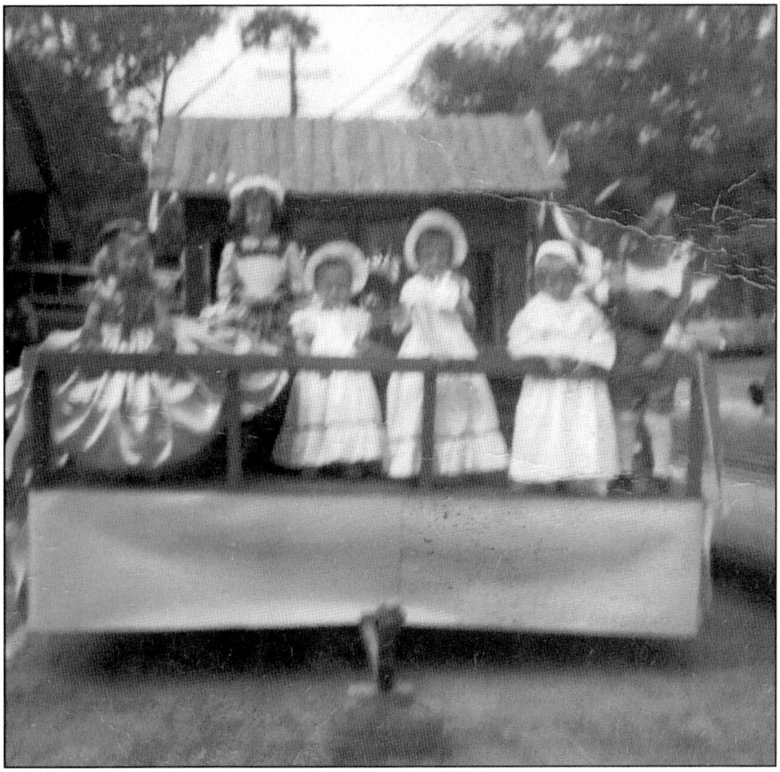

The Eagle Fire Company entered a float in the Fourth of July parade in 1964. The log cabin was built by Les Gallagher, and some children of the firefighters rode on the float displaying their costumes that were handmade by their parents. After the parade, the log cabin was auctioned off to raise funds for the Eagle Fire Company. (Courtesy of Ruth McCullen.)

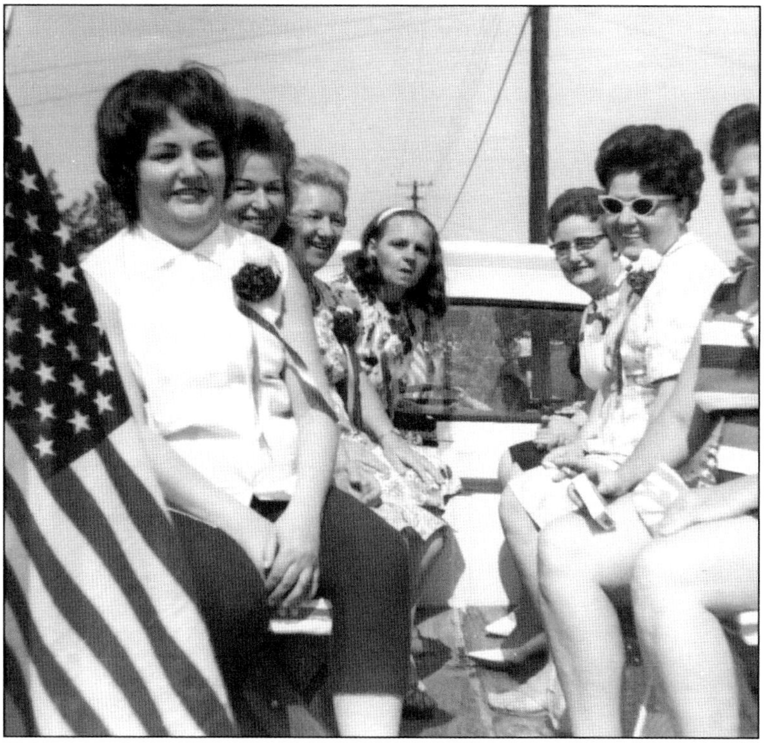

The Pine Hill Service Club rides on the back of a pickup during the 1967 Fourth of July parade. On the left of the truck from front to back are Ruth, Fran, Mary, and Honey; on the right side from front to back are Charlotte, Mildred, and Larraine. (Courtesy of Mary Gallagher.)

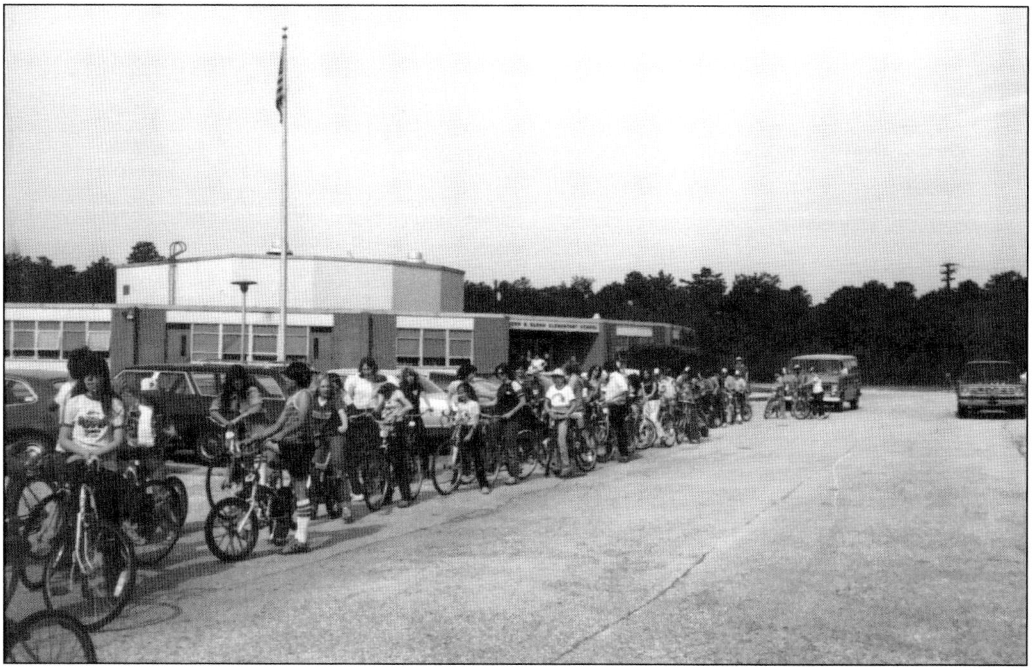

In 1970, the sixth grade students of the John H. Glenn and Dr. Albert Bean schools are lined up for a fun day. The day will begin with a long bike hike to Berlin Park and end with a barbeque and games; celebrating the beginning of summer and the end of elementary school. (Courtesy of Peggy Steelman.)

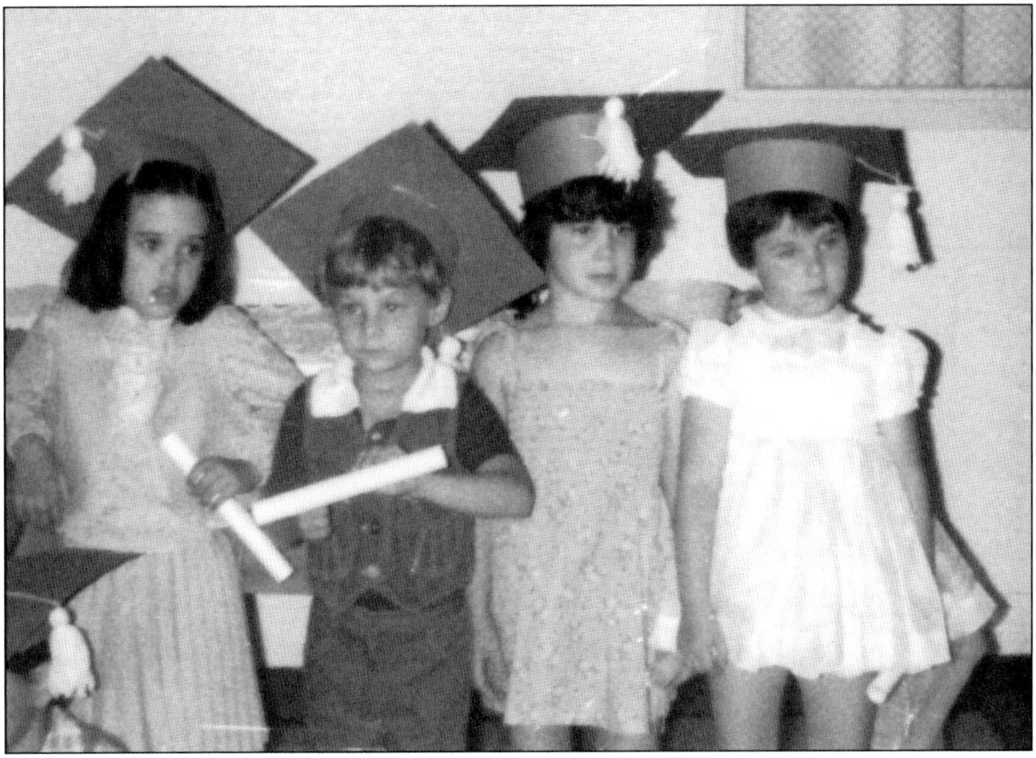

In 1970, Overbrook Senior High School on Turnersville Road in Pine Hill opened its doors to preschool students. Kathleen Morgan was the teacher, and high school students would assist as part of their studies. Kathleen Maguire Chiavallotti, standing second from the right, was one of the first graduates. (Courtesy of Natalie Maguire.)

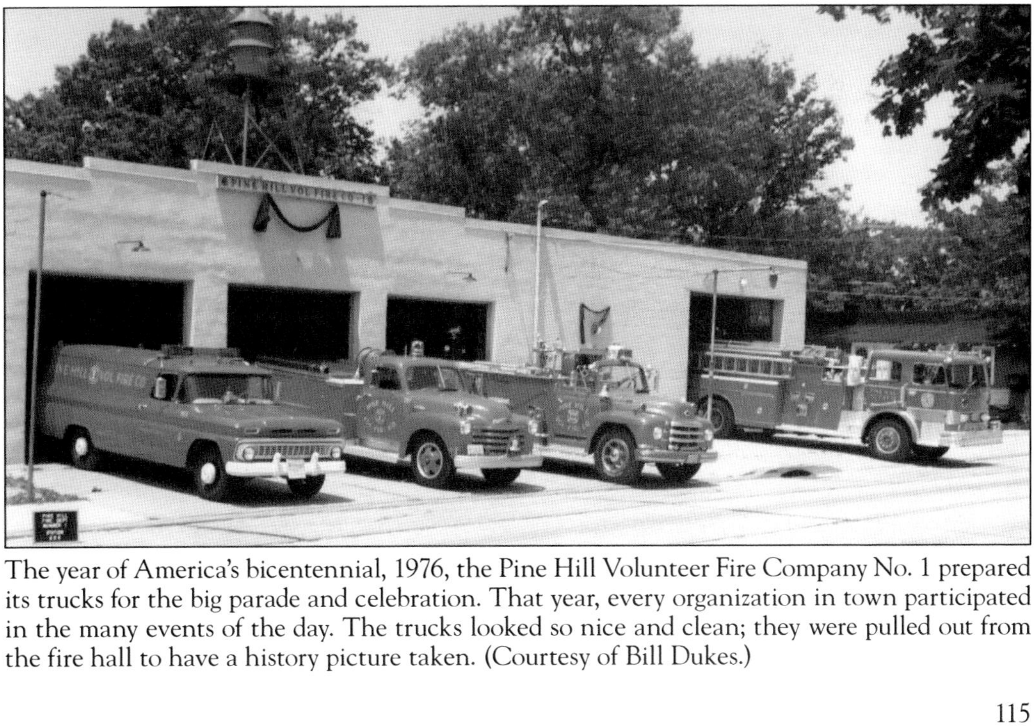

The year of America's bicentennial, 1976, the Pine Hill Volunteer Fire Company No. 1 prepared its trucks for the big parade and celebration. That year, every organization in town participated in the many events of the day. The trucks looked so nice and clean; they were pulled out from the fire hall to have a history picture taken. (Courtesy of Bill Dukes.)

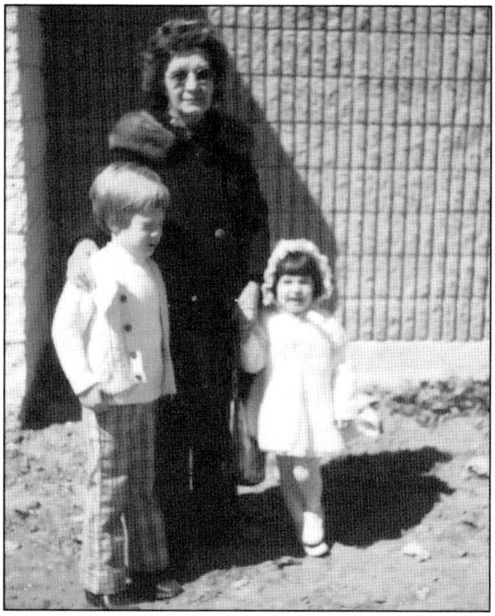

Rose Henshke and her grandchildren Johnnie Maguire and Katie Maguire stand outside of Saint Edwards Church in May 1977. The church was under construction that year. The old one was torn down due to the many repairs that were needed, and the congregation was growing. (Courtesy of Natalie Maguire.)

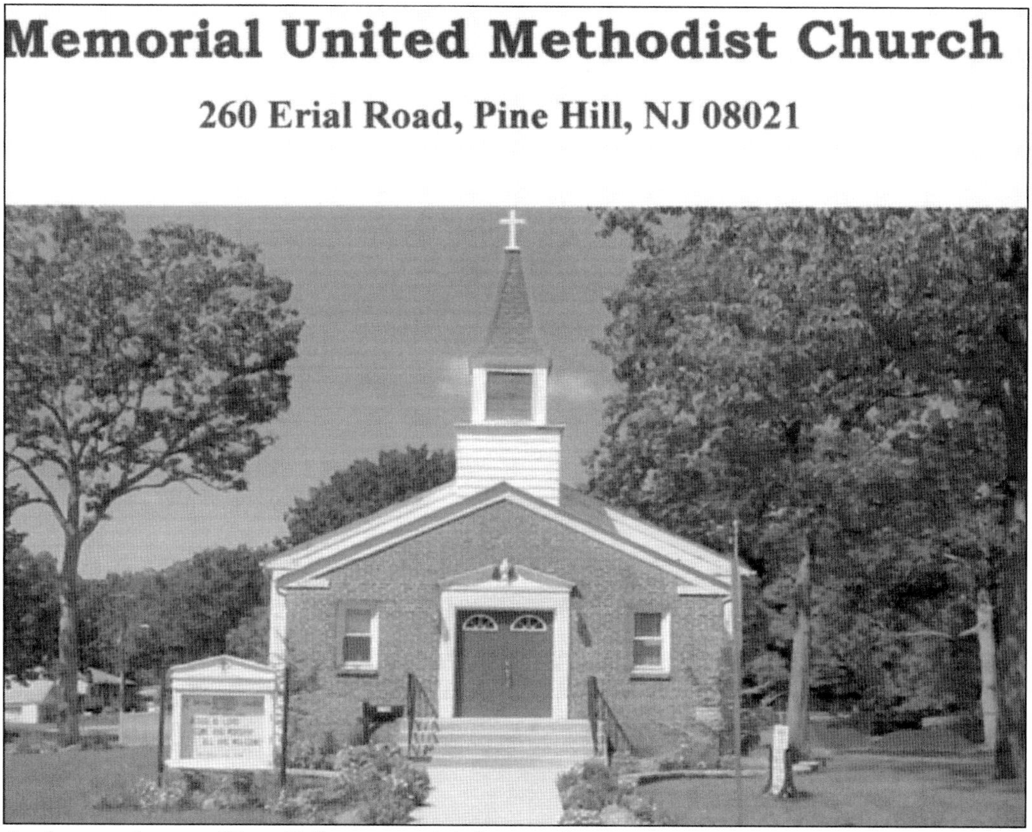

As the population of Pine Hill grew, so did the membership of the Memorial United Methodist Church. The original building was a wood structure and needed a lot of work, so the Parish family chipped in and erected the new church. When the new church was constructed, it was also at a new location on Fourth Avenue and Erial Road on a larger property. (Courtesy of Ida Fieger.)

In 1981, the Memorial United Methodist Church, under the direction of Rev. Charles Thorne, celebrated the 25th anniversary of its construction at Fourth Avenue and Erial Road. Twenty-six years prior, it had to be moved from First Avenue and Erial Road, because the building was falling apart and was too small for the growing congregation. (Courtesy of Ida Fieger.)

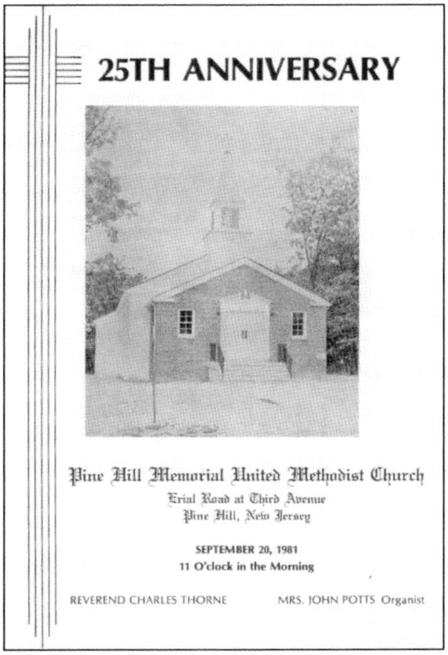

25TH ANNIVERSARY

Pine Hill Memorial United Methodist Church
Erial Road at Third Avenue
Pine Hill, New Jersey

SEPTEMBER 20, 1981
11 O'clock in the Morning

REVEREND CHARLES THORNE   MRS. JOHN POTTS Organist

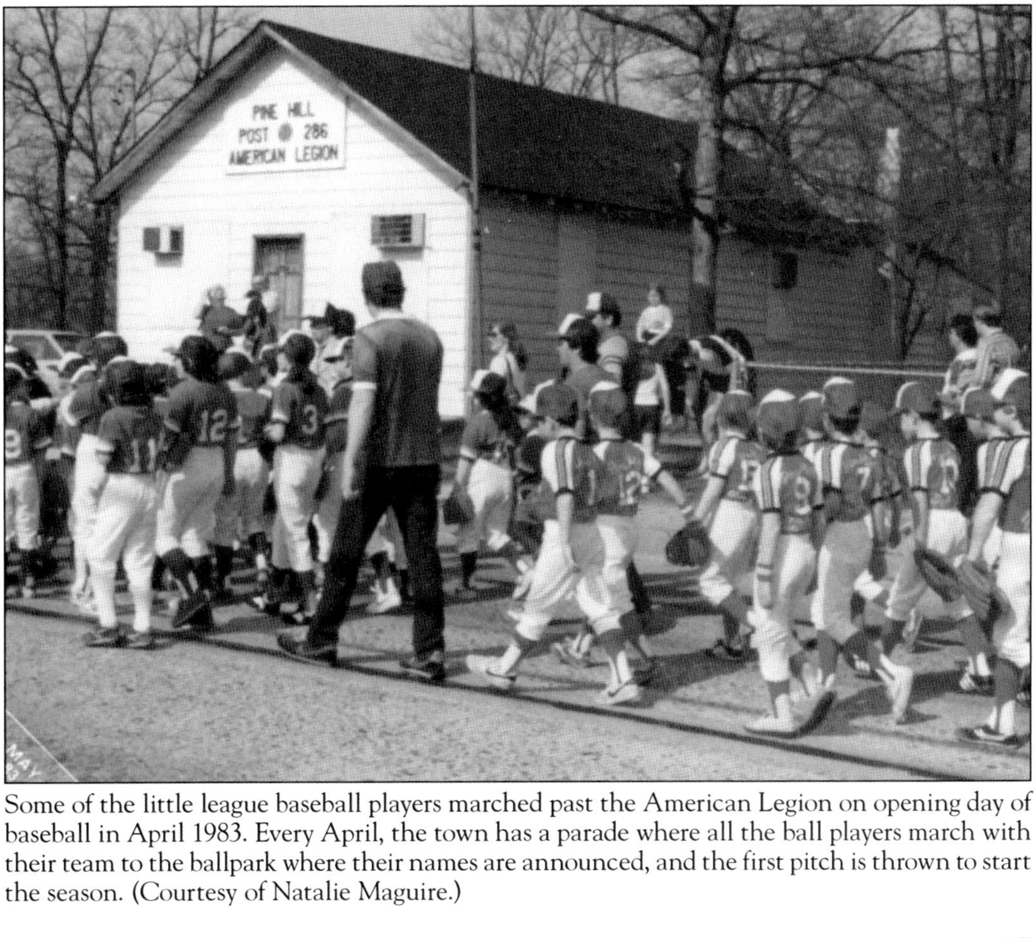

Some of the little league baseball players marched past the American Legion on opening day of baseball in April 1983. Every April, the town has a parade where all the ball players march with their team to the ballpark where their names are announced, and the first pitch is thrown to start the season. (Courtesy of Natalie Maguire.)

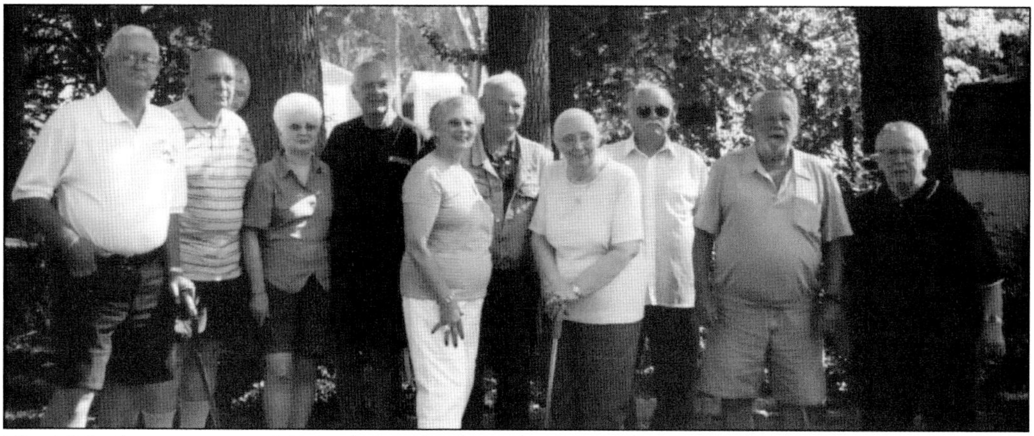

The 57th class reunion of the eight grade class of 1952 was held in the summer of 2009. Pictured from left to right are Les Gallagher Sr., Earl Shone, Dottie Barbour Cook, Ken Scheller, Veda Mathis Drummond, Bill Marck, Glen Osborne Suydam, Norman Hamilton, John Jones, and Alex Cole. (Courtesy of Glen Osborne.)

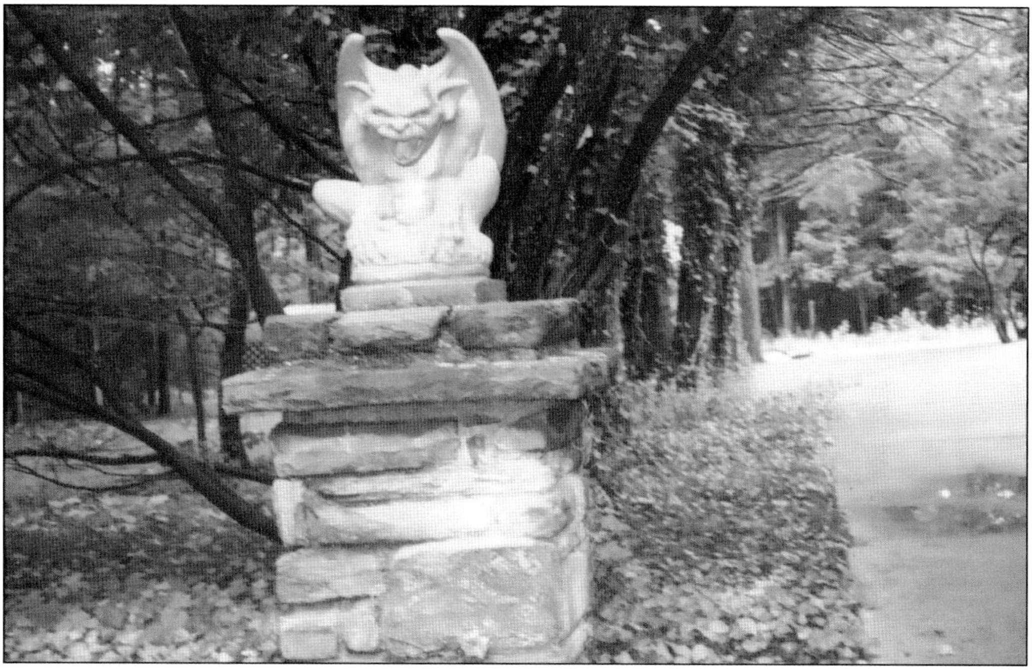

The gargoyle stands guard at the entry to the Blue Berry Mansion on Fifth Avenue. During the late 1950s, many movie stars held private parties here or just spent the night after a long day on the golf course at Pine Valley. Many of the teens of the town would stand at the end of the drive to catch a glimpse of a star or for a chance to be a caddy for the day. (Courtesy of Les Gallagher Jr.)

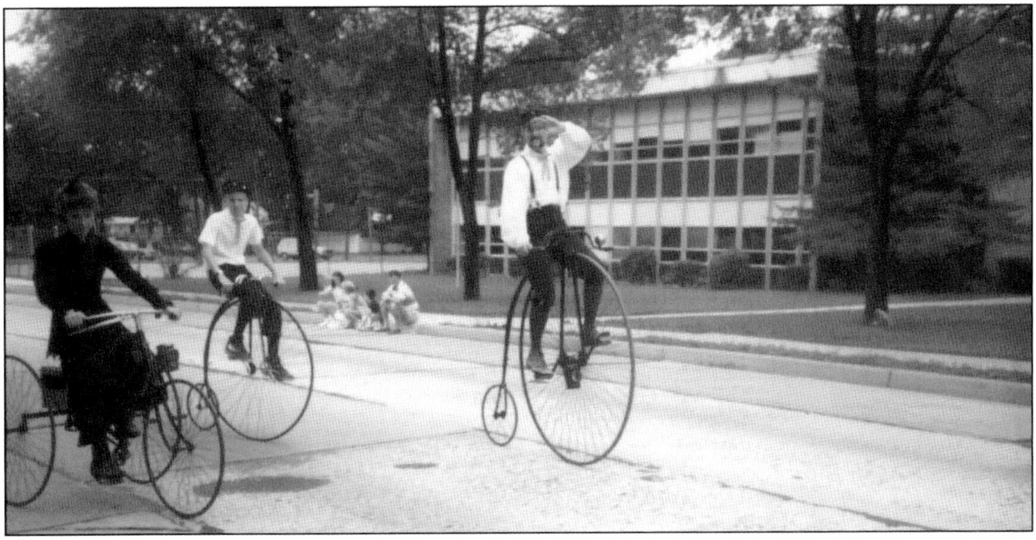

The Fourth of July participants in the parade pass the Saint Edwards School on the way to the Dr. Albert Bean School. Everyone had fun that year, and participants came from all over, like this antique bike club. The parade route was long, but the anticipation of hot dogs and drinks provided by the mayor and council kept everyone moving. (Courtesy of Les Gallagher.)

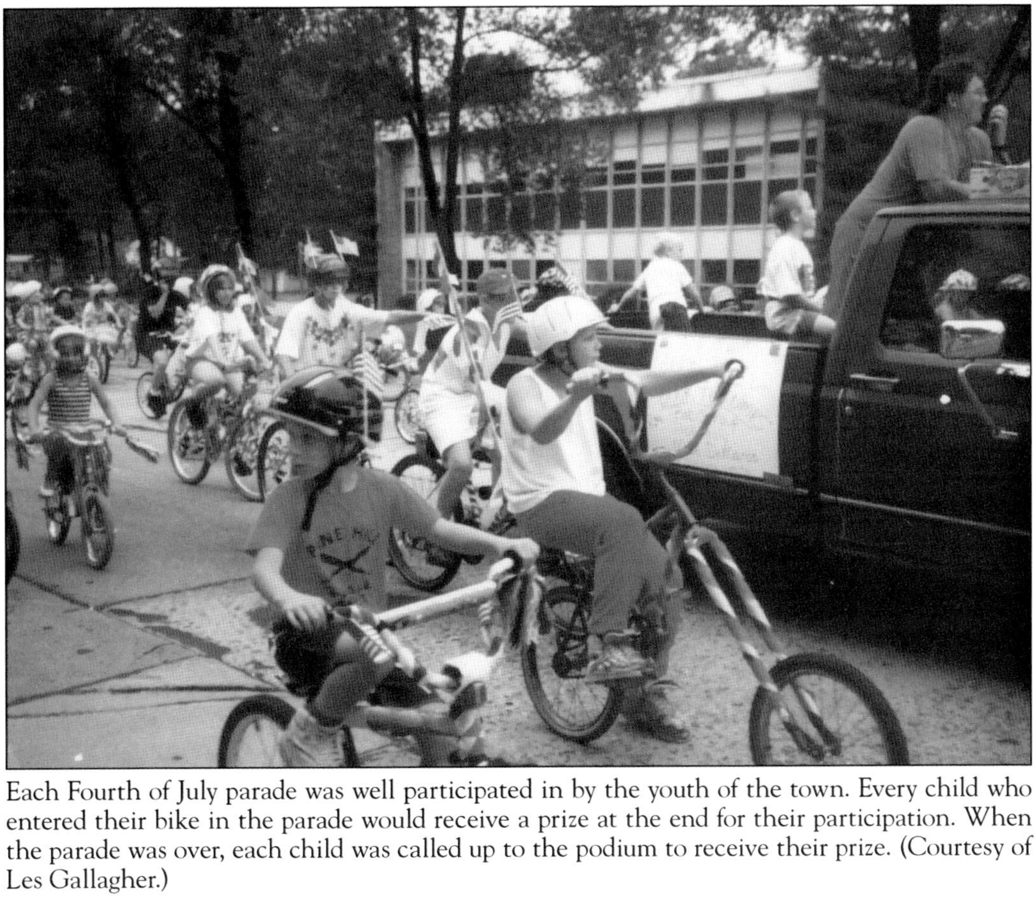

Each Fourth of July parade was well participated in by the youth of the town. Every child who entered their bike in the parade would receive a prize at the end for their participation. When the parade was over, each child was called up to the podium to receive their prize. (Courtesy of Les Gallagher.)

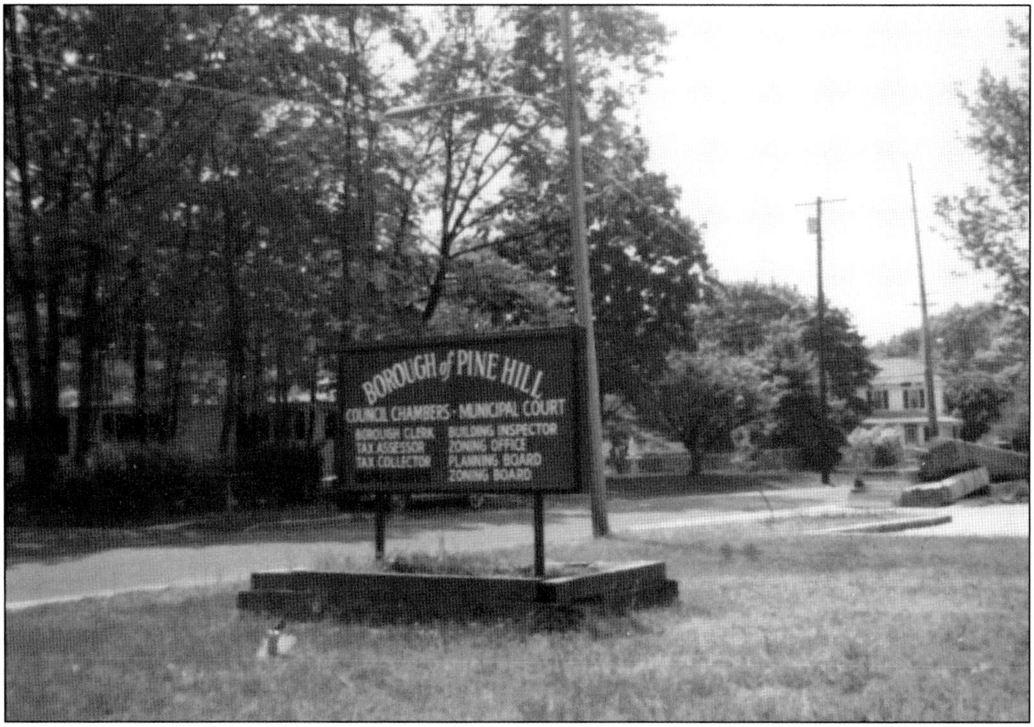

The sign at the borough hall shows the offices that are located inside the building. The building was still under construction at this time, and some of the lumber is in the background. The old structure is no longer economical to house the local government; they constructed a new building on the other side of the property on Seventh Avenue. (Courtesy of Peg Stillman.)

This badge was worn by the vice chairman of economic development commission, Les Gallagher. Members of the commission wore these badges when performing their official duties. The commission is responsible for bringing new business into town, as well as improvements and the redevelopment of the downtown area. (Courtesy of Les Gallagher.)

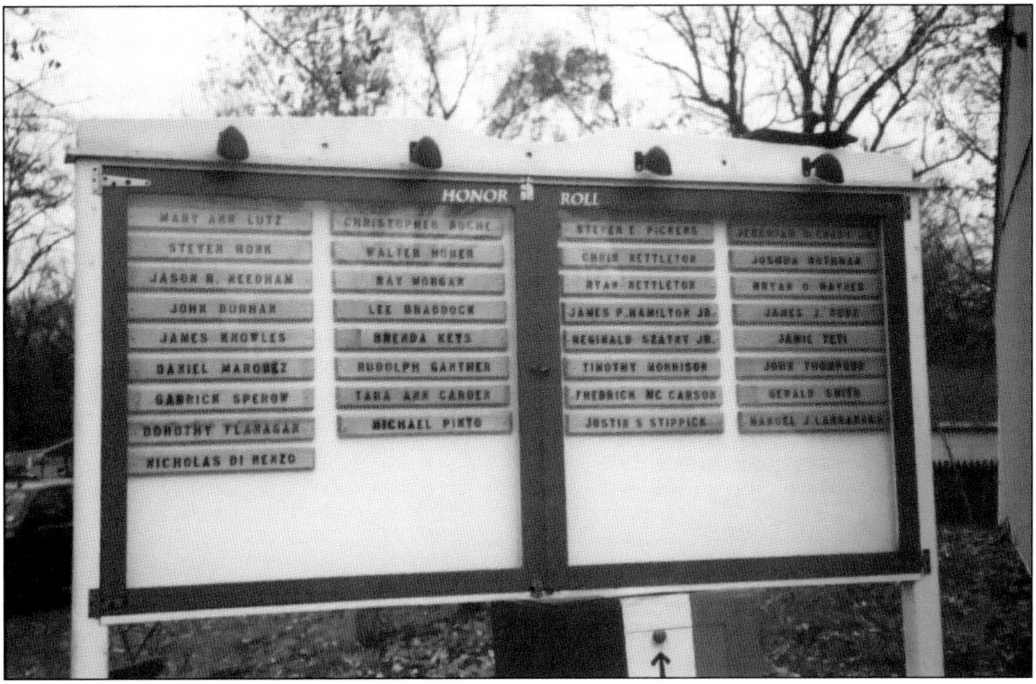

This honor roll board stands at the front door of the American Legion and VFW on Erial Road. The names on the board are members of town who are serving in a war zone or on active duty outside of a war zone. It was placed at the door so all entering the building would pause, read, and reflect on the sacrifices the town's military members were making. (Courtesy of Ronnie Gallagher.)

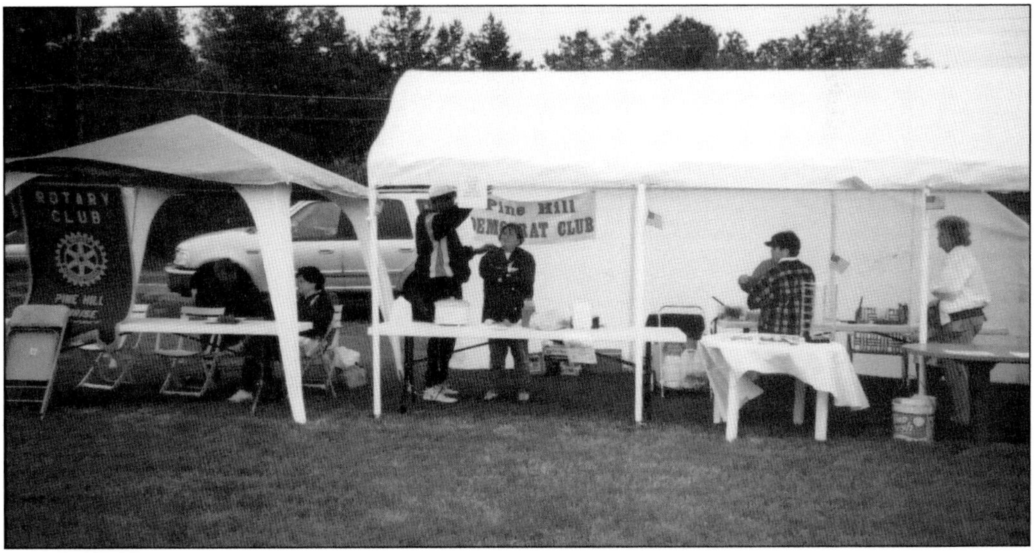

Pine Hill Day was set aside by the mayor and council for all the clubs and organizations to pitch in to create a day of fun and food the entire town to enjoy. Everyone would help out, and there would be games and rides for the children, food for all, and of course, special entertainment. (Courtesy of Natalie Maguire.)

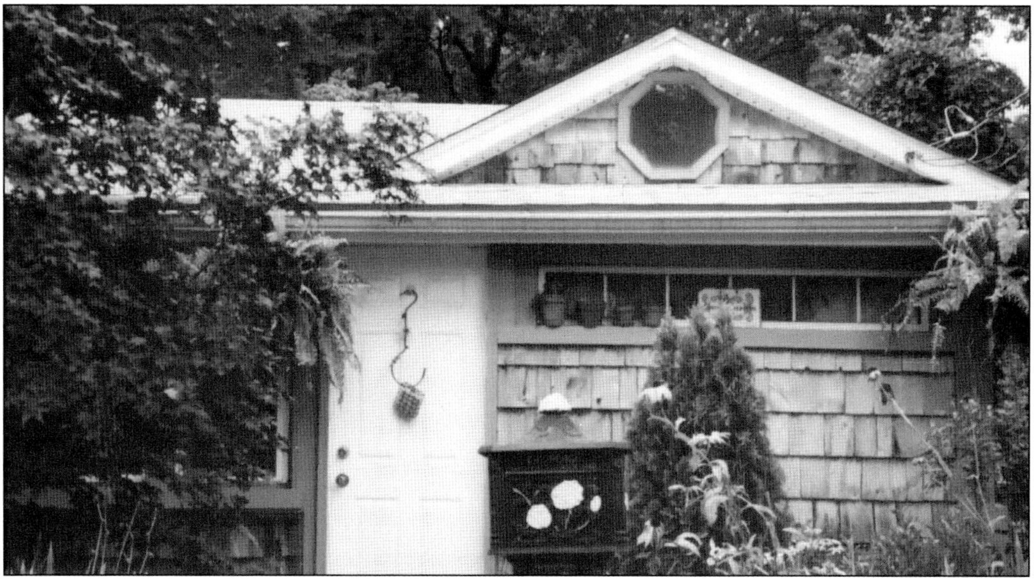

This house, located on the corner of Spring Avenue and Oak Avenue, is what the summer cottages looked like before they were modernized or torn down. This house is located by some of the old underground springs right through the woods, thus the name Spring Avenue. (Courtesy of Les Gallagher.)

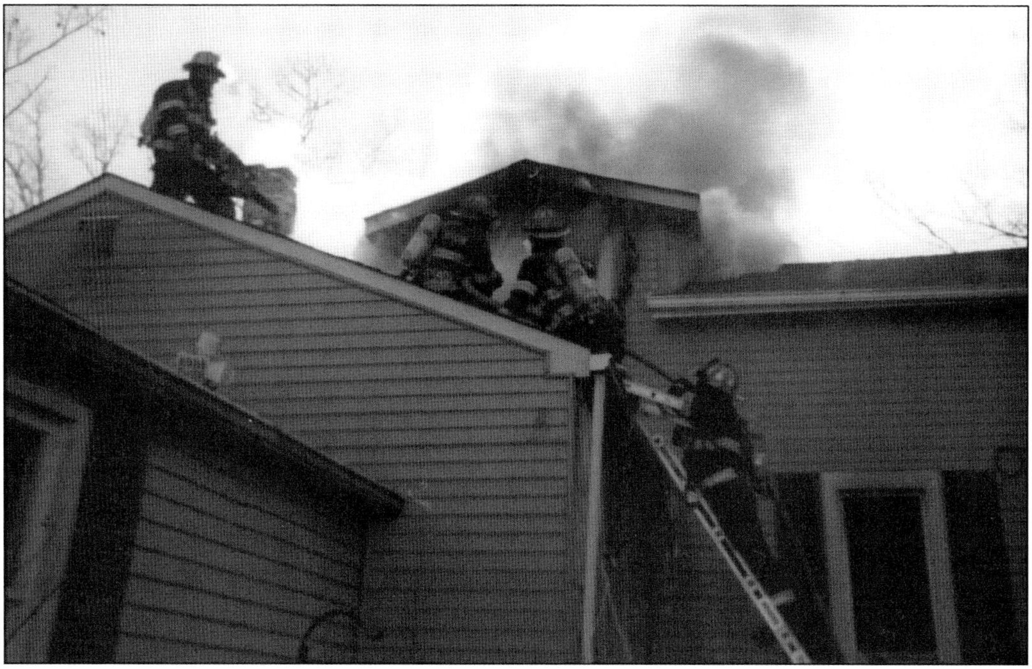

Joint efforts from all three of Pine Hill's fire companies were able to save this house from destruction. This was one of the older homes that had been added on to over the years to make room for more of the modern conveniences. The town's well-trained firefighters were able to get the fire under control without any injuries. (Courtesy of Bill Dukes.)

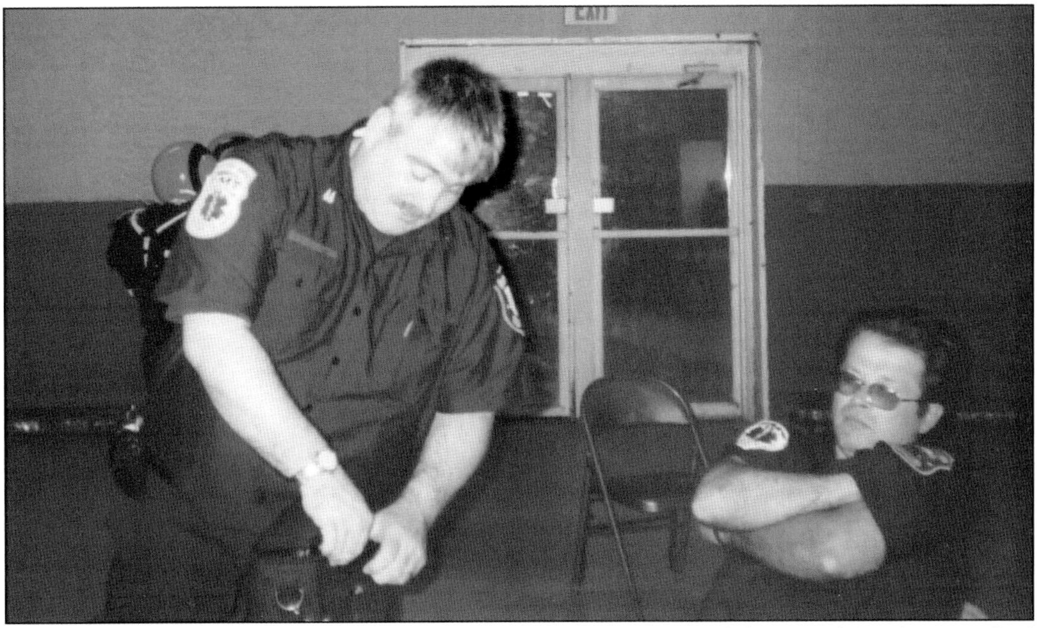

Fire-prevention-week preparations are well underway as some of the members that are dual certified, as emergency medical technicians and firefighters, get ready for the week's activities. Chuck Warrington (left) prepares some of the medical equipment that will be on display as Bill Erdwien keeps a keen eye on him. (Courtesy of Bill Dukes.)

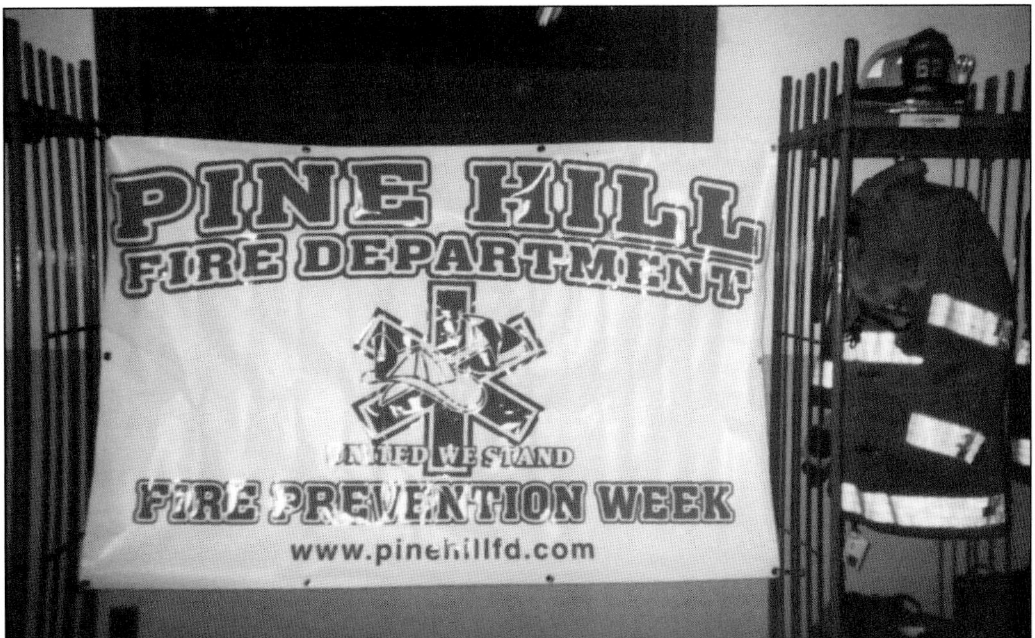

During the first week of each October, fire prevention week is held, and the members of Pine Hill display this banner to remind the people of town that the time is here. The local fire department has an open house and visits the schools to show what to do in a fire and how the trucks work. (Courtesy of Bill Dukes.)

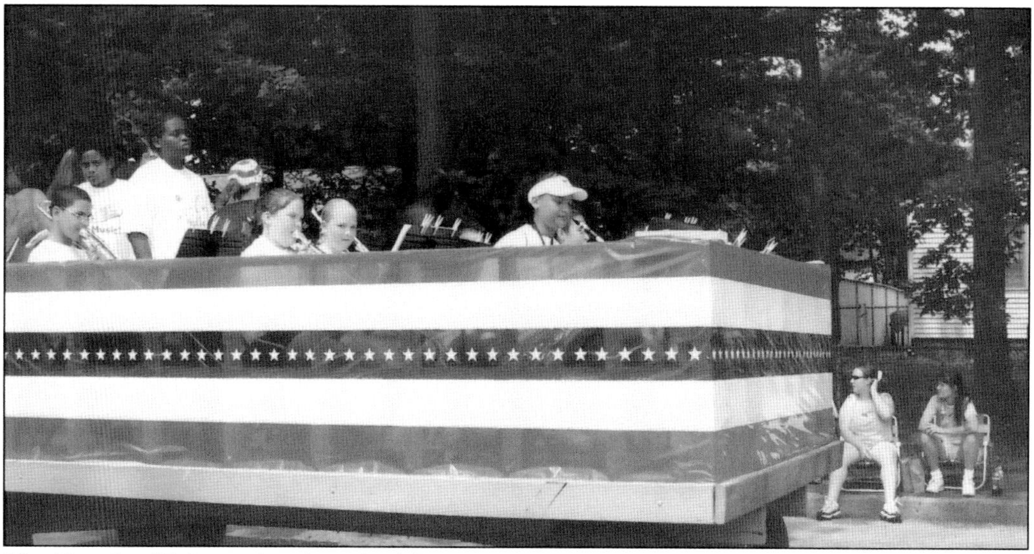

The Fourth of July is a big day of celebration in town, and everyone comes out to participate. The local schools join in the parade every year with the middle school band, and every year, the band gets bigger. This year they had two trailers to hold all the members. (Courtesy of Natalie Maguire.)

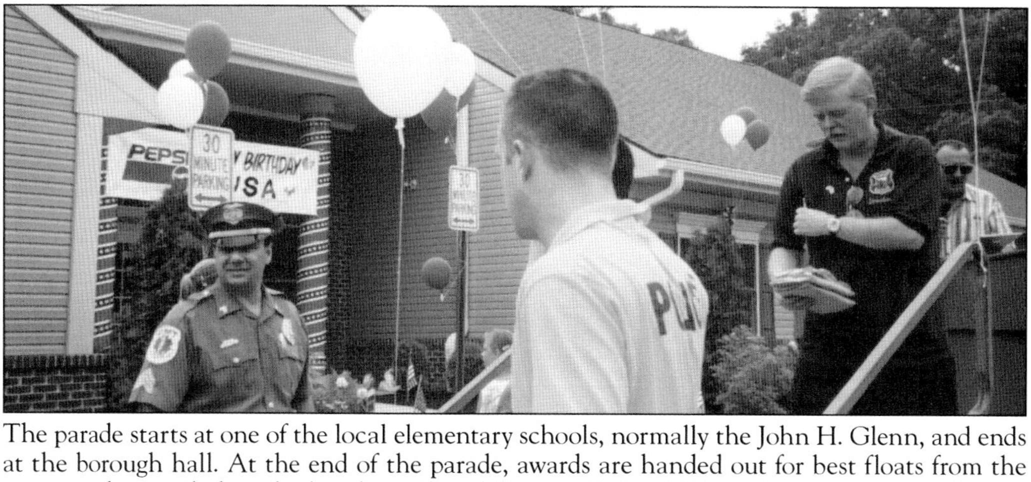

The parade starts at one of the local elementary schools, normally the John H. Glenn, and ends at the borough hall. At the end of the parade, awards are handed out for best floats from the mayor and council, they also hand out silver dollars to all the children who participate with their decorated bikes. (Courtesy of Natalie Maguire.)

Membership of the local American Legion Post No. 286 is growing every year due to the fact of continued military activity and the outreach that the local post has into the community. Each of the members is very active in the community and puts in the extra effort to reach out to fellow veterans. (Courtesy of Post No. 286.)

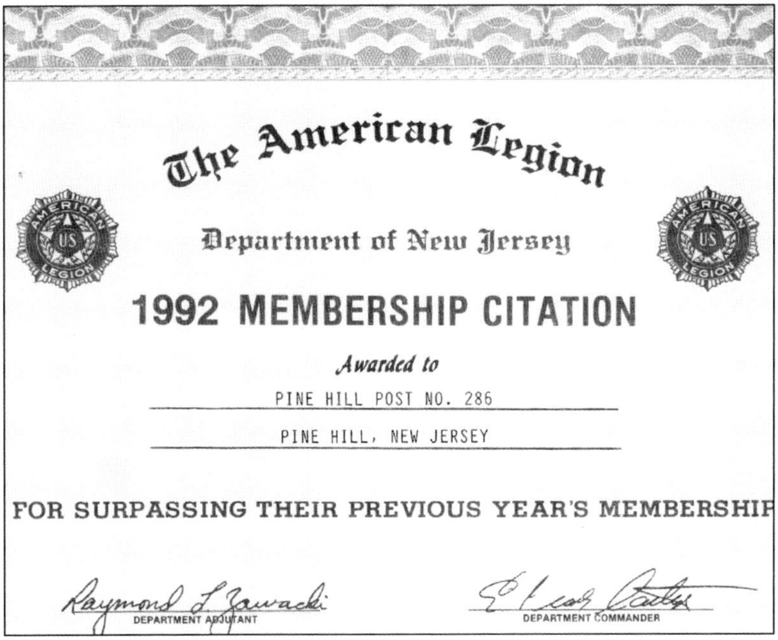

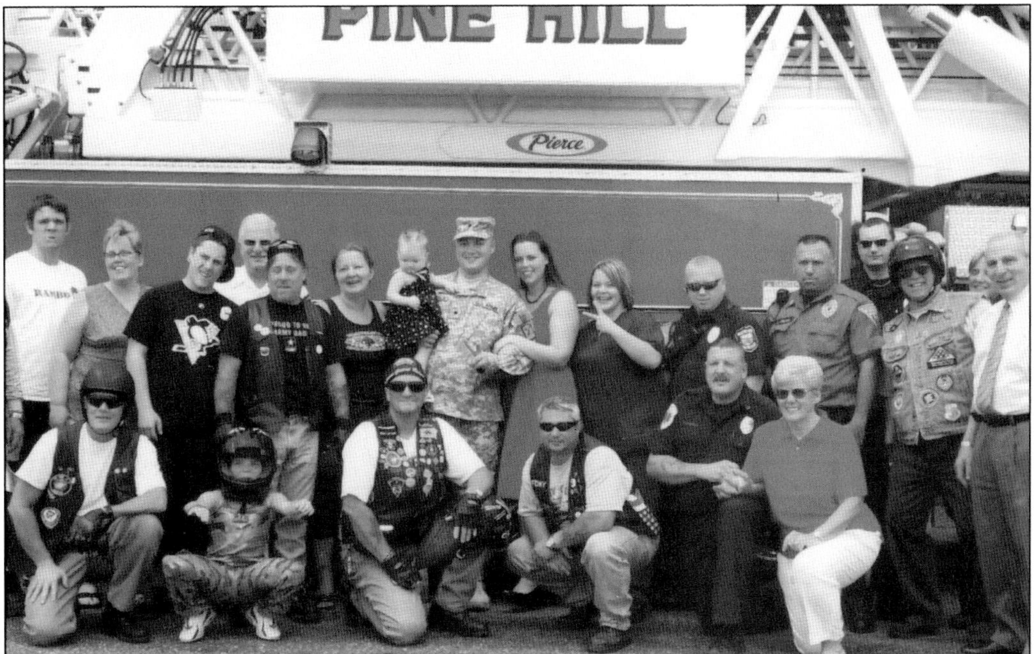

One of the local military members arrives home to a hero's welcome. Army specialist Steven M. Copestick of 38 West Branch Avenue had a motorcade escort when he arrived home on leave from the war zone. Pictured with Steven is his mother, wife, and daughter as well as local firefighters, mayor, council members, and the motorcycle veterans group that let the motorcade. (Courtesy of Bill Dukes.)

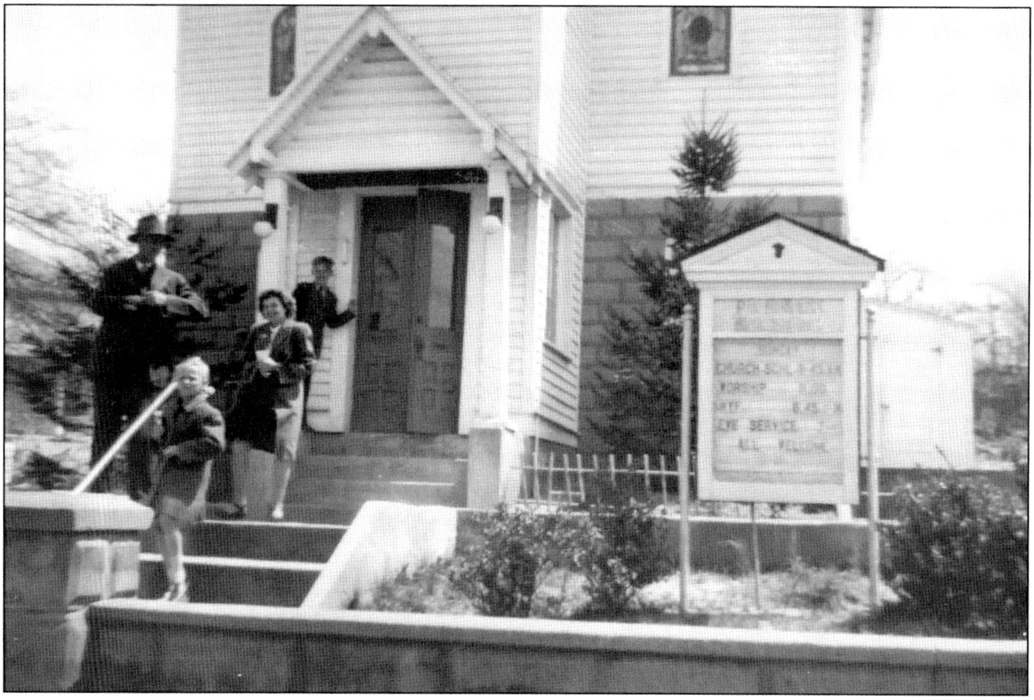

The original Memorial United Methodist Church was located at a triangle where East First Avenue and Lakeview Avenue meet Erial Road. The wall in front of the church stood for many years after the building was torn down. Now known as Freedom Triangle, the town had a small garden planted and two park benches put in place. (Courtesy of Ellen Kerby.)

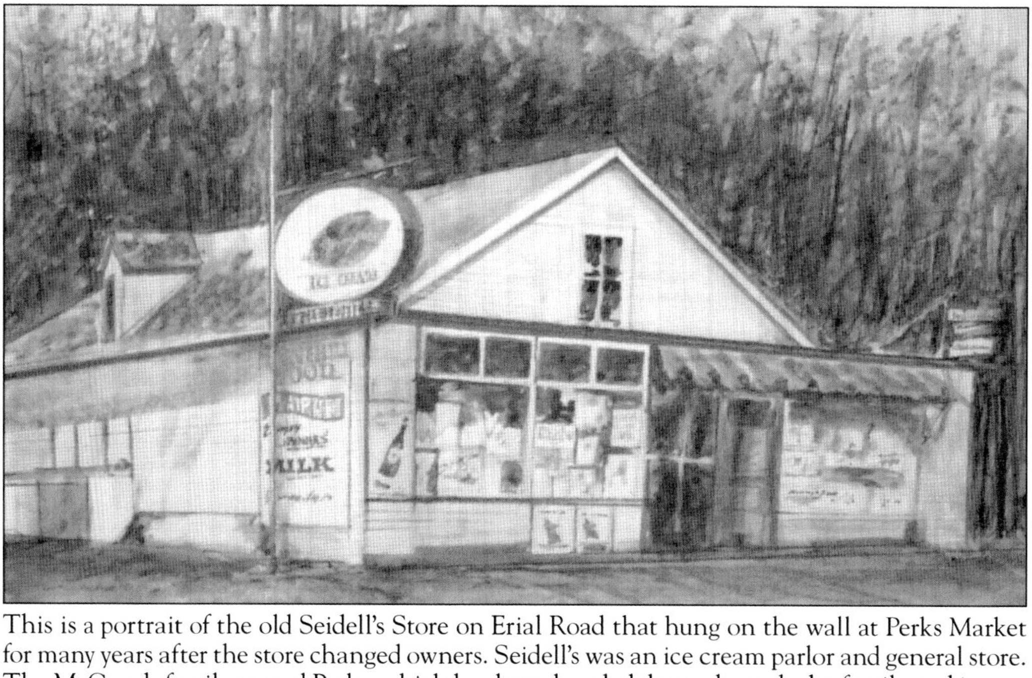

This is a portrait of the old Seidell's Store on Erial Road that hung on the wall at Perks Market for many years after the store changed owners. Seidell's was an ice cream parlor and general store. The McCouch family owned Perks, which has been handed down through the family and is now a grocery store. (Courtesy of Tom McCouch.)

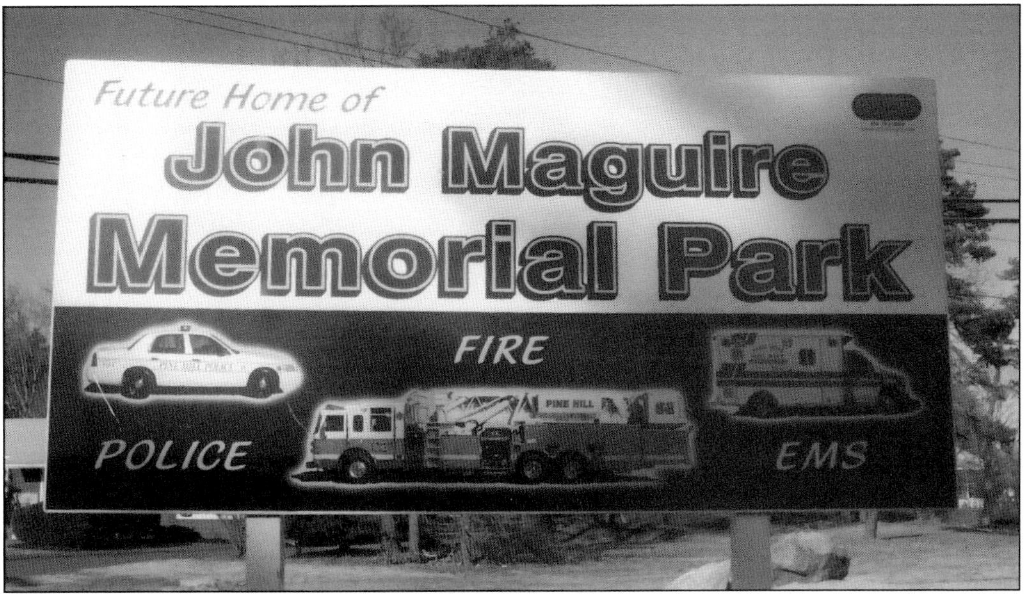

John Maguire Memorial Park is dedicated to the honor of the town's first responders and is located on Turnersville Road and Cross Keys Road. John Maguire was a longtime council member who served as president of council, director of public safety, and was one of the town's first fire commissioners before he passed away. (Courtesy of Natalie Maguire.)

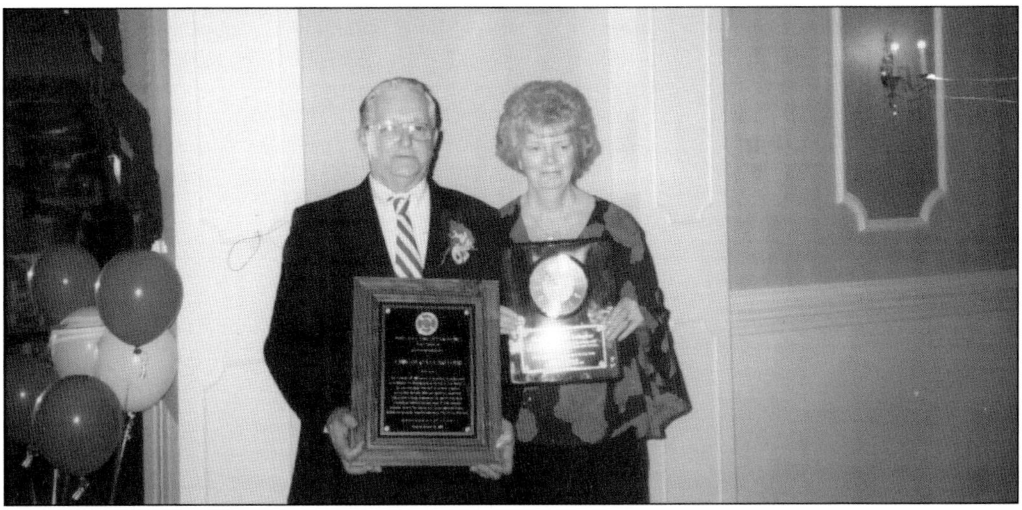

Les Gallagher and his wife, Ronnie, stand holding the clock and commendation that Les received for his many years of service to the fire community. As one of the town's first fire commissioners and the first chairman, he served many years helping the local fire district run smoothly and efficiently. (Courtesy of Les Gallagher.)